P9-CRL-792

THE NEW
SONOMA
COOKBOOK™

THE NEW SONOMA COOKBOOK™

INTERNATIONAL BEST-SELLING AUTHOR
Connie Guttersen, RD, PhD

SONOMA PHOTOGRAPHY
Faith Echtermeyer

RECIPE PHOTOGRAPHY
Annabelle Breakey

STERLING

New York / London
www.sterlingpublishing.com

10 9 8 7 6 5 4 3 2 1

Published by Sterling Publishing Co., Inc.
387 Park Avenue South, New York, NY 10016

© 2011 by Connie Guttersen, RD, PhD

Food Stylist: Karen Shinto; *Prop Stylist:* Emma Star Jensen

Distributed in Canada by Sterling Publishing
c/o Canadian Manda Group, 165 Dufferin Street
Toronto, Ontario, Canada M6K 3H6
Distributed in the United Kingdom by GMC Distribution Services
Castle Place, 166 High Street, Lewes, East Sussex, England BN7 1XU
Distributed in Australia by Capricorn Link (Australia) Pty. Ltd.
P.O. Box 704, Windsor, NSW 2756, Australia

Manufactured in the United States of America

Sterling ISBN 978–1–4027–8119–3

For information about custom editions, special sales, premium and corporate purchases, please contact Sterling Special Sales Department at 800–805–5489 or specialsales@sterlingpublishing.com.

CONTENTS

Acknowledgments

Many thanks and much gratitude are due to the individuals who made this book a reality. Their vision, energy, and remarkable talents are a big part of the Sonoma Way to better living with delicious meals. You have all inspired me with your talents and friendship throughout this project.

I appreciate the tremendous motivation and drive my late father, Bruno Peraglie, MD, instilled in me to explore the science of nutrition as a way to help others attain better health, an idea that today comes to life as we understand how foods and lifestyle can impact our health and happiness. I would also like to thank my mother, Paola, for providing me with a lifetime of lessons on how to prepare and enjoy delicious meals. Her philosophy of simple preparations with wholesome ingredients and a touch of creativity is woven into these recipes.

Thank you to the entire Sonoma team at Sterling Publishing; your partnership has been essential in this amazing journey. Thank you, Marcus Leaver and your team for your extraordinary vision: Jason Prince, Michael Fragnito, Karen Patterson, Susan Lavington, and Jennifer Williams for supporting and believing in my endeavors. A special thanks to Elizabeth Mihalste, Jeff Batzli, Leigh Ann Ambrosi, and Anwesha Basu for your long hours and dedication to the project.

Thank you to the *www.NewSonomaDiet.com* team at Everyday Health, especially Dan Wilmer, Sarah Hutter, Vince Errico, and Mike Keriakos for seeing the future. Your continuing effort to provide supportive information to our community of readers is invaluable.

To the Culinary Institute of America, thank you for many years of inspiration and learning and for the ongoing experience of keeping the science and nutrition in perspective with the enjoyment of wholesome, flavorful foods. A special thanks to my dear friend, mentor, and colleague of almost twenty years, Chef Toni Sakaguchi, whose passion and creativity are beyond praise.

Thank you to Lary Rosenblatt, Laurie Lieb, Susan Elkin, and Fabia Wargin for sharing your excitement and vision. The engaging language and organization of information owe much to your hard work and close attention. So much effort went into finding that perfect cover shot of the beautiful wine country—thank you, Faith Echtermeyer, for capturing the essence of the amazing California wine country. Thanks to Annabelle Breakey for her amazing food photography, Karen Shinto and Emma Star Jensen for their artistic touches.

To Vicki Saunders, thanks for the many hours of tedious dietary calculations and nutrient analysis.

Thank you to our Sonoma friends who contributed the "Taste of the Wine Country" recipes—to name a few, St. Francis Winery, Kobrand Corporation, Cole's Chop House, The Sonoma Mission Inn, California Avocado Board, BUSH's Beans. To the dynamic Sonoma KRUPP team led by Heidi and Darren Lisiten: David Thalberg, Chanel Graham, Rebecca Silver, and Alexa Breslin—everything is possible with your talents and vision. A special thanks to my friend and agent, Heidi Krupp Lisiten, whose ideas set the course for an amazing future.

Finally, to Shawn, my husband, and our children, Gigi and William: without your patience, support, and inspiration, this project would not have been possible. The love and respect that stem from family are the foundation of health, success, and happiness.

From the Author

The coastal region of Sonoma County in northern California is home to an artisan community of bread bakers, cheese makers, small farmers, organic produce growers, and winemakers who have cultivated a new way of appreciating food and the people with whom they share it. Inspired by the culinary delights of the region, these people have changed the culinary culture of the entire nation. Behind all of these growers is a story of how they came to appreciate the quality of the food they produce and the importance of sharing it with others.

The experience of living in the wine country of California has had an immense impact on my professional and personal endeavors as well. It has reminded me of the value of dining as a family and making memories out of the meals we share. In my twenty-five years of studying the art and science of food, I have seen the research reveal new and exciting discoveries, from the heart-healthy attributes of omega-3 fatty acids and olive oil to the miraculous secret of dark chocolate for a healthier heart. But with this fuller under-standing of nutrition comes the realization that it can become easy to misinterpret the meaning of "healthy" or, for that matter, even the word "diet," to the point that it diminishes the simple pleasures a meal can bring. As our knowledge of nutrition continues to grow, I believe we need a nutrition philosophy that strives to incorporate the broader strokes of what it takes to eat and live healthy. Wholesome meals, enjoyed as a special celebration or as part of our daily routine, are an important aspect of the art of living. Embracing this concept could spell the end of what we have long known as "diets."

The New Sonoma Cookbook™ invites you to explore more than 200 new recipes, culinary tips,

If you are using this book as a companion to *The New Sonoma Diet*™, you will find many more options and meal ideas for your Wave 1, 2, and 3 eating plans. Is your goal to lose some extra body weight, especially around your waist? Then start with ten days of Wave 1 plate guidelines and continue through the different waves as described in *The New Sonoma Diet*™. For your ten days of Wave 1, select from the wide variety of recipes in this book that have the lowest glycemic index numbers and calorie counts. If you are looking to stay healthy, trim, and keep your energy levels up, just follow the balanced plate recommendations for The Sonoma Smart Plate, also known as Wave 3, and enjoy all of these wonderful recipes.

For more information on how easy it is to follow the different wave plans, refer to *The New Sonoma Diet*™.

The supportive online community at *www.NewSonomaDiet.com* can enhance the experience of learning to eat the Sonoma way. Our website offers encouraging tips on staying the course for better diet and health, additional nutrition information, and even more meal plans. Interacting online with others who are following the Sonoma plan can provide accountability and support. Inspiring stories from members and local chefs and wine producers offer insight into the art of healthy and happy living. At *www. NewSonomaDiet.com* you will become part of a community making a difference in how Americans think about food and health.

and seasonal variations that bring the California wine country's sun-drenched flavors and vibrant lifestyle into your home. It was important to me to bring the Sonoma Way into your home so that you can create simple, flavorful meals for the entire family to enjoy. Whether you choose spice-rubbed, cedar plank roasted salmon with grilled artichokes or roasted wine country beef with whole-grain mustard and mushrooms, these recipes include easily found ingredients, fragrant spices and herbs, and an emphasis on local seasonal bounty. And when you choose to enjoy a glass of wine, look for recipes that suggest a wine pairing.

It is my hope that this cookbook will make it easier and more enjoyable for you to feed your family and friends with a clearer idea of how delicious "healthy" can be and with the confidence that you can have a meal ready in minutes for your family to enjoy, even on your busiest days. My philosophy in this book centers on the idea that better nutrition for everyone begins with simple, nutritious meals that, above all, create a quality of life that inspires you and your family.

— CONNIE GUTTERSEN, RD, PhD

RETURN TO SONOMA

Welcome to a coastal California way of eating that rediscovers the culinary delights of fresh, health-inducing ingredients, vibrant flavors, and innovative yet simple preparations.

It has been five years since *The Sonoma Diet*® was released, leading a food, flavor, and health renaissance that continues to sweep across America. Just recently, the publication of *The New Sonoma Diet*™ has continued that renaissance. *The New Sonoma Cookbook*™ is a perfect companion to *The New Sonoma Diet*™, a plan that brings together the latest in nutrition and well-being with a celebratory, pleasure-packed approach to healthy eating inspired by the cuisine and lifestyle of one of the most beautiful and inspirational places on earth.

California coastal cuisine conjures up images of food brought from sun-drenched farms right to the table, complemented by wine pressed from the bountiful grapes growing throughout this region. California coastal cuisine, the fusion of culinary inspirations from the Mediterranean, Asia, and Latin America, is widely recognized as a healthy and flavorful alternative to the "Western diet" so many of us have become accustomed to. Meals are often enjoyed with a glass of wine, celebrating the seasons, family, and friends. The Sonoma way of eating is part of a healthy lifestyle. With emphasis on simplicity, innovative cuisine, fresh foods, flavorful ingredients, and streamlined cooking techniques, *The New Sonoma Cookbook*™ is about better nutrition and getting both the science and the flavors right. It embraces the newest theories in food consumption, including the local food movement, which encourages us to eat and prepare food that is grown locally and in season. Eating locally is good for the environment,

supports local economies, nourishes our communities, and happens to taste delicious. There is great satisfaction in knowing where your food comes from.

Not surprisingly, learning to cook the Sonoma way has the added benefit of making it easy to lose weight and feel your best while enjoying delicious and satisfying meals. *The New Sonoma Cookbook*™ brings you a new repertoire of creative recipes bursting with flavor yet true to the principles of maintaining a healthy weight and body. Each bite captures the Golden State's wealth of epicurean richness—the coast's abundant seafood and local ingredients such as olive oil, berries, avocados, dates, figs, almonds, citrus, wine, and more. None of this requires drastic changes in our eating habits. In fact, by just changing a few of our shopping and cooking habits, we can improve our own health and the health of our communities and environment. We have more healthy choices available to us than ever. Where we choose to buy our food and how we choose to prepare it can make a positive difference in how we think about food and ultimately influence our well-being for years to come.

This cookbook includes more than 200 new recipes, tips, and seasonal variations for preparing your favorite meals. Also featured are *Sonoma Express* recipes for quick preparation, and a new concept, *Cook Once/Eat Twice* recipes, to make better use of your time. *Culinary Notes* and *Variations* will help you keep your meals fresh and interesting. There are also recipes for gluten-free eating and more family-style meals. The updated Smart Sonoma pantry and kitchen setup will help you stay organized and ready to make a delicious meal in minutes.

Many of these recipes were inspired by the talented chefs I have met as a nutrition instructor at the Culinary Institute of America at Greystone, my good fortune to live in the beautiful wine country of northern California, and the everyday life lessons I have gained from my family, children, and friends. I am especially excited to include a collection of recipes, "Taste of the Wine Country," from local chefs, restaurants, and wineries. I am sure you will agree that the Sonoma style of cuisine is varied, flavorful, healthy, yet amazingly quick and simple to prepare.

The new frontiers of nutrition look to an integrative, whole-body health approach to food and how it affects your mood. Nutrients and foods such as omega-3 fatty acids, dark chocolate, vitamin D, probiotics, whole grains, and wine continue to play an important role. Anti-inflammatory nutrients from colorful fruits and vegetables, nuts, seeds, and plant oils continue to top the lists with amazing benefits for heart health, anti-aging, and protection against Alzheimer's disease, diabetes, and even certain forms of cancer. With this in mind, I have increased the number of Sonoma Power Foods from ten to twelve, with citrus and beans as the new additions. Taking advantage of dream team combinations for these power foods is key to designing menus that make the most of your calories.

20% Whole Grains
30% Lean Protein
50% Colorful Vegetables

THE SONOMA SMART PLATE

The New Sonoma Cookbook™ is not about obsessive calculations or micromanaging the foods you eat each day. The Sonoma Smart Plate makes it easy to keep tabs on portions and eat the smartest combinations of the Sonoma Power Foods. The emphasis is a shift in focus, so that more vegetables and grains take center stage in the company of lean meats. A nine-inch plate would be divided into 30% lean protein, 20% whole grain, and 50% colorful vegetables—for example, a grilled shrimp salad with a citrus vinaigrette, served with colorful leafy greens and veggies with a whole-grain pita or half a cup of toasted quinoa.

A summary of the Sonoma Smart Plate is illustrated above to help you stay mindful of the choices and amounts of foods you will be eating with the new recipes you will be trying.

COOKING WITH WINE

Cooking with wine is a great way to enhance, accent, and intensify the flavors of any dish. Wine can release flavors in your food that otherwise would not be experienced. As with any seasoning, a careful balance to enhance and not overpower is important.

Wine has three main roles in cooking: as a marinade ingredient, as a cooking liquid such as in poaching, and as a sauce. To put it simply, as the alcohol in wine evaporates during cooking, the flavor remains and concentrates, leaving behind a pleasant acidity and sweetness. The amount of alcohol that remains in the dish depends on the manner and length of cooking. For example, after fifteen minutes of simmering wine, about 40% of the alcohol remains in the dish.

One of the most important rules in cooking is to use only wines that you would drink. An expensive wine is not necessary; there are many moderately priced good-quality wines. If you choose a wine of poor quality or one with unpleasant flavors, these will be intensified by cooking.

For best results, wine should not be added to a dish just before serving. The wine needs to simmer with the food or sauce to develop flavor and allow the alcohol to evaporate. Allow the wine to simmer for at least ten minutes before you add other liquids or seasonings to the sauce. Do not cook in aluminum or cast iron when cooking with wine. Stick with nonreactive cookware such as stainless steel and enamel.

Marinating with wine: Wine is a wonderful addition to marinade ingredients, which would typically include a vinegar, oil, and seasonings such as herbs and spices. Wine adds moisture to the meat while the acids and alcohol in wine help tenderize it.

Poaching with wine: When recipes call for water or broth as a cooking liquid, you can replace some of the water or broth with wine. Typically, you would select a dry white wine or sparkling wine as it is more subtle for this delicate way of cooking. One of my favorites for poaching seafood is to use white wine infused with fresh dill, basil, whole coriander seeds, and lemon juice. Keep in mind that poaching is a gentle cooking technique; the poaching liquid should not reach boiling temperatures.

Creating a sauce with wine: You can create an intense and complex sauce by deglazing with wine. Deglazing means loosening that wonderful layer of flavor left in a pan after meat has been sautéed or vegetables have been roasted. After removing the cooked meat from the pan, add wine to the remaining meat juices and caramelized bits. Heat uncovered over a low flame. Almost immediately, those bits of flavor become loose and the bottom of the pan clears. Cook long enough to reduce the volume by half. The flavors of the wine combine with these bits to produce a base for the sauce for the meat. The longer the liquid is cooked, the richer it becomes. Add stock or juice to the reduction to create a more flavorful sauce. This sauce can then be strained and adjusted for seasonings.

THE NEW TOP 12 SONOMA POWER FOODS

The first step to better nutrition is knowing what foods will give you the maximum amount of flavor and the widest array of health benefits. The recipes in this cookbook make good use of "power foods," a category that has expanded since the first edition of *The Sonoma Cookbook*. Many foods stack up as power foods, but these twelve are exceptionally beneficial, delivering maximum nutrition with minimal calories. As miraculous as these power foods are on their own, they become extraordinary when paired together to boost their protective health benefits. *The New Sonoma Cookbook*™ will show you how you can incorporate these foods into the meals you prepare everyday for yourself and your family.

Almonds provide the right combination of protein, fat, fiber, vitamins, and minerals to curb hunger and decrease heart disease. The dream team of almonds and dark chocolate provides a combination of protective nutrients known as antioxidants. Bring out the flavor, richness, and crunch of almonds the Sonoma way. Toast almonds for a few minutes in a warm oven or in a skillet on the stove. They make a great addition to almost any recipe.

Beans contain more protein and fiber than other vegetables. Beans are extremely versatile and easy to include in many recipes. They add color, texture, and richness to your favorite salads, dips, soups, and sauces.

The power of **bell peppers** is right in their beautiful colors—green, purple, red, yellow, and orange. Heart-healthy, cancer-preventive, sight-saving benefits abound with any of their hues. Roasting peppers is a perfect way to enjoy them. Place peppers on a sheet pan in a preheated 450°F oven. Bake until the skins brown. Rotate the peppers periodically for even browning. Once they're browned but not too soft, place them in a bowl and cover with plastic wrap or a towel so they steam for ten to fifteen minutes. This step will make it easier to peel the peppers. Peel the peppers; then cut in half lengthwise and remove the stems, ribs, and seeds.

Blueberries rank at the top of the fruit list for antioxidant content. Known for protecting your heart, blueberries also slow down and maybe even reverse the memory decline that comes with aging. Sweet blueberries dropped into whole-grain cereals, topped with nonfat yogurt, or added to salads are all great ways to eat more of this fruit. Purchase blueberries with a light "bloom" on them. This natural bloom is the blueberries' protection from the elements and is a sign that the blueberries are fresh.

Broccoli is one of the best sources of vitamin C and calcium. It is also known as a great detoxifier, clearing away potentially cancerous toxins. Broccolini, known as baby broccoli, is a cross between broccoli and Chinese kale. Cook this tasty green with your favorite extra-virgin olive oil, a bit of garlic, and some red pepper flakes, and finish it with a squeeze of fresh lemon juice and a pinch of kosher salt.

Citrus contains vitamin C to boost the immune system and decrease risks associated with cardiovascular disease, cancer, and stroke. Citrus fruits provide anti-inflammatory benefits and may even decrease high blood pressure. Maximize the health benefits of citrus by pairing it with other nutrient-rich ingredients: for example, lemon juice with green tea increases the staying power of the tea's antioxidants. Citrus fruits, at their peak in the winter months, add an enticing fragrance and introduce the palate to brightness, especially when the complement to heavy, rich ingredients. Use the juice and zest to add aroma and flavor to dishes. When selecting citrus, look for fruits that are heavy for their size.

The Romans and Greeks considered **grapes** a gift from the gods. The hillsides of northern California's wine country are covered with vineyards, their ripening fruit gleaming green and purple in the preharvest sun. Grapes deliver virtually all the nutrients that wine does. The deep blue and purple hues hint at the powerful antioxidants in their skins and seeds. Research suggests that these anti-inflammatory compounds promote strong hearts and healthy minds.

Extra-virgin olive oil is a staple of the Sonoma kitchen. Rich in monounsaturated fat and anti-inflammatory antioxidants, it provides health benefits beyond a healthy heart. Exciting research suggests a strong role in preventing obesity, type 2 diabetes, and Alzheimer's disease. "Extra-virgin" simply means that the oil comes from the first pressing of the olives and therefore retains the most beneficial nutrients and flavor compounds. It also has by far the most delicate and pleasing taste. Olive oils are delicate oils that are best used quickly after opening. Look for

A GLASS OF WINE encourages you to relax and savor your meal, a critical element of a healthy lifestyle. Compelling evidence finds that a glass of wine may be a powerful means of avoiding risk factors associated with heart disease, Alzheimer's disease, and diabetes. Wine drinkers tend to live longer, eat healthier foods, smoke less, and exercise more as part of their lifestyle.

bottles with a date on them, and purchase the most recent harvest available. Oils are usually pressed during the winter, so look for new oils in February. Once the bottle is opened, try to use olive oil within six months. Enemies of extra-virgin olive oil are heat, light, and oxygen, so store it in a cool cupboard, away from the light.

Spinach is especially rich in folate, calcium, vitamin K, and anti-inflammatory compounds that fight an array of diseases, including osteoporosis and Alzheimer's disease, and have more recently been linked with healthier eyes and better vision as we age. Use the small, tender leaves in salad and quick sautés, and the larger, tougher leaves for soups and braises.

The health-enhancing effects of **strawberries** are surpassed only by their taste! Rich in vitamin C and antioxidants, strawberries offer anti-inflammatory protection that decreases the risk for many different diseases. The best season for strawberries is late spring and early summer. Select strawberries that are a deep red color, with a shiny surface and bright green tops. Avoid fruit with white or green shoulders. If you are trying to eat locally and don't live in an area of the country where strawberries grow year-round, try freezing them or buy frozen berries so you can enjoy them every month.

Tomatoes are the pride of the kitchen, providing a base for countless recipes. Eat tomatoes fresh, canned, or as a sauce or paste. Heirloom tomatoes are a great way to experience the widest array of flavor profiles. All forms are rich in a powerful, protective

SONOMA POWER PAIRINGS

Mixing and matching the Sonoma Power Foods will enhance flavor as well as magnify health benefits. When you fill your plate with a rainbow of fruits and vegetables, the food acts synergistically to multiply each nutrient's health benefits. These plant-based power foods are part of the Sonoma whole-health approach to looking and feeling your best, including losing those extra pounds around your waist. Science is behind the scenes so you can focus on preparing easy, delicious meals full of flavor, without studying a textbook.

antioxidant, lycopene, which reduces the risk of several cancers. Lycopene is what gives the tomato its beautiful red color.

Whole grains contain all three parts of the grain: bran, endosperm, and germ. Whole grains reduce the risk of stroke, diabetes, heart disease, obesity, and certain cancers. Look for the many different choices of whole grains, including barley, buckwheat, bulgur, farro, oats, quinoa, wild rice, and other exotics like purple forbidden rice or Chinese red rice. I can't imagine a healthy way of eating that does not include an abundance of whole grains every day.

FOR MORE FLAVOR IN YOUR COOKING

Each recipe in *The New Sonoma Cookbook*™ is meant to give you more flavor and taste in your meals. Flavor and taste are actually two separate entities. Flavor is the aroma, texture, temperature, and often the beauty in foods. Taste is centered on the four sensations of bitter, sweet, salty, and sour. There is also a fifth taste, umami, which is described as the savory taste and satisfying quality of certain foods. Umami-rich ingredients give a fuller, richer depth of flavor to dishes. Use dried porcini or shitaki mushrooms, soy sauce, parmesan cheese, sun-dried tomatoes, anchovies, and prosciutto in recipes that call for slow cooking methods, such as braising. It is also helpful to use umami-rich ingredients when making broths and stocks for use in other recipes. When combined with other tastes, umami creates a synergy that enhances the other flavors in foods.

VINAIGRETTES

Salads can be a simple side dish in a meal or they can take center stage. Look to the seasons for inspiration for adding many different ingredients. In the summer, colorful fruits and delicate greens make for a refreshing and light salad. Try pears, green apples, persimmons, pomegranates, hazelnuts, and blue cheese in the fall, and citrus and bitter greens in the winter.

Oils and vinegars are the primary components of the salad's dressing. Explore the many different acidic components, from sherry vinegar, balsamic vinegar, and champagne vinegar to sweet muscat wine; and try the many flavorful infusions of plant oils beyond olive oil and nut oils. The Sonoma ratio of acid to oil in salad dressings is about 1 to 1 or 1 to 2.

There are some key techniques in making a delicious and smooth dressing. Pungent shallots, onions, or garlic can be combined with the vinegar and a pinch of salt. Allow them to macerate (also known as blooming)—that is, to sit in the vinegar for ten minutes to pickle slightly and add another layer of flavor to the dressing. Emulsifying the ingredients is another technique that will yield a smooth, well-blended dressing: Add the oil in a slow drizzle to the other dressing ingredients and whip the oil into the dressing with a wire whisk. You can add bean purees, mustard, or fruit purees to help emulsify as well.

The following ingredients will add interest and flavor to vinaigrettes:

Bright ingredients to add depth: diced shallots, finely diced red onions, scallions, snipped chives, pickled onions (with their juice)

Sharp and salty ingredients: capers, olives, green peppercorns, salty cheeses, miso

Pungent ingredients: grated fresh ginger, fish sauce, anchovies, Worcestershire sauce, black and white pepper, fresh garlic (mashed to paste or finely chopped)

Smoky ingredients: smoked Spanish paprika, roasted peppers (including the liquid), chipotle in adobo sauce (this also adds heat)

Spicy ingredients: fine dice of fresh red or green chiles: jalapeños, serranos, habaneros, Thai birds (remove the seeds and core for less heat), red chile flakes, sriracha hot sauce, Tabasco, Tapatio hot sauce

Rich ingredients: yogurt, buttermilk, cooked egg yolks, low-fat sour cream

Citrus: orange, lemon, lime, grapefruit, blood oranges, tangerines, tangelos. Citrus zest adds freshness and brightens flavors. Use a microplane to grate the zest of lemons, limes, grapefruits, oranges, and tangerines into finished dishes. Zest adds the aroma and flavor of citrus without the excessive acidity of the juice.

Nose-tingling ingredients: dry mustard, Dijon mustard, whole-grain mustard, horseradish, wasabi

Exotic ingredients: pomegranate molasses, preserved lemons, porcini or shiitake mushroom powders, ancho chile powder, saffron (for best extraction, warm saffron in a dry sauté pan, then add to acidic ingredient; let steep for 20 minutes)

Interest and spice: ginger, cumin, coriander, fennel (ground or crushed), paprika, curry powder

Bright and grassy ingredients: all fresh herbs

Sweet and fruity ingredients: fruit purees (mango, papaya, plum, peach), reduced fruit juices (grape, pomegranate, orange, grapefruit)

SALT SAVVY

The average American consumes about 4,000 milligrams of sodium a day (that's about two teaspoons of salt). Depending on your age, that's two or three times the amount recommended in U.S. dietary guidelines. Don't throw out the salt shaker yet, however. Used correctly, salt brings out the natural flavors of herbs and spices, the bright flavors of citrus, and the rich flavors of vegetables. Brined olives, strong-flavored cheeses, capers, and soy sauce can be used sparingly to add layers of flavors to complement their salty attributes.

You can also introduce your taste buds to a variety of salts beyond ordinary table salt. Kosher salt, for example, is a flaked salt that offers less sodium and more flavor than equal amounts of iodized (or table) salt. It has a clean taste and dissolves clearly in food. Sea salt (fleur de sel) is an unrefined salt that is obtained by evaporating sea water collected in man-made pools near a protected shoreline. It contains the minerals and trace elements that are refined out of table salt. With a slightly earthier taste than table salt, sea salt is ideal for salads, cooked fresh vegetables, and grilled meats. Gourmet salts like sel gris (gray salt), pink salt, and black salt get their color from various minerals found where the salts are mined. They can be used as finishing touches to infuse flavor into recipes without introducing a lot of sodium.

SONOMA MADE SIMPLE

COOK 1X · EAT 2X   The Cook Once/Eat Twice symbol alerts you to creative recipes that will provide planned leftovers to cover more than one meal. Wholesome, home-cooked meals take about ten minutes longer to prepare, on average, than serving processed or ready-made food. If you make enough for leftovers and follow our Sonoma recipe guidelines for Cook Once/Eat Twice, you will save time in the long run.

SONOMA EXPRESS   These recipes have fewer than 10 ingredients and can be completed in 30 minutes or less—including cooking time.

GLUTEN FREE   A variety of recipes feature whole grains, from quinoa and wild rice to buckwheat, for delicious, gluten-free options.

GOING GLYCEMIC

One of the exciting new features of this cookbook and *The New Sonoma Diet* ™ is the emphasis on the quality of the carbohydrate and those foods that slowly trickle blood sugar (glucose) into your bloodstream, thereby keeping your

energy levels up and your hunger under control. More importantly, choosing low glycemic foods helps your body lose those extra pounds around your waist and decreases your risk factors for inflammation, type 2 diabetes, and heart disease.

The rate at which your body converts food into blood sugar is measured by the glycemic index, which can be found with the other nutrition facts for each recipe; it is also identified by this symbol. The glycemic index, developed by the University of Sydney, is based on nearly thirty years of scientific experience. While counting numbers is not critical, it is useful to know the different ranges that the glycemic index uses to categorize these foods.

> Low glycemic index: 55 or less
> Medium glycemic index: 56 to 69
> High glycemic index: 70 or higher

Becoming familiar with the glycemic response of foods will help you make smarter choices within food groups. The idea is not for you to get too focused on the numbers, but rather have confidence that these recipes are designed with your best health in mind, using the best combinations of wholesome foods with low glycemic responses. The goal is not to eliminate carbohydrates and breads from your daily diet, but to include nutrient-rich choices of whole grains and colorful fruits and vegetables that will promote health and are linked with higher energy levels, satisfying meals, better sleep patterns, and happier moods.

COOKING VEGETABLES FOR PERFECTION

Sonoma cooking features a wide array of tasty, colorful vegetables. To get the most out of this abundance, buy local vegetables in season and use the appropriate cooking methods.

A natural and easy way to move forward to better health and weight control is to eat locally raised food harvested at the pinnacle of ripeness. Calorie for calorie, locally grown food may offer more nourishment and flavor than foods that have traveled thousands of miles around the globe.

The New Sonoma Cookbook™ offers versatile tips to include seasonal variations as substitutions in many recipes. A risotto, for example, might call for wild mushrooms and barley in the winter but offer summer variations with zucchini and tomatoes. Look for these helpful notes in many of the recipes and see how easy it is to expand a few menus into a lifetime of healthy eating.

In **spring**, choose artichokes, arugula, asparagus, beets, Blue Lake green beans, chard, morel mushrooms, mustard greens, peas, snap peas, snow peas, radishes, rhubarb, and zucchini.

In **summer**, go for basil, green beans, shell beans, berries, chard, corn, eggplant, melons, peppers, porcini mushrooms, stone fruits, summer squashes, and tomatoes.

In **fall**, your best choices are apples, green beans, lima beans, broccoli, broccoli rabe, Brussels sprouts, cabbages, cauliflower, celery root, chanterelle mushrooms, cranberries, fennel, figs, pears, persimmons, pomegranates, pumpkins, radicchio, tangerines, and winter squashes.

In **winter**, in-season produce includes broccoli, Brussels sprouts, cabbages, celery root, citrus, endive, escarole, collard greens, mustard greens, parsnips, radicchio, rutabaga, and winter squashes.

Each vegetable has its own distinct personality when it comes to cooking. Pairing the right vegetable with the right type of cooking method brings out the best flavor and texture. In many instances, cooking vegetables properly preserves their maximum nutrient benefits. For example, overcooking a stir-fried veggie can deplete delicate B and C vitamins. In other recipes, the slow roasting of carrots, sweet potatoes, and eggplant develops more flavor and natural sweetness without compromising their nutrient benefits.

The examples below suggest the best-performing veggies for the specific type of cooking to retain their best flavor, texture, and nutrition.

Stir-frying: bell peppers, broccoli, carrots, green beans, mushrooms, Napa cabbage, peas, scallions, snow peas, spinach, sugar snap peas, zucchini

Sauteing, stewing, or braising: bell peppers, chard, collard greens, fennel, eggplant, green beans, kale, leeks, mushrooms, mustard greens, summer squash, tomatoes

Crisp and raw: baby field greens: arugula, endive, radicchio, spinach; bell peppers, broccoli, carrots, celery, fennel, mizuna, summer squashes

Grilling and broiling: asparagus, chard, mushrooms, peppers, radicchio, sweet potatoes, tomatoes, zucchini

Roasting: asparagus, beets, carrots, corn, eggplant, mushrooms, onions, potatoes, pumpkins, squash, tomatoes, turnips

WHEN TO TOSS

Good for 6 months

- Baking soda and baking powder
- Nuts
- Nut butters
- Oil
- Rice

Good for 1 year

- Canned goods
- Dried beans
- Flour (stored in airtight containers)
- Grains (stored in airtight containers)
- Sugar
- Vinegar

THE SONOMA PANTRY

A smart pantry, stocked with wholesome grains and pastas, spices, beans, flavorful oils, different vinegars, and a few more pantry essentials, will make it easier to prepare delicious meals and snacks on even the busiest days of the week. Here is a starting point for the essentials to include in your Sonoma pantry.

ON THE SHELF

Artichoke hearts

Beans, canned, low-sodium (black beans, cannellini, garbanzo, kidney, pinto)

Broth, low-sodium (beef, chicken, vegetable)

Chipotle chiles in adobo sauce

Chunk light tuna

Tomatoes, diced, fire-roasted (a popular brand is Muir Glen)

Tomatoes, low-sodium (diced, whole, sauce, paste)

GRAINS AND FLOUR

Whole-wheat flour

Buckwheat flour

All-purpose flour

Oatmeal: old-fashioned and/or steel-cut oats

Whole-wheat bread crumbs

Bulgur wheat

Quinoa

Pearl barley

Lentils

Rice (brown, brown basmati, wild, and more)

Whole-wheat couscous

Whole-wheat pasta

Whole-wheat tortillas, corn tortillas

OILS AND VINEGARS

Extra-virgin olive oil (splurge on a really great-tasting oil to be drizzled as a flavor booster; cook with an average-priced oil)

Canola oil

Toasted sesame oil

Nonstick cooking spray

Balsamic vinegar

Cider vinegar

Red wine vinegar

Rice vinegar

Sherry vinegar

White wine vinegar (a favorite is muscatel sweet wine vinegar)

Flavored sea salts

SPICES AND DRY HERBS

Bay leaves

Chili powder

Coriander seed

Cumin seed

Curry powder

Dried mint

Dried oregano

Dried thyme

Fennel seeds

Ground allspice

Ground cinnamon

Paprika (try the smoked sweet paprika)

Whole nutmeg

Your favorite spice (also herb rubs or pastes)

DRIED FRUITS, NUTS AND SEEDS

Dried fruit (apricots, cherries, cranberries, raisins)

Assortment of shelled, unsalted nuts and seeds (almonds, peanuts, pine nuts, pistachios, walnuts, pumpkin seeds, sesame seeds, sunflower seeds)

Nut butters (almond, peanut)

SONOMA FLAVOR BOOSTERS

Canola mayonnaise

Inexpensive cooking wine

Low-sodium soy sauce

Salsa

Capers

Olives

Roasted red peppers

Parmesan cheese

Kosher salt

Coarse ground black pepper or peppercorns to grind

Prepared hummus

Prepared mustards

Prepared pesto

SWEETENERS

Agave syrup

Brown sugar

Dark chocolate (60–70 percent cocoa solids)

Honey

Maple syrup

Sugar

Unsulfured molasses

Unsweetened cocoa powder

PERISHABLES

Basil

Cilantro

Garlic

Italian parsley

Lemons

Onions

Shallots

Eggs

Plain nonfat yogurt

Milk

FREEZER

Fruit (berries and peaches)

Assorted vegetables (artichoke hearts, corn, lima beans, peas, spinach, squash, pureed squash)

Shrimp

Shelled edamame

RULES OF THE KITCHEN

- Set up your cooking station and have everything within reach—knives, ingredients, containers for all cut ingredients, and a place for waste.

- Gather and measure all ingredients before you start to cook.

- Place a damp towel underneath your cutting board to keep it from sliding on the counter.

- Write a prep list of what you are cooking and the order in which you need to prepare it. Start with the items that will take the most amount of time. If you have to cook pasta or blanch vegetables, place a covered pot of water on the stove first. Preheat the oven if necessary.

- Place your ingredients on a tray in the order that they go in the pan.

- Keep your work area free of clutter. Once you cut something, place it in a container and move it off the cutting board.

- As you are cooking, wash dishes and keep the sink area clear.

SONOMA KITCHEN ESSENTIALS

Knives: Good knives are worth splurging on. Look for knives made of high carbon steel and forged, meaning that the metal has been compressed and formed into its shape. Choose a six-, eight-, or ten-inch chef's knife (depending on the size of your hands) for slicing meats and poultry and chopping vegetables, nuts, and herbs. Use a three- to four-inch paring knife for smaller, more precise tasks that require greater control (peeling, cutting, and carving fruit; mincing herbs or garlic; scoring meat), and use a serrated knife for slicing bread and tomatoes.

Mandolin: This machine easily slices, juliennes, and waffle-cuts vegetables.

Food processor: Great for chopping vegetables faster than a knife, grating hard cheeses, emulsifying dressings, pureeing soups, and kneading pizza dough. Select one that has a heavy base and a large tub. Attachments can be added for other functions, such as juicing and whipping.

Steaming basket

Good-quality pots and pans: Heavy-bottomed pans prevent burning. The best have a copper or an aluminum core that goes all the way up the sides for quick and even heating. Interiors can range from stainless steel to nonstick surfaces.

To get started, you will need two- and four-quart saucepans, an eight- to ten-inch skillet, and a twelve- to fourteen-inch skillet. A two- to three-quart sauté pan is a nice addition, but you can get away with using a large skillet with a lid for poaching fish. You will use your two-quart saucepan for sauces and small batches of vegetables or rice; your four-quart saucepan for soups, stews, steaming vegetables, and cooking pasta. If you are buying pieces separately, you have the flexibility to pick and choose from a wide variety. I would suggest also getting a small nonstick skillet (for omelets) and a regular larger skillet (for getting a nice sear on meats and fish).

Meat thermometer, measuring spoons and cups, cookie sheets

Blender: A powerful blender is versatile and effective for a wide range of uses.

Immersion blender: Hand-held immersion blenders do double or even triple duty, blending soups and smoothies, chopping fruits and vegetables, even whipping egg whites or heavy cream. They allow you to work right in the prep bowl or cooking pot, without dirtying additional bowls or equipment. Look for one with a push-button control for continuous or pulsed action.

Gratin dish: This shallow round or oval dish is used to cook thin layers of foods in the oven at high temperatures. It can be made of anything from enameled cast iron to glazed ceramic to metal.

Grilling tools: Every grill chef should own a set of grilling tools. Tongs, spatulas, brushes, fish baskets, vegetable grill baskets, and gloves will get you started.

THE SONOMA WAY

EAT WHOLESOMELY . . . by choosing natural, unprocessed foods. The more a food is processed, the more nutrients and natural flavors are lost.

EAT SEASONALLY . . . because the growing seasons can inspire your menus and give you flavorful rewards.

EAT LOCALLY & SUSTAINABLY . . . as much as possible. Just knowing where your food comes from and how it's produced makes you a more mindful eater.

EAT WITH A GLASS OF WINE . . . because, unless you don't drink alcohol at all, a glass of wine enhances your enjoyment of a healthy meal, is heart-friendly in and of itself, and embodies the Sonoma spirit.

BREAKFAST

Start the morning by adding these delicious quiches, stratas, and frittatas to your everyday favorites of eggs, whole grains, and fruits. Many of these recipes include different variations using fabulous seasonal ingredients or simply your own creative touch. Sonoma omelets, Oatmeal Pancakes with Blueberry Compote, and a Yogurt and Fruit Parfait with crunchy Crumble Topping are just a few to try.

Oatmeal Pancakes
with Blueberry Compote

A favorite in my home on Sunday mornings are these whole-grain pancakes
with blueberries—although you can use any other seasonal berries.
Whole grains in the morning are known to satisfy hunger and provide
key nutrients to keep your blood sugars in healthy ranges.
These are some of the best pancakes I have ever had.

Start to Finish: 30 minutes   Yield: 4 servings, 2 pancakes each

½	cup oat flour
¼	cup brown rice flour
2	teaspoons baking powder
¼	teaspoons kosher salt
½	teaspoon ground cinnamon
1½	cups cooked oatmeal, slightly warm (gluten-free)
½	cup milk (or soy milk, for dairy-free pancakes)
1	tablespoon agave syrup
1	teaspoon vanilla
2	eggs, beaten well
	Nonstick pan spray as needed
	Blueberry Compote (following page)

CULINARY NOTES

- These are moist, dense pancakes with the texture of creamy oatmeal in the center.

- If you are making your own oat flour, place dry oatmeal in a spice grinder or blender and grind until dust.

- If the oatmeal is hot, adding the cold milk will cool it slightly.

- If using leftover oatmeal, microwave it until it is just warm to the touch.

- It is important to have the dry ingredients mixed and ready because when the eggs are added to the oatmeal mixture, they will start to cook. If the eggs are just poured in without stirring, they will start to cook and scramble.

1. Preheat pancake griddle on medium.

2. Combine oat flour, rice flour, baking powder, salt, and cinnamon. Set aside.

3. Combine oatmeal, milk, agave syrup, and vanilla. Stir in beaten eggs. Stir in dry ingredients.

4. Spray the griddle with nonstick pan spray. Pour ¼ cup batter on griddle in a 4-inch circle. Let sit until bubbles start to appear on top and the bottoms are golden brown. Flip pancakes and cook 1 minute on other side. Serve hot topped with Blueberry Compote.

Variations

- Add ½ cup chopped ripe bananas, blueberries, or raspberries.
- Serve with ½ cup fresh blueberries or strawberries and ¼ cup plain nonfat yogurt.

Nutrition Facts per Serving: 250 calories, 8 g protein, 5 g total fat (1 g saturated fat), 32 g carbohydrate, 3.5 g fiber, 90 mg cholesterol, 400 mg sodium, 52 weighted glycemic index

Blueberry Compote

Fruit compote, a dessert dating back to the seventeenth century, is made from fruit gently cooked over low heat until it becomes a thick, rich sauce. There are many creative ways to flavor a compote, such as different fruits, vanilla, orange peel, and cinnamon. Add this compote to yogurts, baked goods, even pancakes. This blueberry recipe has much less sugar than traditional jams and even more natural blueberry fruit flavor.

Start to Finish: 15 minutes   Yield: 2 cups, 8 servings, ¼ cup each

1½	cup blueberries, frozen
½	cup water
2½	tablespoons agave syrup
½	teaspoon vanilla extract
1	pinch salt
½	teaspoon lemon juice
1	teaspoon cornstarch
2	teaspoons water

1. Combine blueberries, ½ cup water, agave syrup, vanilla, and salt in a small saucepan. Bring to a low simmer. Cook 5 minutes or until the water takes on a rich purple color and the blueberries are warmed through. Stir in lemon juice.

2. In a small bowl, combine cornstarch and 2 teaspoons water. Stir into the blueberries. Bring to a low simmer; cook for 1 minute. If it is too thin, add a little more cornstarch mixed with water.

CULINARY NOTES

- Do not boil the blueberries or cook too long or they will burst.

- The cornstarch and water mixture is called a slurry. It's an easy way to quickly thicken a sauce. It must be stirred just before adding because the two ingredients separate when left to sit. Stir slurry into a simmering liquid, stirring constantly. If it is poured into a hot sauce without stirring, it can form lumps.

Variations

- Replace frozen blueberries with fresh blueberries. Cook for less time.

- Replace half of the blueberries with raspberries.

- Replace three-quarters of the blueberries with peeled, chopped nectarines or mangos.

Nutrition Facts per Serving: 45 calories, 0 g protein, 0 g total fat, (0 g saturated fat), 12 g carbohydrate, 1 g fiber, 0 mg cholesterol, 20 mg sodium

Sautéed Broccoli and Red Onion Scramble

Eggs happen to be one of the most versatile ingredients in your kitchen. You will be surprised by the great flavors of this recipe when you prepare eggs with broccoli. Another great opportunity to start your day with a nutrient-rich meal loaded with vitamins, antioxidants, fiber, and protein.

Start to Finish: 30 minutes   Yield: 4 servings

1	tablespoon extra-virgin olive oil	1	tablespoon water
½	cup red onions, sliced thin	2	teaspoons garlic, chopped
2	cups broccoli florets, cut in ½-inch to ¾-inch pieces	8	eggs, beaten
2	tablespoons low-sodium soy sauce	2	tablespoons scallions, sliced thin

1. Heat olive oil in a 10-inch nonstick pan over medium heat. Add red onions and sauté until golden brown. Add broccoli and cook for 5 minutes, stirring to brown slightly. Add soy sauce and water. When the water has evaporated, add the garlic and cook 30 seconds.

2. Stir in eggs and continue to cook until the eggs are soft and creamy. Stir in scallions. Adjust seasoning.

Variation

- Replace broccoli with sliced mushrooms; add ½ cup chopped red peppers.

CULINARY NOTE

- The soy sauce and water cause the broccoli to steam quickly without becoming too brown.

- For a vegan version, replace the eggs with 1 pound firm tofu broken into chunks.

Nutrition Facts per Serving: 198 calories, 14 g protein, 13 g total fat (3.5 g saturated fat), 6 g carbohydrate, 2 g fiber, 400 mg cholesterol, 300 mg sodium, 11 weighted glycemic index

Canadian Bacon and Egg Pockets

Enjoy this simple sandwich-style breakfast and you'll meet both your grain and protein recommendations to start your morning off right. Canadian-style bacon is a lean alternative to bacon, yet gives the dish intensified flavor.

Start to Finish: 15 minutes   *Yield: 4 servings*

4 egg whites	Nonstick cooking spray
2 eggs	2 ounces reduced-fat cheddar cheese, shredded (½ cup) (optional)
3 tablespoons water	2 large whole-wheat pita bread rounds, cut in half
⅛ teaspoon kosher salt	
3 ounces Canadian bacon, chopped	
2 tablespoons sliced scallions (optional)	

1. In a medium bowl combine egg whites, eggs, water, and salt. Beat with a wire whisk or rotary beater until well mixed. Stir in Canadian bacon and, if desired, scallions.

2. Lightly coat an unheated large nonstick skillet with nonstick cooking spray. Preheat over medium heat. Add eggs to skillet. Cook, without stirring, until mixture begins to set on the bottom and around edges.

3. Using a spatula or a large spoon, lift and fold the partially cooked eggs so the uncooked portion flows underneath. Continue cooking for about 2 minutes or until eggs are cooked through but still glossy and moist. Remove from heat immediately. Fold in cheese.

4. Open pita halves to form a pocket. Fill pita halves with eggs.

CULINARY NOTE

For more tender eggs, replace water with 3 tablespoons low-fat or nonfat milk.

Variations

Smoked Salmon and Asparagus

Replace Canadian bacon with smoked salmon, chopped in 1-inch pieces. Add 1 cup cooked asparagus, cut in ½-inch pieces. Replace cheddar cheese with low-fat cream cheese cut in ½-inch cubes; fold in just before placing in pita breads.

Artichoke, Roasted Peppers, and Feta

Replace Canadian bacon with 1 cup sliced artichoke hearts, ½ cup diced roasted red peppers, and 1 tablespoon chopped basil. Replace cheddar cheese with feta cheese; fold in just before placing in pita breads.

Nutrition Facts per Serving: 200 calories, 18 g protein, 6 g total fat, (2 g saturated fat), 19 g carbohydrate, 2.5 g fiber, 120 mg cholesterol, 300 mg sodium, 57 weighted glycemic index

Yogurt and Fruit Parfait

This is a quick and easy recipe with layers of healthy colors and flavors. It's sure to be a favorite with your kids, especially on busy mornings or as an after-school snack.

Start to Finish: 15 minutes   Yield: 1 serving

½ cup assorted cut-up fruit and berries
   Light drizzle of agave syrup (optional)
   Pinch salt

½ cup nonfat plain yogurt
2 tablespoons toasted Crumble Topping (following page)

1. Combine fruit, agave syrup, and salt in a bowl. Let sit for 5 minutes.

2. Place ¼ cup of the fruit in the bottom of a parfait cup. Add ¼ cup yogurt and 1 tablespoon crumble topping. Repeat layers, finishing with the crumble topping.

Variation

• Toss fruit with ¼ teaspoon vanilla or a sprinkle of cinnamon or dark chocolate mini chips.

CULINARY NOTE

Use a combination of raspberries, blueberries, strawberries, mango, peach, pineapple, nectarine, grapes, figs, banana, or any seasonal fruit.

Nutrition Facts per Serving: 175 calories, 9 g protein, 6 g total fat (3 g saturated fat), 25 g carbohydrate, 4 g fiber, 2.5 mg cholesterol, 90 mg sodium, 26 weighted glycemic index

Crumble Topping

Wholesome oatmeal, almonds, and a touch of brown sugar and cinnamon make for a wonderful crumble that is delicious baked on winter fruits like apples and pears or your favorite summer berries. Its crisp bite is a nice combination with almost any fruit. Use it to top your favorite pies or baked muffins or simply add to yogurt.

Start to Finish: 30 minutes   Yield: 2¼ cups, 20 servings, 2 tablespoons per serving

2	tablespoons brown sugar	¼	teaspoon ground cinnamon
½	cup almonds	1	pinch salt
2	cups oatmeal, old-fashioned style	4	tablespoons coconut oil
4	tablespoons oat bran		Parchment paper

1. Preheat oven 325°F.

2. Place brown sugar and almonds in a spice grinder or food processor. Grind to a fine powder. Combine almond mixture, oatmeal, oat bran, cinnamon, and salt. Stir in coconut oil until well distributed. Leave clumps.

3. At this point you can either bake the mixture and use as a topping or leave uncooked and bake on a crumble or fruit. If you bake it now, place mixture in a parchment-lined sheet pan. Bake in preheated oven for 8 minutes, stirring periodically for even browning. Cool.

CULINARY NOTE

Grinding the almonds with sugar prevents them from becoming almond butter.

Variations

- Replace oat bran with wheat bran.
- Replace coconut oil with safflower oil or canola oil.
- This recipe will be gluten-free if you use gluten-free oats and oat bran.

Nutrition Facts per Serving: 90 calories, 2 g protein, 6 g total fat (3 g saturated fat), 9 g carbohydrate, 2 g fiber, 0 mg cholesterol, 0 mg sodium, 13 weighted glycemic index

Omelet

Once you have the technique for making light and fluffy omelets, it becomes easy to try different flavor variations. You will never get bored with this recipe.

Start to Finish: 15 minutes   Yield: 4 servings

8 large eggs, beaten	2 cups vegetable filling (see filling variations on the next pages)
2 tablespoons milk	Nonstick cooking spray as needed
2 teaspoons butter	Salt and pepper to taste
2 tablespoons parmesan cheese	

1. Combine eggs and milk. Season well with salt and pepper.

2. Heat a nonstick 8-inch egg pan over medium-low heat. Spray well with nonstick cooking spray and add ½ teaspoon butter. Let butter melt; then pour in 2 ounces of eggs (approximately 2 eggs). Tilt pan to evenly distribute the eggs. Stir gently for 30 seconds as the eggs start to set; then spread over the bottom of the pan in an even layer. Sprinkle with parmesan cheese.

3. Spread warm filling on one side of the eggs. When the eggs are just set and a little runny, fold the side of the egg without the filling over the side with the filling. Slide onto a warm plate.

CULINARY NOTES

- Cook the omelet over medium-low heat to keep the eggs tender and moist. Use any of the frittata fillings for the omelets.

- To make the omelets even lighter, use a total of 6 egg whites and two whole eggs. Whip the eggs to add even more volume and lightness to the omelets.

Nutrition Facts per Serving: 175 calories, 14 g protein, 13 g total fat (5 g saturated fat), 2 g carbohydrate, 5 g fiber, 350 mg cholesterol, 200 mg sodium, 15 weighted glycemic index

Artichoke and Red Pepper

Start to Finish: 30 minutes   Yield: 4 servings

1	tablespoon olive oil
¼	cup red onion, julienne
1½	cup artichoke hearts, frozen, thawed
2	teaspoons garlic, chopped
½	cup roasted red peppers, diced
1	tablespoon basil, chopped
	Salt and pepper to taste

1. Heat a sauté pan over medium-high heat. Add olive oil, red onion, and artichokes. Season with salt and pepper. Sauté until slightly brown.

2. Add garlic and red peppers. Cook until garlic is aromatic. Stir in basil.

3. Use filling in omelet; fold over and serve.

Nutrition Facts per Serving: 240 calories, 15 g protein, 15 g total fat (5 g saturated fat), 11 g carbohydrate, 6 g fiber, 430 mg cholesterol, 250 mg sodium, 17 weighted glycemic index

Broccoli, Oven-Dried Tomatoes, and Feta

Start to Finish: 30 minutes   Yield: 4 servings

1	tablespoon olive oil
2	cups broccoli, broken into small florets
1	tablespoon water
1	tablespoon garlic, chopped
½	cup Oven-Dried Tomatoes (page 263), diced
1	tablespoon oregano
2	ounces feta cheese, crumbled
	Salt and pepper to taste

1. Heat a sauté pan over medium-high heat. Add olive oil and broccoli. Season with salt and pepper. Sauté until slightly brown; add water and let steam.

2. Add garlic and tomatoes. Cook until garlic is aromatic. Stir in oregano.

3. Use filling in omelet; top with feta cheese and fold over.

Nutrition Facts per Serving: 270 calories, 18 g protein, 18 g total fat (6 g saturated fat), 9 g carbohydrate, 2.5 g fiber, 430 mg cholesterol, 265 mg sodium, 26 weighted glycemic index

Smoked Salmon and Green Onion

Start to Finish: 30 minutes   Yield: 4 servings

4   ounces smoked salmon, sliced thin (2 slices per omelet)

¼   cup scallions, sliced thin

4   tablespoons low-fat cream cheese
    Black pepper to taste

1. Place salmon on one half of the eggs in the pan.

2. Sprinkle with scallions and top with cream cheese. Sprinkle with black pepper. Fold over and serve.

Nutrition Facts per Serving: 275 calories, 19 g protein, 15 g total fat (6 g saturated fat), 3 g carbohydrate, 1 g fiber, 440 mg cholesterol, 450 mg sodium, 6 weighted glycemic index

Southwest Omelet

Start to Finish: 30 minutes   Yield: 4 servings

1   tablespoon extra-virgin olive oil

½   cup red onions, diced

½   cup green pepper, diced

1   tablespoon garlic, chopped

1   tablespoon chile powder

½   cup tomatoes, chopped

1   cup black beans, canned, drained

1   tablespoon cilantro, chopped

2   ounces cheddar cheese, crumbled
    Salt and pepper to taste

1. Heat a sauté pan over medium-high heat. Add olive oil, red onion, and green pepper. Season with salt and pepper. Sauté until slightly brown.

2. Add garlic and chile powder; cook until aromatic. Stir in tomatoes and beans. Adjust seasoning with salt and pepper. Finish with chopped cilantro.

3. Use filling in omelet; top with cheddar cheese and fold over.

Nutrition Facts per Serving: 280 calories, 20 g protein, 16 g total fat (6 g saturated fat), 15 g carbohydrate, 5 g fiber, 430 mg cholesterol, 410 mg sodium, 23 weighted glycemic index

Southwest Breakfast Strata

The word "strata" refers to many layers. This multilayered, brightly colored dish is loaded with flavor boosters to give your taste buds a wake-up call.

Start to Finish: 40 minutes   Chill: 4 to 24 hours   Yield: 6 servings

Nonstick olive oil cooking spray

6 slices rustic country-style whole-grain bread

6 eggs

2 tablespoons canned diced green chile peppers

⅛ teaspoon freshly ground black pepper

2 slices Canadian bacon, cut into thin strips, or ½ cup chopped cooked ham

2 Roma tomatoes, thinly sliced

2 ounces reduced-fat Monterey Jack cheese, shredded (½ cup)

1 tablespoon chopped fresh cilantro

1. Lightly coat a 2-quart rectangular baking dish with nonstick cooking spray. Cover the bottom of the dish with bread slices, cutting to fit.

2. In a medium bowl, whisk together eggs, chile peppers, and black pepper until well mixed. Pour eggs evenly over bread. Sprinkle with Canadian bacon or ham. Top with tomato slices and cheese. Cover and refrigerate 4 to 24 hours.

3. Preheat oven to 350°F. Bake, uncovered, about 25 minutes or until a knife inserted near center comes out clean. Sprinkle with cilantro.

CULINARY NOTES

- Letting the strata sit for at least 4 hours allows the eggs to soak into the bread, giving the strata a custardy texture, similar to a bread pudding.

- For a more tender strata, add ¼ cup low-fat or nonfat milk.

Nutrition Facts per Serving: 245 calories, 15 g protein, 9 g total fat (3 g saturated fat), 25 g carbohydrate, 3 g fiber, 220 mg cholesterol, 420 mg sodium, 70 weighted glycemic index

Variations

Summer Strata

Replace green chiles, tomatoes, Monterey Jack cheese, and cilantro with the following ingredients: 1 cup mushrooms sautéed with 1 teaspoon garlic; 1 cup sautéed zucchini, cut in quarters lengthwise, then cut in ¼-inch pieces; ¼ cup sliced scallions; ½ cup cream cheese; and ½ cup cheddar cheese.

Broccoli and Cheddar Strata

Replace tomatoes with 1 cup cooked, drained broccoli florets (½-inch pieces). Replace cilantro with parsley, thyme, basil, or oregano.

Mediterranean Breakfast Strata

Replace green chiles, tomatoes, Monterey Jack cheese, and cilantro with 1 cup roasted eggplant (½-inch pieces); ½ cup diced roasted red peppers; ½ cup feta cheese; and 1 tablespoon chopped basil or oregano.

Winter Vegetable Strata

Replace green chiles and tomatoes with 1 cup leftover roasted vegetables (butternut squash, carrots, parsnips, or potatoes). Replace cilantro with parsley, thyme, rosemary, or oregano.

Asparagus, Ham, and Swiss Strata

Replace green chiles, tomatoes, Monterey Jack cheese, and cilantro with 1 cup chopped cooked asparagus, ¼ cup chopped scallions, ½ cup Swiss cheese, and 1 tablespoon chopped thyme, parsley, and tarragon.

CULINARY NOTES

- If preparing the frittata for a party, you can finish the cooking in a 350°F oven. Make sure you are using a nonstick pan with a metal handle. After you have whisked the eggs in step #2, add the artichokes and cheese. Pour the eggs into the pan with the shrimp and lift the edges so the uncooked portion flows underneath a couple of times; place the frittata in the oven and bake for 10 minutes or until the center is cooked through.

- For a more tender frittata, stir 1 tablespoon low-fat or nonfat milk into the eggs.

Shrimp-Artichoke Frittata

Add some crustacean character to your basic frittata by including shrimp,
a great source of tryptophan and selenium.

Start to Finish: 25 minutes   Yield: 4 servings

4 ounces fresh or frozen shrimp in shells	⅛ teaspoon garlic powder
Kosher salt	⅛ teaspoon freshly ground black pepper
Freshly ground black pepper	Nonstick olive oil cooking spray
½ 9-ounce package of frozen artichoke hearts	3 tablespoons finely shredded parmesan cheese
8 eggs	Sliced scallions (optional)
¼ cup nonfat or low-fat milk	Fresh flat-leaf parsley (optional)
¼ cup thinly sliced scallions	

1. Thaw shrimp, if frozen. Peel and devein shrimp. Rinse shrimp; pat dry with paper towels. Halve shrimp lengthwise; season with kosher salt and pepper. Set aside. Meanwhile, cook artichoke hearts according to package directions; drain. Cut artichoke hearts into quarters; season lightly with kosher salt and pepper. Set aside.

2. In a large bowl, whisk together eggs, milk, ¼ cup scallions, garlic powder, and ⅛ teaspoon pepper; set aside.

3. Lightly coat an unheated large nonstick skillet with nonstick cooking spray. Preheat over medium heat. Add shrimp to hot skillet; cook for 1 to 3 minutes or until shrimp are opaque. Reduce heat to medium-low.

4. Pour eggs into skillet; do not stir. As eggs set, run a spatula around the edge of the skillet, lifting eggs so uncooked portion flows underneath. Continue cooking and lifting edges until eggs are almost set (surface will be moist).

5. Remove skillet from heat; sprinkle artichoke pieces evenly over the top. Sprinkle with parmesan cheese. Cover and let stand for 3 to 4 minutes or until top is set. Loosen edge of frittata. Transfer to a serving plate; cut into wedges to serve. If desired, garnish with additional sliced green onions and fresh parsley.

Spring Frittata

Replace shrimp with 1 cup asparagus sliced in ½-inch pieces and ½ cup diced red peppers; sauté in oil until tender. Add ½ cup defrosted peas, quartered artichokes, and 1 tablespoon chopped parsley. Pour eggs into skillet and continue with the recipe.

Roasted Red Pepper, Spinach, Caramelized Onions, and Feta Cheese

Replace shrimp with 1 cup julienne onions; sauté over medium heat until golden brown. Add ½ cup diced roasted red peppers and 2 cups baby spinach or chopped spinach. Sauté until wilted. Drain excess liquid in a colander. Return to sauté pan. Add eggs; when eggs start to set, sprinkle in teaspoon-size pieces of feta cheese (¼ cup total). Cook until eggs are set.

Nutrition Facts per Serving: 210 calories, 21 g protein, 11 g total fat (4 g saturated fat), 5 g carbohydrate, 2 g fiber, 450 mg cholesterol, 300 mg sodium, 22 weighted glycemic index

Tomato and Basil Frittata

Loaded with nutrients and phytochemicals, this egg-based dish includes basil, a key herb in Mediterranean cooking, for enhanced flavor.

Start to Finish: 25 minutes   Yield: 2 servings

5 egg whites	1 cup chopped fresh spinach
1 egg	2 scallions, sliced
1 tablespoon chopped fresh basil or ½ teaspoon dried basil, crushed	1 clove garlic, minced (½ teaspoon minced)
⅛ teaspoon kosher salt	1 small tomato, chopped
Dash freshly ground black pepper	1 ounce reduced-fat cheddar cheese, shredded (¼ cup)
Nonstick olive oil cooking spray	

1. Preheat oven to 350°F. In a medium bowl, lightly beat together egg whites and whole egg. Stir in basil, kosher salt, and pepper; set aside.

2. Coat an unheated 8-inch oven-going skillet with nonstick cooking spray. Preheat the skillet over medium heat. Add spinach, scallions, and garlic. Cook for 1 to 2 minutes or until spinach begins to wilt. Remove skillet from heat; drain, if necessary.

3. Pour eggs over spinach in the skillet. Bake for 6 to 8 minutes or until eggs are set. Sprinkle with chopped tomato and cheese. Bake for 1 to 2 minutes more or until the cheese melts. Cut the frittata into wedges to serve.

Variation

Broccoli, Canadian Bacon, and Cheddar Frittata

Replace spinach with 1 cup blanched broccoli florets. Heat a sauté pan over medium heat. Add chopped garlic and 1 teaspoon olive oil; sauté until aromatic. Add broccoli and ½ cup chopped Canadian bacon; sauté until warmed through. Pour in eggs and continue with the recipe.

Nutrition Facts per Serving: 130 calories, 18 g protein, 4 g total fat (1.5 g saturated fat), 6 g carbohydrate, 1.5 g fiber, 110 mg cholesterol, 400 mg sodium, 16 weighted glycemic index

Tomato and Asparagus Pizza

With this unique dish, flash back to the days when pizza for breakfast was commonplace. The inclusion of tomatoes, asparagus, garlic, and herbs means you get plenty of vitamins and beneficial phytochemicals.

Start to Finish: 20 minutes   *Makes: 6 servings*

1 12-inch whole-wheat Italian bread shell (such as Boboli brand)	1 cup fresh asparagus bias-cut into 1-inch pieces
1 tablespoon grated parmesan cheese	1 clove garlic, minced (½ teaspoon minced)
6 eggs	1 tablespoon extra-virgin olive oil
⅓ cup low-fat milk	1 large tomato, halved and sliced
2 teaspoons chopped fresh tarragon or oregano	Chopped fresh tomato (optional)
⅛ teaspoon kosher salt	Chopped fresh tarragon (optional)
⅛ teaspoon freshly ground black pepper	

1. Preheat oven to 450°F. Place bread shell on a 12-inch pizza pan. Sprinkle with parmesan cheese. Bake for 8 to 10 minutes or until heated through.

2. Meanwhile, in a medium bowl beat together eggs, milk, 2 teaspoons tarragon, kosher salt, and pepper.

3. In a large nonstick skillet, cook asparagus and garlic in hot oil over medium heat for 3 minutes. Pour eggs over asparagus in skillet. Cook over medium heat, without stirring, until mixture begins to set on the bottom and around the edge.

4. Using a spatula, lift and fold the partially cooked eggs so the uncooked portion flows underneath. Continue cooking for 2 to 3 minutes or until eggs are cooked through but still glossy and moist. Remove from heat immediately.

5. Arrange tomato slices evenly around the edge of the baked bread shell. Spoon scrambled egg mixture in the center. If desired, garnish with additional chopped tomato and tarragon. Cut into wedges; serve immediately.

Nutrition Facts per Serving: 250 calories, 13 g protein, 10 g total fat (2.5 g saturated fat), 27g carbohydrate, 2 g fiber, 212 mg cholesterol, 390 mg sodium, 53 weighted glycemic index

Southwest Breakfast Pizza

CULINARY NOTE

Toasting the bread shell until golden brown prevents it from becoming soggy once the tomatoes are placed on top.

Omit tarragon and asparagus. Add 1 to 2 teaspoons chile powder to egg mixture. Sauté 2 tablespoons chopped green chiles, 1 tablespoon chopped garlic, ¼ cup chopped scallions, and ½ cup drained black beans. Add egg mixture and cook until just set; add ½ cup cheddar cheese. Garnish with fresh tomato salsa, or chopped tomatoes and cilantro with lime juice.

Smoked Salmon and Asparagus Breakfast Pizza

Fold in ½ cup smoked salmon cut in ½-inch pieces and ¼ cup sliced scallions when the eggs are almost done.

Crustless Feta and Cheddar Quiche

The mingling of cheeses in this savory quiche gives it a full, rich flavor you'll want to let linger on your taste buds.

Start to Finish: 65 minutes   Yield: 8 servings

Nonstick olive oil cooking spray	⅛ teaspoon kosher salt
4 beaten eggs	1½ cups low-fat cottage cheese (12 ounces)
⅓ cup whole-wheat pastry flour	
4 cloves garlic, minced (2 teaspoons minced)	1 10-ounce package frozen chopped broccoli, cooked and drained
1 tablespoon chopped fresh dill, thyme, or mint	1 cup crumbled feta cheese (4 ounces)
¼ teaspoon freshly ground black pepper	1 cup shredded reduced-fat cheddar cheese (4 ounces)

1. Preheat oven to 350°F. Lightly coat a 9-inch pie plate with cooking spray.

2. In a medium bowl combine eggs, pastry flour, garlic, dill, pepper, and kosher salt. Stir in cottage cheese, broccoli, feta, and cheddar. Spoon into the prepared pie plate.

3. Bake for 40 to 45 minutes or until a knife inserted near center comes out clean. Cool on a wire rack for 5 to 10 minutes before serving.

CULINARY NOTE

The quiche will be easier to cut once it is allowed to rest for 5 to 10 minutes after removing from the oven.

Nutrition Facts per Serving: 350 calories, 34 g protein, 15 g total fat (8 g saturated fat), 16 g carbohydrate, 4 g fiber, 245 mg cholesterol, 900 mg sodium, 42 weighted glycemic index

Variations

Spinach, Roasted Pepper, and Feta

Replace dill with basil. Replace broccoli with 10 ounces cooked, drained spinach, squeezed dry. Add ½ cup diced roasted red pepper; omit cheddar cheese.

Artichoke and Sun-Dried Tomato

Replace dill with oregano. Replace broccoli with 10 ounces cooked artichoke hearts. Add 2 tablespoons Sun-Dried Tomato Pesto (page 392) and replace cheddar cheese with 1 cup diced fresh mozzarella cheese.

Roasted Red Pepper, Caramelized Onions, and Goat Cheese

Replace dill with basil. Replace broccoli with 1 cup roasted red peppers and 2 cups caramelized onions. Replace feta cheese with goat cheese; replace cheddar with grated mozzarella.

Roasted Vegetable

Replace dill with parsley. Replace broccoli with 10 ounces of cooked leftover roasted vegetables.

SOUPS, SALADS, SANDWICHES

Sonoma-inspired ideas for a really great lunch start with tempting, wholesome soups, colorful salads brimming with crunchy fresh produce and nuts, and many varieties of grains and sandwiches packed with flavorful ingredients. Look to our COOK 1X · EAT 2X ideas for easy-to-make lunch menus the entire family will enjoy.

Black-Eyed Pea, Smoked Turkey, and Chard Soup

Black-eyed peas are lucky to eat for the New Year's Eve celebration; they are also a good source of folic acid, fiber, and protein. These are important nutrients to keep you healthy and strong any time of the year.

Start to Finish: 75 minutes   Yield: 12 servings, 1 cup each

1	tablespoon olive oil	1	bay leaf
2	cups onions, chopped	7	cups water
1	cup celery, chopped	7	cups low-sodium chicken stock
1	cup carrots, chopped	8	ounces smoked turkey leg
1	tablespoon garlic, chopped	4	cups chard, chopped
1	tablespoon thyme, chopped		Salt to taste
1	14.5-ounce can of diced tomatoes		Ground black pepper
1	pound black-eyed peas, rinsed		

1. Heat large soup pot over medium heat. Add olive oil, onions, celery, and carrots. Sauté over low heat until translucent. Add garlic and thyme and cook until aromatic.

2. Add tomatoes, peas, bay leaf, water, chicken stock, and turkey leg; bring to a simmer and cook until the peas are tender, but still hold their shape, about 1 hour.

3. Remove the turkey leg; remove the bone and chop the meat. Add chard and chopped turkey to soup. Season with salt and pepper.

Variations

- Replace thyme with oregano.
- Replace chard with spinach.

CULINARY NOTES

- Cook the peas until they have lost their starchy flavor, but still hold their shape.

- Season the soup at the end of the cooking. Salt toughens the skin coat on beans.

Nutrition Facts per Serving: 225 calories, 18 g protein, 4 g total fat (1 g saturated fat), 30 g carbohydrate, 5.5 g fiber, 15 mg cholesterol, 350 mg sodium, 29 weighted glycemic index

Carrot Soup

Indulge in this Asian-inspired soup with a velvety finish to its rich flavors. It also happens to be an excellent source of beta carotene. Using a hand blender gives it a creamy texture and makes preparing this soup very easy.

Start to Finish: 50 minutes   *Yield: 4 servings, 1 cup each*

1 teaspoon extra-virgin olive oil	1 teaspoon red curry paste
¼ cup onion, sliced	1 tablespoon lemon grass, chopped
½ teaspoon garlic, chopped	1 cup coconut milk
½ teaspoon ginger, chopped	1 tablespoon fish sauce
¼ pound carrots, peeled, sliced thin	1 tablespoon lime juice
½ cup low-sodium chicken stock	1 tablespoon cilantro, chopped
1 tablespoon canola oil	Salt and pepper to taste

1. Heat a small saucepan. Add olive oil and onion; cook over low heat until translucent. Add garlic and ginger; cook until aromatic. Add carrots and chicken stock. Bring to a simmer. Cook for 20 minutes or until the carrots are tender.

2. Drain off ¼ cup of liquid. Set aside.

3. Puree the remaining carrots and liquid until smooth. Set aside.

4. Heat a 1-quart saucepan over medium heat. Add canola oil, curry paste, and lemon grass. Cook 1 minute or until aromatic. Add reserved carrot liquid, carrot puree, and coconut milk. Bring to a simmer. Cook for 10 minutes.

5. Stir in the fish sauce and lime juice. Adjust seasoning with salt and pepper. Garnish with cilantro.

Nutrition Facts per Serving: 175 calories, 2.5 g protein, 7 g total fat (5 g saturated fat), 7 g carbohydrate, 1.5 g fiber, 0 mg cholesterol, 400 mg sodium, 50 weighted glycemic index

Chicken, Pear, and Walnut Salad

This lively salad is great for using up any leftover chicken you might have on hand and tempting enough that you'll gladly make a trip to the grocery store for more. Champagne vinegar lends mild delicacy to the dressing while Dijon mustard adds tang.

Start to Finish: 30 minutes   Yield: 6 servings

12	ounces cooked chicken breast, shredded	2	tablespoons chopped fresh basil
4	cups torn mixed greens	2	tablespoons chopped fresh mint
4	cups torn arugula leaves	¼	cup champagne vinegar
4	ounces provolone cheese, cut into thin strips, or 2 ounces Gorgonzola cheese	2	tablespoons extra-virgin olive oil
		1	tablespoon Dijon mustard
2	medium-ripe pears, cored, halved, and thinly sliced	⅔	cup chopped walnuts, toasted
		2	scallions, thinly sliced

1. In a very large bowl, combine chicken, greens, arugula, cheese, pear slices, basil, and mint. Set aside.

2. In a screw-top jar, combine champagne vinegar, olive oil, and mustard. Cover and shake well. Drizzle over chicken mixture. Toss to coat. Top individual servings with walnuts and scallions.

Variations

- Replace pears with Asian pears or apples.
- Replace pears with figs.
- Replace champagne vinegar with red wine vinegar.

CULINARY NOTE

If possible, slice the pears just before serving so they do not discolor. If you have to slice the pears in advance, rinse them in a mixture of 1 tablespoon lemon juice to 2 cups water. Do not soak the slices in the lemon water or they will lose their flavor.

Nutrition Facts per Serving: 345 calories, 25.5 g protein, 20 g total fat (5 g saturated fat), 17 g carbohydrate, 4 g fiber, 60 cholesterol, 280 mg sodium, 31 weighted glycemic index

Creamy Broccoli Soup

White beans give this soup a rich and creamy texture without all the cream. This soup just happens to provide a dream team combination of two Sonoma Power Foods: beans and broccoli.

Start to Finish: 45 minutes   Yield: 4 servings, 1 cup each

2 cups broccoli florets	3 cups low-sodium chicken stock
1 tablespoon extra-virgin olive oil	1 bay leaf
1 cup onion, chopped	1 teaspoon thyme, chopped
½ cup celery, chopped	½ cup canned white beans, drained
1 teaspoon garlic, chopped	1 tablespoon sour cream
1 cup broccoli stems	

1. Fill a mixing bowl halfway with ice and enough water to cover it. Bring a pot of water to a boil and cook the broccoli florets until they're tender. Using a slotted spoon, transfer the florets from the pot to the ice bath. Remove when they're cold, in about 1 minute. Set aside.

2. Heat a soup pot over medium heat. Add olive oil, onion, and celery. Cook for 4 minutes until translucent. Add garlic and cook until aromatic. Add broccoli stems and cook for 10 minutes over low heat until soft.

3. Add chicken stock, bay leaf, thyme, and beans. Bring to a simmer.

4. Add broccoli florets. Simmer for 5 minutes or until warm.

5. Remove bay leaf. Pour soup into blender and blend until completely smooth. Adjust seasoning and stir in sour cream.

Nutrition Facts per Serving: 145 calories, 9 g protein, 5.5 g total fat (1.2 g saturated fat), 18 g carbohydrate, 4 g fiber, 1.5 mg cholesterol, 95 mg sodium, 21 weighted glycemic index

Barley Minestrone Soup

Take time to savor this version of the Italian classic.
A delightful blend of fresh herbs, vegetables, ham, and barley,
this soup will satisfy your soul as well as your stomach.

Start to Finish: 75 minutes   Yield: 6 servings

2 tablespoons extra-virgin olive oil	1 ½ cups sliced carrots
2 cups chopped onion	2 tablespoons chopped fresh flat-leaf parsley
6 cloves garlic, minced (1 tablespoon minced)	2 teaspoons chopped fresh marjoram
1 tablespoon chopped fresh rosemary	2 teaspoons chopped fresh oregano
1 cup sliced celery	1 tablespoon lemon juice
1 cup chopped cooked ham (about 5 ounces)	2 tablespoons shredded parmesan cheese
¾ cup regular barley (not quick-cooking), rinsed	Cracked or freshly ground black pepper
8 cups reduced-sodium chicken broth or chicken stock	

1. In a 4- to 6-quart Dutch oven, heat oil over medium heat. Add onion; cook until lightly golden brown, stirring occasionally. Add garlic and rosemary; cook and stir for 1 minute. Add celery, ham, and uncooked barley; cook for 4 minutes, stirring occasionally.

2. Add chicken broth. Bring to boiling; reduce heat. Cover and simmer for 30 minutes. Stir in carrots, parsley, marjoram, and oregano. Cover and simmer for 15 to 20 minutes more or until carrots and barley are tender.

3. Stir in lemon juice. Sprinkle individual servings with parmesan cheese and cracked pepper.

CULINARY NOTE

As the barley cooks, it will absorb liquid and give the soup a rich, creamy texture. Thin the soup if necessary during the simmering with chicken or vegetable stock or water.

Variations

- Replace ham with leftover roasted chicken. Add 1 cup defrosted frozen peas, 1 teaspoon lemon zest, and 1 pinch chile flakes at the end of cooking.

- Add 2 cups baby spinach leaves at the end of cooking.

Nutrition Facts per Serving: 260 calories, 16.5 g protein, 9.5 g total fat (2.2 g saturated fat), 30 g carbohydrate, 6 g fiber, 15 mg cholesterol, 250 mg sodium, 21 weighted glycemic index

Tuscan Tomato and Bread Soup

This soup has such a rich, delicious base that you'll think it was made from cream. But it's really made from pureed tomatoes and vegetables. The bread makes a fun, crunchy topper.

Start to Finish: 1 hour   Yield: 6 servings

1 tablespoon extra-virgin olive oil	1 tablespoon extra-virgin olive oil
3 pounds fresh tomatoes, cored and coarsely chopped, or three 14 ½ ounce cans diced tomatoes, undrained	4 cups chopped zucchini and/or yellow summer squash
12 cloves garlic, minced (2 tablespoons minced)	2 tablespoons chopped fresh oregano
¼ to ½ teaspoon crushed red pepper	2 tablespoons chopped fresh flat-leaf parsley
2 14-ounce cans chicken broth	Kosher salt
6 slices whole-grain bread	Freshly ground black pepper
	1 ounce parmesan cheese, shaved

1. In a 4-quart Dutch oven, heat 1 tablespoon olive oil over medium heat. Reserve 1 cup of the chopped fresh tomatoes or, if using canned tomatoes, reserve 1 can of tomatoes. Add remaining fresh tomatoes or undrained canned tomatoes, garlic, and crushed red pepper to hot oil in Dutch oven. Bring to boiling; reduce heat. Cover and cook for 15 to 20 minutes or until tomatoes are very tender, stirring occasionally. Add chicken broth. Bring to boiling; reduce heat. Cover and simmer for 15 minutes. Cool slightly.

2. Meanwhile, preheat oven to 350°F. Cut or tear bread into 1-inch pieces. Place in a shallow baking pan. Bake for 10 to 15 minutes or until toasted, stirring occasionally. Set aside.

3. In a large skillet, heat 1 tablespoon olive oil over medium heat. Add zucchini; cook for 3 to 5 minutes or until lightly browned and crisp-tender. Set aside.

4. Transfer half of the tomato and broth mixture to a blender or food processor. Cover and blend or process until smooth.

Repeat with remaining half of the mixture. Return all to Dutch oven.

5. If using canned tomatoes, drain the reserved can. Add reserved fresh or canned tomatoes, the cooked zucchini, oregano, and parsley to pureed mixture. Season to taste with kosher salt and pepper. Heat through.

6. Divide soup among six soup bowls. Top with bread pieces; garnish with cheese.

Variations

- Replace the zucchini with hearty greens such as chard or kale. Simmer the soup until the greens are tender.

CULINARY NOTES

- Use day-old whole-grain bread for this recipe—the more rustic and hearty the bread, the better. Tearing the bread by hand gives it a rustic appearance. Make sure that the bread is well toasted and dry. This keeps it from becoming too soggy in the soup.

- A favorite way to serve this soup is to place the bread in the bottom of the bowl and sprinkle it with grated parmesan cheese. Pour the soup on top and finish with a drizzle of extra-virgin olive oil.

WINE SUGGESTION: *Sauvignon blanc*

Nutrition Facts per Serving: 270 calories, 11.5 g protein, 9.5 g total fat (2 g saturated fat), 39 g carbohydrate, 6.5 g fiber, 3 mg cholesterol, 280 mg sodium, 55 weighted glycemic index

Wild Rice Chicken Soup

This easy-to-make, hearty soup uses an abundance of tomatoes. Cooking them enhances their sweetness and activates their cancer-preventing properties.

Start to Finish: 75 minutes   Yield: 6 servings, 1 cup each

½ cup wild rice	2 cups chopped cooked chicken breast
2 cups water	1 cup finely chopped zucchini
½ cup long-grain brown rice	¼ teaspoon freshly ground black pepper
2 14-ounce cans chicken broth	1 tablespoon chopped fresh thyme
4 cloves garlic, minced (2 teaspoons minced)	1 tablespoon Madeira or dry sherry (optional)
4 cups chopped fresh tomatoes or two 14 ½-ounce cans diced tomatoes, undrained	

1. Rinse wild rice well; set aside. In a large saucepan, bring the water to boiling. Add wild rice and brown rice. Return to boiling; reduce heat. Cover and simmer for 40 to 45 minutes or until rice is tender and most of the liquid is absorbed. Remove from heat; set aside.

2. Meanwhile, in a 4-quart Dutch oven, combine chicken broth and garlic; bring to boiling. Stir in tomatoes, chicken, zucchini, and pepper. Return to boiling; reduce heat. Cover and simmer for 5 minutes. Stir in cooked rice, thyme, and, if desired, Madeira. Heat through.

WINE SUGGESTION: *Cabernet sauvignon*

Nutrition Facts per Serving: 230 calories, 22 g protein, 3.5 g total fat, (0 g saturated fat), 30 g carbohydrate, 3 g fiber, 40 mg cholesterol, 85 mg sodium, 37 weighted glycemic index

Variations

Latin-Style Soup

Stir in 1 teaspoon chipotle in adobo sauce with the garlic. Finish soup with 1 tablespoon chopped cilantro and 1 tablespoon lime juice.

Wild Rice Chicken Soup with Pesto

Add 2 tablespoons pesto and 1 teaspoon lemon zest at the end. Finish with a teaspoon of red wine vinegar or lemon juice.

- Wild rice is actually a grass, not a rice. It requires quite a bit of water to cook, so if the rice is not tender and the water has evaporated, add more water. You can always drain off the excess. Wild rice can also be cooked by the pasta method: in a large pot of simmering water, add the wild rice and simmer until tender. Drain off excess liquid.

- Soaking the brown rice and wild rice in water will expedite the cooking process. Rinse the rice varieties separately and place each in a large bowl. Add water to cover by 3 times. Cover and let sit for several hours or overnight. Drain the liquid and add the rice to recipes as required.

Creamy Vegetable Soups

Start to Finish: 45 minutes   *Yield: 8 servings, one cup each*

1 tablespoon extra-virgin olive oil	3 cups low-sodium chicken stock or vegetable stock
1 cup onion, chopped	1 bay leaf
½ cup celery, chopped	1 teaspoon thyme
1 teaspoon garlic, chopped	1 teaspoon mint
1 teaspoon ginger, chopped	½ cup canned white beans, drained
3 cups vegetables, peeled, chopped (see variations following)	1 tablespoon sour cream, cream, or silken tofu (optional)

CULINARY NOTES

- Green vegetables such as broccoli, asparagus, spinach, peas, and greens will discolor after prolonged cooking. In soups using these vegetables, the tender part of the vegetables (asparagus tips and broccoli florets, peas, leafy greens) should be added during the last 10 minutes of cooking, cooked until just wilted, and then pureed in the soup.

- If the green vegetables are cooked too long or with a lot of acid (lemon, vinegar, tomatoes), they will become olive green in color. To retain their bright green color, use lemon zest to add flavor and finish with a tiny bit of lemon juice just before serving.

- When pureeing the soup, do not fill the blender container more than halfway and start it on low, gradually turning up the speed. Hold the blender lid in place using a towel underneath your hand. If you start the blender on high, the soup may spray out of the top and burn your hand. Puree the mixture until completely smooth, with no visible particles. For the creamiest texture, strain the soup through a mesh strainer after blending. Use a small ladle to push the soup through the strainer. If the soup comes out watery with a lot of particles left in the strainer, reblend everything again until the soup is smoother.

Nutrition Facts per Serving: 95 calories, 4.5 g protein, 2.5 g total fat (.5 g saturated fat), 15 g carbohydrate, 2.5 g fiber, 0 mg cholesterol, 45 mg sodium, 21 weighted glycemic index

1. Heat a soup pot over medium heat. Add olive oil, onion, and celery. Cook for 4 minutes until translucent. Add garlic and ginger; cook until aromatic. Add choice of vegetables; cook for 20 minutes on low heat until soft and tender.

2. Add chicken stock, herbs, and beans. Bring to a simmer. Simmer for 10 minutes or until warm. Remove bay leaf. Pour soup into blender and blend until completely smooth. Adjust seasoning and stir in sour cream.

Long-Cooking Vegetables

Cut these vegetables into 1-inch pieces. They should be added after the aromatics and cooked until they are tender, about 25 minutes depending on size of cut.

VEGETABLE	AROMATIC	SPICES / HERBS
Carrots	ginger	cinnamon
Carrots	ginger	lemon and mint
Cauliflower	ginger	garam masala or curry
Cauliflower	ginger	lemon, parsley
Celery root	garlic	parsley, thyme, bay leaf
Fennel	garlic	thyme, fennel seeds, lemon, finish with pesto
Sweet potatoes	ginger	cinnamon, or ginger and chai spice, lemon, and mint
Beets	orange and mint, finish with orange salsa	
Roasted eggplant	garlic	cumin and cilantro or parsley
Mushrooms	garlic, deglaze with madeira	thyme and parsley
Mushrooms	garlic and chile	cilantro and lime
Butternut squash	ginger	cinnamon and parsley
Butternut squash	ginger	soy sauce, lemon and parsley
Butternut squash	ginger, garlic, chile	curry powder and coriander, cilantro and lemon
Garlic	lemon and parsley	

Medium-Cooking Vegetables

Cut these vegetables into 1-inch pieces. The fibrous stems of these vegetables can be cooked with the onions. The tender parts (broccoli florets, asparagus tips) should be blanched and added after the stock has simmered for 15 minutes and cooked until they are tender, about 10 minutes.

VEGETABLE	AROMATIC	SPICES / HERBS
Asparagus	garlic	nutmeg, parsley
Asparagus	leek or shallot	tarragon
Artichokes, fresh	garlic	pesto, mint, basil
Broccoli	garlic	nutmeg, finish with sun-dried tomato pesto (page 392)
Celery	garlic	savory or rosemary, lemon
Tomatoes	garlic	basil
Tomatoes	garlic	sherry, thyme
Corn	garlic	cumin, cilantro, finish with salsa
Red or yellow peppers	garlic	cumin, cilantro
Red or yellow peppers	garlic	basil, lemon

Short-Cooking Vegetables

Cut these vegetables into 1-inch pieces.
They should be added after the aromatics and cooked briefly.

VEGETABLE	AROMATIC	SPICES / HERBS
Peas	leek or shallot	mint, lemon zest
Greens: spinach, chard	garlic, chiles	parsley, chives, tarragon, sorrel
Peppers, roasted	garlic, chiles	basil, lemon

Summer Squash Soup

The delicate flavor, soft shell, and creamy white flesh of summer squash make a perfect addition to any summer meal. Once only available in the summer, summer squash are now available throughout the year; however, between May and July, when they are in season, they are at their best and most readily available. Summer squash is an excellent source of vitamin C, another reason to enjoy this wonderful soup.

Start to Finish: 30 minutes   Yield: 4 servings, 1 cup each

1 tablespoon extra-virgin olive oil	1 pinch chile flakes
1 cup onions, diced	5 cups low-sodium chicken stock
1 tablespoon garlic, chopped	1 cup chard, cut in 1-inch pieces
4 cups yellow squash or zucchini	1 tablespoon Italian parsley, chopped
1 cup tomato, diced	Salt and pepper to taste

1. Heat a 2-quart saucepan over medium heat. Add extra-virgin olive oil, onions, and garlic. Sauté for about 5 minutes, or until the onions are slightly brown. Add squash or zucchini and sauté for 1 minute. Add tomato and chile flakes; sauté 5 minutes.

2. Add chicken stock and simmer for 10 minutes or until the squash is tender and the flavors meld.

3. Stir in chard; simmer 5 minutes. Season with salt and pepper. Add parsley.

WINE SUGGESTION: *Chardonnay*

Nutrition Facts per Serving: 125 calories, 8.5 g protein, 5.5 g total fat (1 g saturated fat), 14 g carbohydrate, 3 g fiber, 0 mg cholesterol, 115 mg sodium, 9 weighted glycemic index

Lentil Soup with Brown Rice

This warming soup is deliciously topped with a sprinkling of
Asiago cheese. Named after Asiago, Italy, the town
where it was developed, it adds rich, nutty flavor.

Start to Finish: 1 hour   Yield: 6 servings

3 tablespoons extra-virgin olive oil	2 cups chopped tomato
1 cup chopped onion	¾ cup dry brown lentils, rinsed and drained
1 cup chopped celery	1 tablespoon lemon juice
6 cloves garlic, minced (1 tablespoon minced)	¼ teaspoon freshly ground black pepper
1 tablespoon chopped fresh thyme	2 tablespoons finely shredded Asiago cheese
1 tablespoon chopped fresh oregano	Fresh thyme sprigs and/or oregano leaves
8 cups reduced-sodium chicken broth or chicken stock	
½ cup long-grain brown rice	

1. In a 4-quart Dutch oven, heat olive oil over medium heat. Add onion, celery, garlic, and herbs; cook about 5 minutes, stirring occasionally, until vegetables are tender. Stir in broth and raw brown rice. Bring to boiling; reduce heat. Simmer, uncovered, for 10 minutes. Stir in tomato and lentils. Return to boiling; reduce heat. Cover and simmer about 30 minutes more or until rice and lentils are tender.

2. Stir in lemon juice and pepper. Top individual servings with Asiago cheese and, if desired, thyme sprigs and/or oregano leaves.

Variations

- Replace chopped tomatoes with canned tomatoes.

- Finish with 1 tablespoon chopped fresh parsley.

- For a spicier version, add 1 teaspoon chopped chipotle in adobo sauce.

Nutrition Facts per Serving: 285 calories, 15.5 g protein, 10 g total fat (2 g saturated fat), 36 g carbohydrate, 9.5 g fiber, 2 mg cholesterol, 140 mg sodium, 32 weighted glycemic index

CULINARY NOTES

- Cook the soup until the lentils are tender without a starchy taste and the broth has thickened slightly.

- Thyme and oregano are considered resinous herbs. These herbs are best added at the beginning of the cooking and infused into the oil.

Manhattan-Style Chowder

Tomato-based clam chowders came about with the new-found popularity of the tomato in the mid-1800s and the large population of Italians in New York and the Portuguese fishing communities of Rhode Island. By the 1930s, this tomato version had come to be called Manhattan clam chowder. This is a much lighter and nutrient-rich version of the cream-based New England clam chowder.

Start to Finish: 45 minutes   Yield: 4 servings, one cup each

1 tablespoon bacon, chopped	1 tablespoon thyme, chopped
1 cup onions, diced	1 cup potatoes, diced into ½-inch pieces
1 cup celery, diced	2 cups low-sodium chicken stock
½ cup carrots, diced	2 10-ounce cans chopped clams and juice
1 cup green bell peppers, chopped	1 shake Tabasco sauce
2 tablespoons garlic, chopped	1 shake Worcestershire sauce
2 cups canned tomatoes, chopped	Salt and pepper to taste
2 cups tomato puree	
1 bay leaf	

1. Heat a saucepan over medium-high heat. Add bacon and cook until browned and fat has rendered.

2. Add onions, celery, carrots, green pepper, and garlic. Sauté for 5 minutes or until the onions are tender.

3. Add tomatoes, tomato puree, bay leaf, and thyme. Bring to a simmer.

4. Add potatoes and chicken stock; simmer until potatoes are tender.

5. Stir in clams and juice; bring to a simmer to warm through. Remove from heat; season with Tabasco sauce, Worcestershire sauce, salt, and pepper.

Nutrition Facts per Serving: 400 calories, 44.5 g protein, 6.5 g total fat (1.5 g saturated fat), 42 g carbohydrate, 6.5 g fiber, 98 mg cholesterol, 400 mg sodium, 40 weighted glycemic index

Variation

- Use 1½ pounds fresh clams. Rinse the clams well; soak in fresh water for 1 hour. Change the water and rinse well. This helps the clams purge sand. Place the clams, 1 clove chopped garlic, and ¼ cup water in the pot. Cover tightly and simmer until the clams open. Remove clams from the shells. Strain liquid through cheesecloth and use in place of clam juice or chicken stock.

WINE SUGGESTION: *Chardonnay*

Spicy Cauliflower Soup

This rich, creamy cauliflower soup is serious comfort food on a cold winter night. It is a much lighter and healthier version of the creamy potato soup.

Start to Finish: 1 hour   Yield: 8 servings, 1 cup each

4 cups cauliflower, chopped into florets	¼ teaspoon turmeric
1 tablespoon canola oil	1 teaspoon chile powder
1 cup onion, chopped	1 pinch chile flakes
½ cup celery, chopped	3 cups low-sodium chicken stock
2 teaspoons ginger, chopped	¼ cup nonfat plain yogurt
½ teaspoon ground cumin	1 tablespoon cilantro, chopped
½ teaspoon ground coriander	Salt, pepper, and lemon juice to taste

1. Bring a small pot of water to a boil. Blanch ½ cup cauliflower florets until tender. Shock in an ice bath for 30 seconds. Reserve for garnish.

2. Heat a saucepan over medium heat. Add oil, onion, celery, and the rest of the cauliflower. Cook until translucent, about 5 minutes. Add ginger and spices; cook until aromatic. Add chicken stock and bring to a simmer. Cook for 20 minutes or until the cauliflower is tender. Stir in the yogurt and adjust seasoning.

3. Place soup in blender and blend until smooth. If the soup is too thick, add a little more hot chicken stock. Add reserved cauliflower as garnish and heat to warm. Stir in cilantro.

Variations

- Replace cauliflower with parsnips or winter squash, such as butternut squash or acorn squash.

- Replace cauliflower with carrots.

- The thickness of the soup is determined by the proportions of cauliflower to water. Because sizes of cauliflower vary, add water to the soup to get the thickness and creaminess you are looking for.

WINE SUGGESTION: *Chardonnay*

CULINARY NOTE

When pureeing the soup, do not fill the blender container more than halfway, and start it on low, gradually turning up the speed. Hold the blender lid in place using a towel underneath your hand. If you start the blender on high, the soup may spray out of the top and burn you. Puree the mixture until completely smooth, with no visible particles. For the creamiest texture, strain the soup through a mesh strainer after blending. Use a small ladle to push the soup through the strainer. If the soup comes out watery with a lot of particles left in the strainer, blend everything again until smoother.

Nutrition Facts per Serving: 65 calories, 4 g protein, 3 g total fat (.5 g saturated fat), 7.5 g carbohydrate, 2 g fiber, 0 mg cholesterol, 65 mg sodium, 11 weighted glycemic index

The Gigi Salad

This is my daughter's favorite salad! She loves the bright colors, flavors, and interesting ingredients, especially the tangy, jeweled pomegranate seeds, delicious California avocado, and crunchy jicama. This is an easy salad to prepare and looks fantastic on the plate. Serve with a flatbread and you have a complete meal that anyone would love to make their favorite too.

The Dietary Guidelines for Americans now recommend that Americans double the amount of fruits and vegetables they currently eat. This recipe is loaded with fruits and vegetables, including California avocado, which is a fruit, naturally sodium- and cholesterol-free, contributing good fats (3 grams of mono- and 0.5 gram of polyunsaturated fat per 1-ounce serving) to your diet. People who eat generous amounts of fruits and vegetables as part of a healthy diet are likely to have reduced risk of chronic diseases, including stroke, type 2 diabetes, some types of cancer, and perhaps even heart disease and high blood pressure. With those benefits in mind, enjoy The Gigi Salad and here's to your health!

Start to Finish: 30 minutes   Yield: 4 servings

2 cups hearts of palms, sliced	¼ cup scallions, thinly cut on the bias
2 cups orange segments	2 cups butter lettuce, cut into strips ½ inch x 2 inches
1 cup jicama, julienne	
1 pound shrimp, peeled and cooked	4 flatbreads (Whole-Wheat Pizza Dough for Flatbreads, page 282)
½ cup Citrus Vinaigrette (page 385)	
½ cup pomegranate seeds	2 tablespoons slivered almonds, toasted
1 California avocado, cut in quarters lengthwise, then in ¼-inch pieces	Salt and pepper to taste

Nutrition Facts per Serving (includes the flat bread and dressing): 530 calories, 35 g protein, 12 g total fat (2 g saturated fat), 75 g carbohydrate, 13 g fiber, 220 mg cholesterol, 600 mg sodium, 50 weighted glycemic index

1. Combine hearts of palm, oranges, jicama, and shrimp in a bowl. Toss with salt and pepper. Dress with 4 tablespoons Citrus Vinaigrette.

2. Gently mix in pomegranate seeds, avocado, scallions, and lettuce. Adjust seasoning.

3. Serve on top of a warm whole-wheat flatbread. Garnish with toasted almonds.

CULINARY NOTE

Vary the ingredients to make this a seasonal favorite. Use oranges and pomegranates in the winter. In the summer, replace oranges with mango, peach, or nectarines. Replace pomegranates with radishes.

Variations

- Use raw shrimp, sautéed over high heat in a nonstick pan with a little oil. Deglaze with 2 tablespoons Citrus Vinaigrette.
- Replace shrimp with chicken breast cut in strips.

Grilled Watermelon Salad

with Prosciutto

A unique salad that combines the sweetness of watermelon with the mellow saltiness of prosciutto. A great salad to entertain with in the summer time.

Start to Finish: 30 minutes   Yield: 4 servings

2 pounds watermelon, peeled, cut in 8 wedges, each 1 inch thick	1 ounce prosciutto, shaved, cut in ¼-inch-wide strips
1 tablespoon extra-virgin olive oil	2 ounces parmesan cheese, shaved
1 tablespoon balsamic vinegar	1 ounce toasted, sliced almonds
3 cups arugula	Salt and pepper to taste

1. Preheat a hot grill.

2. Season the watermelon with salt and pepper. Grill over high heat to mark the watermelon, but not cook it. It should still be cool in the center of the slice. Chill.

3. Combine the extra-virgin olive oil and balsamic vinegar. Toss with the arugula.

4. Place 2 wedges of watermelon on a plate. Top with a portion of the arugula. Top with prosciutto and parmesan cheese. Sprinkle with almonds.

Variations

- Serve with figs, cut in half and grilled.
- Drizzle with a little fig or agave syrup if desired.

WINE SUGGESTION: *Sauvignon blanc*

CULINARY NOTES

- When grilling the watermelon, use a hot grill. You want to give the smoky, charred flavor of the grill to the watermelon without cooking it. Chill it immediately after grilling to stop the cooking.

- The prosciutto should be sliced as thinly as possible. You want to give only a hint of meat and salt. It will be more delicate when it is thinly sliced.

Nutrition Facts per Serving: 220 calories, 10 g protein, 12 g total fat (3.5 g saturated fat), 25 g carbohydrate, 2.7 g fiber, 18 mg cholesterol, 400 mg sodium, 64 weighted glycemic index

Sonoma Chicken Salad in Lettuce Cups

Tender shredded chicken breasts and California veggies marinated in a
tangy red wine vinaigrette take on tremendous flavor. When served on top
of a leaf of lettuce and sprinkled with parmesan cheese,
this simple salad becomes an elegant entrée.

Start to Finish: 30 minutes   Chill: 1 to 24 hours   Yield: 6 servings

4 cups coarsely shredded cooked chicken breast (about 1¼ pounds)	2 tablespoons chopped fresh flat-leaf parsley
1 15-ounce jar roasted red and yellow bell peppers, drained and cut into strips	2 tablespoons capers, rinsed and drained
1 6-ounce jar marinated artichoke hearts, drained and coarsely chopped	1 recipe Red Wine Vinaigrette (below)
¼ cup thinly sliced red onion	6 large butterhead (Bibb or Boston) lettuce leaves
¼ cup chopped almonds, toasted	2 ounces parmesan cheese, shaved

1. In a large bowl, combine chicken, roasted bell peppers, artichoke hearts, red onion, almonds, parsley, and capers. Drizzle with Red Wine Vinaigrette; toss gently to coat. Cover and chill for 1 to 24 hours.

2. To serve, place a lettuce leaf on each of six dinner plates. Spoon chicken salad onto lettuce leaves. Sprinkle with Parmesan cheese.

RED WINE VINAIGRETTE: In a small bowl, combine 2 tablespoons red wine vinegar and 1 tablespoon finely chopped shallot. Let stand for 5 minutes. Whisk in 1½ teaspoons Dijon mustard. Add 2 tablespoons extra-virgin olive oil in a thin, steady stream, whisking constantly until combined. Stir in ⅛ teaspoon kosher salt and ⅛ teaspoon freshly ground black pepper. Makes about ⅓ cup.

Variations

- Toss the cooked chicken with 1 tablespoon pesto or Sun-Dried Tomato Pesto (page 392).
- Replace chicken with sliced cooked pork tenderloin.

Asian Chicken Salad in Lettuce Cups

Replace artichoke hearts with 1 cup cooked broccoli, sugar snap peas, or snow peas. Replace roasted pepper with raw, julienned red and yellow peppers. Replace parsley with cilantro; replace Red Wine Vinaigrette with Soy Sesame Vinaigrette (page 391). Add 1 tablespoon chopped pickled ginger (optional) and garnish with 1 teaspoon toasted sesame seeds. Omit the parmesan cheese.

WINE SUGGESTION: *Sauvignon blanc*

Nutrition Facts per Serving: 340 calories, 35 g protein, 17 g total fat (4 g saturated fat), 8 g carbohydrate, 1.2 g fiber, 85 mg cholesterol, 450 mg sodium, 22 weighted glycemic index

Mediterranean Steak Salad

with Lemon Vinaigrette

A savory, zingy midday meal is the perfect rejuvenator on a long day.
The contrasting textures and flavors of sirloin steak, fresh veggies, and
crumbled feta complement each other and provide variety for your palate.

Start to Finish: 45 minutes   *Yield: 4 servings*

1	pound boneless beef sirloin steak, cut 1 inch thick	1	cup halved cherry or grape tomatoes
	Kosher salt	1	cup canned cannellini beans (white kidney beans), rinsed and drained
	Freshly ground black pepper	½	cup crumbled feta cheese (2 ounces)
4	cups torn romaine	1	recipe Lemon Vinaigrette (below)
1	small cucumber, sliced		Fresh flat-leaf parsley (optional)
½	small red onion, thinly sliced and separated into rings		

1. Preheat broiler. Trim fat from steak. Season steak with kosher salt and pepper. Let sit for at least 15 minutes. Place steak on the unheated rack of a broiler pan. Broil 3 to 4 inches from the heat until desired doneness, turning once. Allow 15 to 17 minutes for medium-rare (135°F) or 20 to 22 minutes for medium (140°F). Let the meat rest for 10 to 15 minutes before slicing. Thinly slice the meat.

2. Divide torn romaine among four dinner plates. Top with sliced meat, cucumber slices, red onion, tomatoes, cannellini beans, and feta cheese. Drizzle with Lemon Vinaigrette. If desired, garnish with parsley.

Variations

- Replace the feta cheese with blue cheese. Replace the Lemon Vinaigrette with Red Wine Vinaigrette.
- Replace cucumber with 1 cup cooked artichoke hearts. Replace Lemon Vinaigrette with balsamic vinaigrette.

LEMON VINAIGRETTE: In a screw-top jar, combine ¼ cup extra-virgin olive oil, ½ teaspoon finely shredded lemon peel, 3 tablespoons lemon juice 1 tablespoon chopped fresh oregano, and 2 cloves garlic, minced (1 teaspoon minced). Cover and shake well. Season to taste with kosher salt and freshly ground black pepper. Makes about ½ cup.

CULINARY NOTE

Letting the steak rest before slicing allows the juices to flow back into the meat. If you cut into the meat immediately after it is removed from the broiler, the juices will run out onto the cutting board, leaving the piece of meat dry.

Nutrition Facts per Serving: 400 calories, 33.5 g protein, 22 g total fat (5.5 g saturated fat), 16.5 g carbohydrate, 5.5 g fiber, 57 mg cholesterol, 350 mg sodium, 29 weighted glycemic index

Spicy Grapefruit, Orange, Avocado, and Radish Salad

Avocados and citrus make this Latin California salad a favorite for entertaining. The avocado's mellow, rich flavors are a delicious flavor pairing with the subtle sweetness and bright flavors of citrus.

Start to Finish: 20 minutes   Yield: 4 servings

2 cups ruby grapefruit segments	¼ cup red onion, sliced thin, rinsed
2 cups orange segments	1 tablespoon mint
1 cup arugula	2 avocados, cut into ½-inch pieces
1 cup frisée or romaine lettuce, shredded	½ cup Spicy Lemon Mint Vinaigrette (page 71)
½ cup radishes, sliced paper-thin	Salt and pepper to taste

1. Segment the oranges and grapefruits. Slice the top and bottom off the orange, exposing the center and providing a stable bottom surface. Place the orange on a cutting board. Using a paring knife, start at the top of the orange where the peel meets the fruit. Cut down and around the orange, removing the skin and pith in a curved motion following the natural curve of the orange. Next, hold the orange in your hand over a bowl to catch the juice. Using the paring knife, cut down between the membrane wall and fruit toward the center of the fruit to loosen the segment. Repeat on the other side of membrane wall until segment is removed. Repeat for grapefruit.

2. Toss arugula and frisée with salt, pepper, and a little vinaigrette.

3. Combine greens with citrus, radishes, red onion, and mint in a large bowl; season with salt and pepper. Gently toss. Add avocados and vinaigrette. Toss just to mix, being careful not to mash the avocados.

Nutrition Facts per Serving: 250 calories, 21 g protein, 5 g total fat (1 g saturated fat), 32 g carbohydrate, 12 g fiber, 19 mg cholesterol, 290 mg sodium, 29 weighted glycemic index

Variation

- Replace oranges or grapefruits with fresh seasonal fruits such as peaches, nectarines, watermelon, or mango during the summer.

Spicy Lemon Mint Vinaigrette

Start to Finish: 10 minutes   Yield: Serves 8   1 tablespoon per serving

¼ cup lemon juice	½ teaspoon jalapeño or serrano chile, chopped fine
1 teaspoon agave syrup	¼ cup canola oil
¼ teaspoon ginger, chopped	1 tablespoon sesame oil
1 tablespoon mint, chopped	Salt and pepper to taste

Combine all ingredients. Whisk well.

Variation

- Try replacing the lemon juice with a Muscat sweet wine vinegar for a sweeter and more delicate flavor.

Nutrition Facts per Serving: 75 calories, 0 g protein, 8 g total fat (0 g saturated fat), 1.5 g carbohydrate, 0 g fiber, 0 mg cholesterol, 0 mg sodium, 17 weighted glycemic index

Spinach, Basil, and Feta Panini

With half of its ingredients on the list of Sonoma Power Foods,
this grilled Italian sandwich packs a nutritional punch.
Spinach is rich in carotenoids, folate, vitamin K, and magnesium.

Start to Finish: 20 minutes   Yield: 4 servings

4   6-inch whole-wheat hoagie rolls,
    split; 8 slices whole-wheat bread;
    or 2 whole-wheat pita bread
    rounds, halved crosswise and
    split horizontally

4   cups fresh baby spinach leaves

8   thin tomato slices
    (1 medium tomato)

¼   teaspoon kosher salt

⅛   teaspoon freshly ground
    black pepper

¼   cup thinly sliced red onion

2   tablespoons shredded fresh
    basil leaves

½   cup crumbled feta cheese (2 ounces)
    Nonstick olive oil cooking spray

1. Place hoagie roll bottoms or 4 of the bread slices or 4 pita pieces on a work surface; divide half of the spinach leaves among them. Top spinach with tomato and sprinkle lightly with kosher salt and pepper. Add red onion slices and basil. Top with feta and remaining spinach. Top with hoagie roll tops, remaining bread slices, or pita pieces. Press down firmly.

2. Lightly coat an unheated panini griddle, covered indoor electric grill, or large nonstick skillet with nonstick cooking spray. Preheat griddle, grill, or skillet over medium heat or heat according to manufacturer's directions. Add sandwiches, in batches if necessary.

3. If using griddle or grill, close lid and grill for 2 to 3 minutes or until bread is toasted.

4. If using skillet, place a heavy plate on top of sandwiches. Cook for 1 to 2 minutes or until bottoms are toasted. Carefully remove plate, which may be hot. Turn sandwiches and top with the plate. Cook for 1 to 2 minutes more or until bread is toasted.

Variation

• Replace feta cheese with sliced fresh mozzarella cheese.

Nutrition Facts per Serving: 315 calories, 12 g protein, 8 g total fat (3 g saturated fat), 53 g carbohydrate, 9 g fiber, 10 mg cholesterol, 500 mg sodium, 57 weighted glycemic index

Portabello, Mozzarella, and Pesto Panini

Spread each sandwich bread with 2 tablespoons pesto. Top with 1 roasted portabello mushroom, 2 slices tomato, 2 slices fresh mozzarella, and 2 ounces Balsamic Red Onions (optional; page 327). Or use leftover grilled vegetables in place of portabellos.

Nutrition Facts per Serving: 358 calories, 22 g protein, 25 g total fat (10 g saturated fat), 20 g carbohydrate, 2.5 g fiber, 40 mg cholesterol, 540 mg sodium, 21 weighted glycemic index

Apple, Ham, and Swiss Cheese Panini

Spread each sandwich bread with 1 teaspoon whole-grain mustard. Top with 2 slices of Black Forest ham (2 ounces per sandwich); 2 slices of a Granny Smith apple, cored; and 2 slices of Swiss or Gruyère cheese.

Nutrition Facts per Serving: 425 calories, 22 g protein, 11 g total fat (4 g saturated fat), 62 g carbohydrate, 7 g fiber, 30 mg cholesterol, 900 mg sodium, 63 weighted glycemic index

Cuban Sandwich

Spread each sandwich bread with 1 teaspoon yellow mustard. Top with 1½ ounces leftover roast pork tenderloin, sliced thin, and ½ ounce Black Forest ham or sliced deli ham. Top with thin slices of Swiss cheese and julienne pickles.

Nutrition Facts per Serving: 380 calories, 24 g protein, 11 g total fat (4 g saturated fat), 49 g carbohydrate, 6 g fiber, 40 mg cholesterol, 700 mg sodium, 72 weighted glycemic index

Heirloom Tomato, Mozzarella, and Caponata Panini

Caponata is the one Sicilian dish most people are familiar with. It is a cooked vegetable salad, typically made with artichokes, eggplant, capers, and celery in a sweet and sour dressing. Try this Sonoma version topped on your favorite grilled fish, in a pasta salad, or as a delicious panini.

Start to Finish: 30 minutes   Yield: 4 servings

2 cups Caponata (page 383)
4 multigrain thin buns
8 slices heirloom tomatoes, ½-inch thick
8 slices fresh mozzarella, ¼-inch thick
4 cups arugula
1 tablespoon lemon juice
Nonstick cooking spray
Salt and pepper to taste

1. Preheat a griddle to medium. Have a large skillet and three 15-ounce cans to use as weights by the stove.

2. Chop the caponata into ½-inch pieces.

3. On the bottom half of each bun, place 2 slices of tomato; season with salt and pepper. Add ½ cup caponata and 2 slices of mozzarella. Top with 1 cup arugula, sprinkled with salt, pepper, and lemon juice. Cover with the top half of the bun.

4. Spray the griddle with nonstick cooking spray. Place sandwiches on griddle; top with empty skillet and the weight of the 3 cans. Cook over medium heat until the bottom of the bun starts to brown. Flip and cook on the other side without the weights until the top is golden brown and the sandwich is warmed through.

Variations

- Add 2 ounces lean beef to each sandwich.
- Replace arugula with watercress.
- Replace caponata with 1 pound grilled vegetables tossed with 2 tablespoons pesto.

Nutrition Facts per Serving: 400 calories, 12 g protein, 10 g total fat (3 g saturated fat), 55 g carbohydrate, 9 g fiber, 10 mg cholesterol, 500 mg sodium, 45 weighted glycemic index

Curried Chicken Wrap

Curry, coriander, and mango combine in this wrap to bring you a taste of the exotic. Chicken may be the meat of the dish, but mango steals the show with its vibrant orange color, amazing aroma, and sweet-tart flavor.

Start to Finish: 55 minutes   Yield: 6 servings

12 ounces skinless, boneless chicken breast halves, cut into ¼-inch-thick slices	1 cup thinly sliced red onion
1 tablespoon extra-virgin olive oil	1 cup chopped mango
1 tablespoon curry powder	2 cups shredded romaine
1 teaspoon ground coriander	1 cup watercress, tough stems removed
½ teaspoon kosher salt	2 tablespoons lemon juice
¼ teaspoon freshly ground black pepper	2 teaspoons extra-virgin olive oil
1 tablespoon extra-virgin olive oil	6 7- to 8-inch whole-wheat flour tortillas

1. In a medium bowl combine chicken, 1 tablespoon olive oil, curry powder, coriander, kosher salt, and pepper. Cover and marinate in the refrigerator for 30 minutes.

2. In a large skillet, heat 1 tablespoon olive oil over medium heat. Add the chicken and red onion; cook and stir for 4 to 6 minutes or until chicken is tender and no longer pink. Add mango; cook and stir until heated through.

3. Meanwhile, in a medium bowl combine romaine and watercress. Drizzle with lemon juice and 2 teaspoons olive oil; toss gently to coat.

4. To serve, divide the chicken mixture and romaine mixture among tortillas. Roll up tortillas. Heating the tortillas in a dry sauté pan over medium heat will make them more pliable and easier to roll up.

Variations
- Replace chicken with shrimp.
- Replace chicken with pork tenderloin cut in ¼-inch pieces.

Nutrition Facts per Serving: 295 calories, 17 g protein, 11 g total fat (1 g saturated fat), 30 g carbohydrate, 4 g fiber, 36 mg cholesterol, 300 mg sodium, 32 weighted glycemic index

Grilled Vegetable and Feta Cheese Wrap

2 cups grilled vegetables, 2 tablespoons balsamic vinaigrette, ½ cup feta cheese, 2 cups arugula, 1 sliced avocado, 1 sliced tomato.

Toss grilled vegetables with balsamic vinaigrette and feta cheese. Divide arugula, avocado, and tomato among 4 warmed tortillas. Top with equal portions of grilled vegetables. Roll up.

Nutrition Facts per Serving: 315 calories, 10 g protein, 12.5 g total fat (3 g saturated fat), 41 g carbohydrate, 8.5 g fiber, 10 mg cholesterol, 540 mg sodium, 24 weighted glycemic index

Chipotle Avocado Wrap

Replace curry powder with 1 teaspoon chipotle in adobo sauce and 2 teaspoons chopped garlic. Replace mango with diced tomatoes. Add 2 tablespoons rinsed, thinly sliced red onions, 1 tablespoon chopped cilantro, and 1 avocado sliced thin. Top with a squeeze of lime juice.

Nutrition Facts per Serving: 310 calories, 17 g protein, 14 g total fat (1.5 g saturated fat), 27 g carbohydrate, 4.5 g fiber, 36 mg cholesterol, 400 mg sodium, 29 weighted glycemic index

Tuscan Chicken with Artichokes Wrap

Replace curry powder and coriander with 1 tablespoon chopped oregano, 1 pinch chile flakes, and 2 teaspoons chopped garlic. Replace mango with cooked chopped artichoke hearts. Add 1 cup chopped roasted red peppers.

Nutrition Facts per Serving: 305 calories, 18 g protein, 11 g total fat (1 g saturated fat), 31 g carbohydrate, 6.5 g fiber, 36 mg cholesterol, 350 mg sodium, 30 weighted glycemic index

Thanksgiving Turkey Wrap

12 ounces shredded roast turkey, ¼ cup cranberry orange relish, ¼ cup rinsed julienned red onions, 2 cups shredded romaine lettuce, 1 cup arugula or watercress, 2 tablespoons red wine vinegar, 2 teaspoons extra-virgin olive oil, 4 whole-wheat tortillas.

Heat tortillas. Spread turkey down the center of each tortilla, spread cranberry relish on turkey, and sprinkle with red onions. Toss romaine, watercress, red wine vinegar, and extra-virgin olive oil with salt and pepper. Lay on top. Wrap up.

Nutrition Facts per Serving: 295 calories, 30 g protein, 6 g total fat (.5 g saturated fat), 26 g carbohydrate, 3 g fiber, 70 mg cholesterol, 215 mg sodium, 35 weighted glycemic index

BEEF ENTRÉES

The rich flavors of beef work so well with the many ideas in this section. Here you will find a culinary adventure of spices, herbs, and wine sauces to complement many different preparations of beef, from the bold Argentine flavors in chimichurri to Mediterranean peperonata sauce and Thai Roast Beef Lettuce Rolls.

Braised Pot Roast

What a great crockpot meal to come home to after a long day.
The long, slow cooking time develops rich, savory flavors with tender beef.
Great dishes create food and flavor memories; this very easy and delicious
recipe is one to rekindle those flavor memories or start a new tradition.

Start to Finish: 6 hours (in a crockpot)   Yield: 10 servings

3 pounds beef top round, lean	1 tablespoon thyme, chopped
1 tablespoon extra-virgin olive oil	1 15-ounce can tomatoes, diced
2 cups onions, diced	1 cup red wine
1 cup celery, diced	1 cup low-sodium chicken stock
1 cup carrots, diced	1 tablespoon low-sodium soy sauce
1 cup mushrooms, cut 1/6 inch thick	1 teaspoon lemon zest
3 cloves garlic	1 tablespoon parsley, chopped
1 tablespoon paprika	½ teaspoon kosher salt
1 teaspoon dry mustard	½ teaspoon ground black pepper

1. Season meat with salt and pepper.

2. Heat a large nonstick sauté pan over medium-high heat. Add olive oil and meat. Sear meat all over until nicely browned. Remove from pan and place in crockpot.

3. Add onions, celery, and carrots to sauté pan; sauté for 5 minutes. Add mushrooms and turn up heat to brown. Add garlic and spices; cook until aromatic. Add tomatoes and red wine; reduce by half. Add chicken stock and soy sauce; bring to a simmer. Pour over meat in crockpot. Turn crockpot on low, cover, and let cook for 6 hours or until the meat is tender.

4. Remove the meat from crockpot. Place on a cutting board. Let sit. Degrease the sauce; adjust seasoning with salt, pepper, and lemon zest. Stir in parsley. Slice the meat. Add to sauce and serve.

Nutrition Facts per Serving: 250 calories, 33 g protein, 6.5 g total fat (1.8 g saturated fat), 8 g carbohydrate, 1 g fiber, 62 mg cholesterol, 300 mg sodium, 39 weighted glycemic index

Variations

Mediterranean

Add 2 tablespoons chopped garlic with the onions. Increase paprika to 2 tablespoons and omit mustard. Add 1 tablespoon chopped basil with the parsley.

Latin

Add 1 chopped chipotle chile and 2 tablespoons garlic with the onions. Add 2 tablespoons chile powder in place of paprika and dry mustard. Replace thyme with Mexican oregano. Finish with a squeeze of fresh lime juice and chopped cilantro in place of parsley.

CULINARY NOTE

The amount of cooking necessary will depend on the shape of the roast. If the roast is long and skinny, it will take less time. The more dense the roast, the longer the cooking time required.

Citrus Ginger Flank Steak

The tangy sweet flavor of pomegranate molasses makes for a delicious marinade for flank steak. The pomegranate is one of the oldest fruits known. It was grown in ancient Egypt and Rome, and it even has a place in Greek mythology. Today, it is also grown in California. Pomegranate seeds add brilliant color and a sweet-sour element to salads or in a salsa. When juiced, they can be reduced to a syrup or molasses to be used in marinades, glazes, rubs, and desserts.

Start to Finish: 25 minutes, plus 1 to 24 hours for marinating   Yield: 4 servings

1 pound flank steak, fat removed	1 tablespoon garlic
1 tablespoon lemon juice	½ teaspoon sesame oil
1 tablespoon soy sauce	2 teaspoons ginger, chopped
½ tablespoon pomegranate molasses or agave syrup	Black pepper

1. Season meat with pepper.

2. Combine remaining ingredients in a Ziploc bag and add flank steak. Place in the refrigerator for 1 to 24 hours.

3. For a charcoal grill, place meat on the rack of an uncovered grill directly over medium coals. Grill for 15 to 20 minutes or until medium doneness (160°F), turning once halfway through grilling. For a gas grill, preheat grill. Reduce heat to medium. Place meat on grill rack over heat. Cover and grill as above.

4. Transfer grilled meat to a cutting board. Cover and let stand for 10 minutes. To serve, slice very thinly across the grain.

Variation

- Replace flank steak with pork chops or chicken.

Nutrition Facts per Serving: 192 calories, 25 g protein, 8.5 g total fat (3.5 g saturated fat), 3 g carbohydrate, 0 g fiber, 40 mg cholesterol, 280 mg sodium, 46 weighted glycemic index

CULINARY NOTE

Since the marinade contains soy sauce, which is salty, there is no need to salt the flank steak. You can purchase pomegranate molasses or make your own: In a saucepan, combine 8 cups pomegranate juice, 2 tablespoons sugar, and 1 tablespoon lemon juice. Cook at medium heat for 45 minutes to 1 hour, until a thick molasses consistency. Store in an airtight container in the refrigerator for up to a month.

The agave syrup or pomegranate molasses will caramelize when cooked, so be careful not to let the steak get too dark and bitter. Medium heat is best to cook sweet marinades. You can always finish the cooking in the oven if the steak is getting too dark.

CULINARY NOTES

- You can marinate the meat in the refrigerator for 1 to 24 hours.
- You can grill or sauté the meat if you do not have a broiler.

Coriander-Studded Tenderloin Steak

Crushed coriander seeds bestow a slightly sweet citrus flavor upon these tender steaks, making them irresistible.

Start to Finish: 25 minutes   Yield: 4 servings

4 3- to 4-ounce beef tenderloin steaks, cut 1 inch thick	2 cloves garlic, minced (1 teaspoon minced)
Kosher salt	½ teaspoon coriander seeds or cumin seeds, crushed
1 tablespoon reduced-sodium soy sauce	½ teaspoon celery seeds
1 tablespoon extra-virgin olive oil	½ teaspoon coarsely ground black pepper
1 tablespoon fresh chives, chopped	

1. Preheat broiler. Trim fat from steaks. Season steaks with kosher salt. In a small bowl, combine soy sauce, olive oil, chives, garlic, coriander seeds or cumin seeds, celery seeds, and pepper. Brush mixture onto both sides of each steak.

2. Place steaks on the unheated rack of a broiler pan. Broil 3 to 4 inches from heat for 12 to 14 minutes for medium-rare doneness (145°F) or 15 to 18 minutes for medium doneness (160°F), turning once halfway through broiling time.

Variation

- Replace extra-virgin olive oil with sesame oil; add 1 tablespoon chopped ginger.

WINE SUGGESTION: *Merlot*

Nutrition Facts per Serving: 156 calories, 22 g protein, 7.5 g total fat (2 g saturated fat), 1 g carbohydrate, 0 g fiber, 60 mg cholesterol, 155 mg sodium, 12 weighted glycemic index

Flank Steak

with Middle Eastern Spice Marinade

The seasoning in this dish takes its flavors from a popular sandwich known as *shawarma* in the eastern Mediterranean or gyro in Greece. Serve with a soft whole-wheat pita bread or a flatbread accompanied by tabbouleh. See page 92 for the best California version of a gyro sandwich using this recipe.

Start to Finish: 25 minutes, plus 1 to 24 hours for marinating   Yield: 4 servings

1	pound beef flank steak, cut in half, lengthwise	½	teaspoon cardamom
1	tablespoon garlic, chopped	½	teaspoon chile flakes
1	tablespoon lemon juice	¼	teaspoon black pepper
1½	teaspoons ground cumin	¼	teaspoon kosher salt

1. Season flank steak with salt and pepper. Let sit 10 minutes.

2. Combine remaining ingredients.

3. Spread spice mix evenly over both sides of the steak; rub in with your fingers. Place steak in a shallow dish. Cover and marinate in the refrigerator for 1 to 24 hours.

4. For a charcoal grill, place meat on the rack of an uncovered grill directly over medium coals. Grill for 17 to 21 minutes or until medium doneness (160°F), turning once halfway through grilling. For a gas grill, preheat grill. Reduce heat to medium. Place meat on grill rack over heat. Cover and grill as above.

5. Transfer grilled meat to a cutting board. Cover and let stand for 10 minutes. To serve, slice very thinly across the grain.

Variations

- Replace cardamom with chopped oregano or rosemary.

- Replace beef with lean cuts of lamb, chicken, or pork.

- This is a COOK 1X · EAT 2X recipe for Grilled Beef Pita Sandwiches with Spicy Tahini Sauce, Tomatoes, and Cucumber (page 92).

Nutrition Facts per Serving: 170 calories, 25 g protein, 6.5 g total fat (2 g saturated fat), 1.5 g carbohydrate, 0 g fiber, 37 mg cholesterol, 65 mg sodium, 21 weighted glycemic index

Spinach and Basil Salad
with Beef

Basil and spinach put a new spin on traditional iceberg- and romaine-based salads while providing a vibrant backdrop for juicy fruits and beef. A unique pear dressing makes this an elegant main-dish salad.

Start to Finish: 25 minutes   Yield: 2 servings

½ small, very ripe pear, cored and peeled	1 cup fresh mushrooms, sliced
1 tablespoon white wine vinegar or cider vinegar	½ cup lightly packed fresh basil leaves
¼ teaspoon Worcestershire sauce for chicken or regular Worcestershire sauce	6 ounces sliced cooked beef, cut into thin strips (about 1 cup)
Dash freshly ground black pepper	2 small oranges, peeled and sectioned, or one 11-ounce can mandarin orange sections, drained
2 cups lightly packed torn fresh spinach	2 tablespoons sliced almonds, toasted

1. For dressing, in a blender or food processor combine the pear, vinegar, Worcestershire sauce, and pepper. Cover and blend or process until smooth.

2. In a bowl toss together the spinach, mushrooms, and basil leaves. Add the beef strips and orange sections. Toss lightly to mix. Add the dressing; toss to mix. Sprinkle each serving with almonds.

Variation
- Replace pear with sweet red apple or Asian pear.

CULINARY NOTE

COOK 1X · EAT 2X for South American Hanger Steak (page 112), Citrus Ginger Flank Steak (page 82), or Mustard-Crusted Beef Tenderloin (page 97).

Nutrition Facts per Serving: 330 calories, 34 g protein, 11.5 g total fat (3 g saturated fat), 24 g carbohydrate, 6 g fiber, 100 mg cholesterol, 65 mg sodium, 37 weighted glycemic index

Grilled Beef Tenderloin
with Quinoa, Green Beans, and Roasted Peppers

Quinoa is a complete protein source because it contains all eight essential amino acids. Its unique texture and delicate flavor perfectly complement this meaty meal.

Start to Finish: 40 minutes   Yield: 4 servings

1 cup water	Freshly ground black pepper
½ cup quinoa	1 cup bottled roasted red and/or yellow bell peppers, drained and chopped
2 cups fresh green beans, bias-sliced into 2-inch pieces	2 tablespoons red wine vinegar
4 beef tenderloin steaks, cut 1 inch thick (about 1 pound total)	1 tablespoon pitted kalamata olives, chopped
1 tablespoon fennel seeds, crushed	2 teaspoons fresh flat-leaf parsley, chopped
2 tablespoons extra-virgin olive oil	
Kosher salt	

1. In a medium saucepan, bring the water to boiling. Add quinoa, season with salt and pepper, and return to boiling; reduce heat. Cover and simmer about 15 minutes or until quinoa is tender and most of the liquid is absorbed. Remove from heat; set aside.

2. Meanwhile, pan steam the green beans: Place green beans in a covered medium saucepan; cook in a small amount of lightly salted boiling water for 5 minutes. Drain; submerse green beans in ice water to stop the cooking process. Drain well. Set aside.

3. Meanwhile, season meat with kosher salt and black pepper; sprinkle with crushed fennel seeds. Drizzle the steaks with 1 tablespoon of the olive oil.

4. For a charcoal grill, place steaks on the rack of an uncovered grill directly over medium coals. Grill 10 to 12 minutes for medium-rare doneness (145°F) or 12 to 15 minutes for medium doneness (160°F), turning once halfway through grilling. For a gas grill, preheat grill. Reduce heat to medium. Place steaks on grill rack over heat. Cover and grill as above.

5. In a large bowl, combine cooked quinoa, green beans, roasted peppers, red wine vinegar, olives, parsley, and the remaining 1 tablespoon olive oil. Season to taste with kosher salt and black pepper.

6. To serve, divide quinoa mixture among four dinner plates. Top with the steaks.

Variations

- Replace beef tenderloin with pork tenderloin.
- Replace green beans with broccoli.
- Replace red wine vinegar with balsamic vinegar.

CULINARY NOTES

- To give the quinoa a nutty flavor, toast for 8 to 10 minutes on a sheet pan in a 350°F oven. The quinoa should have a light brown color.

- Season the quinoa cooking liquid with salt and pepper before covering the saucepan. The seasoning will be absorbed into the quinoa so less salt and pepper will be needed to season the final dish.

- If the quinoa is prepared in advance, season again before serving.

WINE SUGGESTION: *Syrah*

Nutrition Facts per Serving: 300 calories, 27 g protein, 13 g total fat (2.5 g saturated fat), 21 g carbohydrate, 5 g fiber, 60 mg cholesterol, 525 mg sodium, 44 weighted glycemic index

Grilled Hanger Steak
with Chimichurri Sauce

A traditional sauce of Argentina, chimichurri is loaded with fresh herbs and seasonings. It's used in Argentina the way Americans use ketchup and is a must on grilled meat, particularly beef.

Start to Finish: 30 minutes   Yield: 4 servings

¼	cup fresh flat-leaf parsley, chopped
2	tablespoons red wine vinegar
2	tablespoons extra-virgin olive oil
2	tablespoons low-sodium beef broth or water
2	tablespoons shallot, finely chopped
1	tablespoon fresh oregano, chopped
4	cloves garlic, minced (2 teaspoons minced)
½	teaspoon lemon juice
¼	teaspoon crushed red pepper
	Kosher salt
1	pound beef hanger steak
	Freshly ground black pepper

1. For chimichurri sauce, in a small bowl combine parsley, red wine vinegar, olive oil, broth, shallot, oregano, garlic, lemon juice, and crushed red pepper. Season to taste with kosher salt. Cover and let stand at room temperature for 1 hour. (Or chill in the refrigerator for up to 48 hours; let stand at room temperature before using.)

2. Trim fat from steak. Score both sides of steak in a diamond pattern by making shallow diagonal cuts at 1-inch intervals. Season meat with kosher salt and black pepper. For a charcoal grill, place steak on the rack of an uncovered grill directly over medium coals.

Grill for 12 to 14 minutes or until medium doneness (140°F). For a gas grill, preheat grill. Reduce heat to medium. Place steak on grill rack over heat. Cover and grill as above. Serve steak with chimichurri sauce.

Variations
- Replace hanger steak with beef skirt steak.
- Replace hanger steak with pork tenderloin.

WINE SUGGESTION: *Pinot noir*

Nutrition Facts per Serving: 230 calories, 25 g protein, 13 g total fat (3.3 g saturated fat), 2 g carbohydrate, 10 g fiber, 37 mg cholesterol, 68 mg sodium, 15 weighted glycemic index

Grilled Beef Pita Sandwiches
with Spicy Tahini Sauce, Tomatoes, and Cucumber

This tasty sandwich is inspired by the Greek gyro sandwich,
also known as *shawarma* in Turkey. Traditionally, the meat is grilled on
a rotating spit in front of a fire for hours.

*Start to Finish: 20 minutes if using prepared Flank Steak with Middle Eastern Spice Marinade
(page 86)   Yield: 4 sandwiches*

½ cup tomato, chopped	8 ounces leftover Flank Steak with Middle Eastern Spice Marinade, sliced (page 86)
½ cup cucumber, chopped	
1 cup romaine lettuce, shredded	2 ounces feta cheese, crumbled
1 tablespoon lemon juice	½ cup Spicy Tahini Sauce (page 93)
4 whole-wheat pita breads	Salt and pepper to taste

1. Toss the tomatoes, cucumber, and lettuce with lemon juice, salt, and pepper.

2. Lightly toast pita bread. Cut each pita in half. Divide the sliced beef among the pitas. Sprinkle ½ ounce of feta cheese in each pita. Divide tomato mixture among the pitas. Drizzle with Spicy Tahini Sauce.

Variations
- Replace the beef with chicken.
- Replace the beef with grilled vegetables.

Nutrition Facts per Serving: 300 calories, 20 g protein, 15.5 g total fat (4.5 g saturated fat), 23 g carbohydrate, 4.5 g fiber, 31 mg cholesterol, 350 mg sodium, 52 weighted glycemic index

Spicy Tahini Sauce

Start to Finish: 5 minutes   Yield: 1¼ cup

1 tablespoon garlic, minced	¼ teaspoon cayenne pepper
½ cup tahini (Middle Eastern sesame paste), mixed well	2 tablespoons extra-virgin olive oil
⅓ cup lemon juice	1 tablespoon cilantro, chopped
¼ cup water	1 tablespoon parsley chopped
½ teaspoon ground cumin	Salt and pepper to taste

Combine garlic, tahini, lemon juice, water, and spices in a food processor. Mix until smooth. Add extra-virgin olive oil; pulse just to mix. Add herbs and salt and pepper. Thin out with more water if necessary.

CULINARY NOTE

The oil in tahini separates as it sits. Stir the tahini well before using. Store in an airtight container upside down in the refrigerator.

CULINARY NOTE

Soaking wooden skewers in water will help prevent them from burning.

Beef Satay with Peanut Sauce

Staying true to its Indonesian roots, this savory beef satay is skewered and served with a warm peanut sauce, perfect for dipping. For simplified preparation, partially freeze the steak to make slicing easier.

Start to Finish: 45 minutes   Yield: 5 servings

1 1- to 1¼-pound beef flank steak	½ medium red onion, cut into thin wedges
⅓ cup light teriyaki sauce	4 scallions, cut into 1-inch pieces
½ teaspoon bottled hot pepper sauce	1 red or green bell pepper, cut into ¾-inch chunks
3 tablespoons peanut butter	Skewers
3 tablespoons water	
2 tablespoons light teriyaki sauce	

1. If desired, partially freeze steak for easier slicing. Trim fat from steak. Cut steak crosswise into thin slices.

2. In a medium bowl, combine ⅓ cup teriyaki sauce and ¼ teaspoon hot pepper sauce. Add steak; toss to coat. Cover and marinate in the refrigerator for 30 minutes. If using wooden skewers, soak them in water for 30 minutes before using.

3. Meanwhile, in a small saucepan, combine peanut butter, water, 2 tablespoons teriyaki sauce, and the remaining ¼ teaspoon hot pepper sauce. Cook and stir over medium heat just until smooth and heated through. Set aside and keep warm.

4. Drain steak, reserving marinade. On wooden or metal skewers, alternately thread steak strips (accordion style), onion wedges, scallion pieces, and bell pepper. Brush with reserved marinade. Discard any remaining marinade.

5. Place skewers on the unheated rack of a broiler pan. Broil 4 to 5 inches from the heat about 4 minutes or until meat is slightly pink in center, turning once.

6. Serve satay with warm peanut sauce.

Variations

- Replace beef with chicken breast or pork tenderloin.

Asian Marinade

½ cup yogurt, ½ teaspoon grated ginger, ½ teaspoon mashed garlic, 2 teaspoons curry powder, 1 pinch cayenne pepper, 1 pinch sugar

Peanut Sauce

½ cup peanut butter, ½ teaspoon grated ginger, 1 tablespoon soy sauce, 1 teaspoon brown sugar or agave syrup, 1 tablespoon lime juice, ¼ cup water. Combine all ingredients; bring to a low simmer for 10 minutes.

WINE SUGGESTION: *Sparkling white or sparkling red*

Nutrition Facts per Serving: 159 calories, 25 g protein, 11 g total fat (3 g saturated fat), 11 g carbohydrate, 2 g fiber, 37 mg cholesterol, 700 mg sodium, 62 weighted glycemic index

Mustard-Crusted Beef Tenderloin

Melt-in-your-mouth beef tenderloin enhanced with the fresh, sharp flavor of mustard makes this a dish you won't soon forget.

Start to Finish: 70 minutes   Yield: 4 servings

¼ cup coarse whole-grain mustard	½ teaspoon orange zest
2 teaspoons honey	½ teaspoon lemon zest
¾ teaspoon dry mustard	1 tablespoon extra-virgin olive oil
¾ teaspoon freshly ground black pepper	1 1-pound beef tenderloin roast

1. Preheat oven to 425°F. In a small bowl, combine whole-grain mustard, honey, dry mustard, pepper, orange zest, and lemon zest; set aside.

2. In a heavy, large skillet, heat olive oil over medium-high heat. Quickly brown the roast on all sides in the hot oil (about 2 minutes total). Transfer meat to a rack set in a shallow roasting pan. Spread mustard mixture over top and sides of roast. Insert an oven meat thermometer into center of roast.

3. Roast the beef for 35 to 45 minutes or until meat thermometer registers 140°F. Cover meat with foil and let stand for 10 to 15 minutes before slicing. The temperature of the meat after standing should be 145°F.

Variation

- Replace beef with pork loin or pork chops.

CULINARY NOTES

Slice the meat against the grain for a tender cut. To find the grain, find the small fibers that are running in the same direction in the meat. This is the grain. Cut against the grain, meaning perpendicular to the grain, to shorten the fibers. Cut at a 45° angle and slice thin (⅛ to 1/16 inch thick).

WINE SUGGESTION: *Merlot*

Nutrition Facts per Serving: 200 calories, 23 g protein, 8 g total fat (2 g saturated fat), 11 g carbohydrate, 1 g fiber, 60 mg cholesterol, 170 mg sodium, 40 weighted glycemic index

Grilled Skirt Steak
with Peperonata

This is a very typical Italian dish that is served at room temperature and with many different pairings, from seafood, topped on toasted country-style bread, or as a side salad. This is a great salad for summer months when so many colorful peppers are available.

Start to Finish: 45 minutes, plus up to 24 hours for marinating   Yield: 8 servings

For marinade
- 2 pounds beef skirt steak, fat removed
- 1 tablespoon extra-virgin olive oil
- 1 tablespoon lemon zest
- 1 tablespoon rosemary, chopped
- 1 tablespoon garlic, mashed to a paste
- 1 pinch red chile flakes
- Salt and pepper to taste

For peperonata
- 1 tablespoon extra-virgin olive oil
- 3 cups red peppers, julienne
- 1 cup onions, julienne, rinsed and drained well
- 1 tablespoon garlic, chopped
- 2 teaspoons oregano, chopped
- 2 tablespoons balsamic vinegar
- 1 teaspoon agave syrup
- 1 tablespoon capers, rinsed well
- Salt and pepper to taste

1. Season meat well with salt and pepper. Let sit for 10 minutes.

2. Combine remaining marinade ingredients in a sealable plastic bag. Add seasoned meat; marinate in refrigerator up to 24 hours.

3. Preheat grill over medium high. Remove meat from refrigerator and bring to room temperature.

4. Remove the meat from the marinade. Brush off any large pieces of garlic or rosemary. Place on clean hot grill. Cook for about 5 minutes or until the juices start to puddle on top; then flip and cook on the other side to an internal temperature of 125°F. Let rest for 15 minutes.

5. Heat a large heavy-bottomed sauté pan over medium-high heat. When hot, add oil and peppers; sauté 2 to 3 minutes over high heat, being careful not to overcrowd the pan. Add onions and sauté 2 minutes until wilted; season with salt and pepper. Add garlic and oregano and cook until aromatic; turn off heat and quickly deglaze with vinegar and agave syrup. The peppers should still be crisp. Stir in capers; adjust seasoning.

6. Slice meat against the grain. Serve on a bed of the peperonata.

Variation

- Replace skirt steak with tri tip, sirloin steak, pork loin chops, or chicken breast.
- Use a mixture of red and yellow peppers.
- Replace the balsamic vinegar with sherry vinegar.

Nutrition Facts per Serving: 245 calories, 25 g protein, 13 g total fat (4 g saturated fat), 6 g carbohydrate, 1.5 g fiber, 65 mg cholesterol, 65 mg sodium, 15 weighted glycemic index

CULINARY NOTE

COOK 1X · EAT 2X : Use leftover roast beef, skirt steak, or flank steak.

Thai Roast Beef Lettuce Rolls

When you're looking for an enticing meal but don't have a lot of time, enjoy these Thai-inspired wraps. Holding true to Thai tradition, they call for fish sauce, an essential Thai ingredient that adds a salty, piquant flavor.

Start to Finish: 30 minutes   Yield: 4 servings

2 tablespoons lime juice	1 pound cooked roast beef, cut into thin strips
1 tablespoon bottled fish sauce	8 leaves red leaf lettuce
1 tablespoon water	1 ½ cups red and/or green bell pepper strips
1½ teaspoons honey	1 ½ cups bite-size carrot strips
2 cloves garlic, minced (1 teaspoon minced)	16 sprigs fresh cilantro and/or mint
1 teaspoon fresh jalapeño or serrano chile pepper, finely chopped	

1. In a medium bowl, whisk together lime juice, fish sauce, water, honey, garlic, and chile pepper. Add beef strips; toss well.

2. Arrange 2 lettuce leaves on each of four dinner plates. Top lettuce with meat strips, pepper strips, carrot strips, and cilantro and/or mint. Drizzle with any remaining lime mixture. Roll up lettuce leaves. Serve immediately.

Variations
- Add julienne cucumbers to the rolls.
- Replace honey with agave syrup.

WINE SUGGESTION: *Rosé*

Nutrition Facts per Serving: 305 calories, 40 g protein, 11 g total fat (3.5 g saturated fat), 10 g carbohydrate, 2.5 g fiber, 135 mg cholesterol, 450 mg sodium, 39 weighted glycemic index

Sicilian-Style Beef Flank Steak

The island of Sicily boasts some of Italy's most elegant and delicious dishes. You can enjoy this Sicilian-style meal from your own kitchen. Italian flat-leaf parsley is used as more than a simple garnish here; it adds color, flavor, and vitamins A and C.

Start to Finish: 40 minutes   Yield: 4 servings

1 pound boneless beef flank steak, cut 1 inch thick	2 teaspoons fresh oregano, chopped
½ teaspoon kosher salt	¼ teaspoon crushed red pepper
¼ teaspoon freshly ground black pepper	1 15-ounce can tomatoes, undrained, diced
2 tablespoons extra-virgin olive oil	¾ cup sliced pitted ripe olives
½ cup finely chopped celery	1 tablespoon capers, rinsed and drained
1 clove garlic, minced (½ teaspoon minced)	2 tablespoons fresh flat-leaf parsley, chopped

1. Trim fat from meat. Season meat with kosher salt and black pepper.

2. In a large skillet, heat olive oil over medium heat. Add meat; cook for 8 to 10 minutes or until browned, turning once. Remove meat from skillet.

3. In the same skillet, cook celery over medium-low heat about 4 minutes or just until tender. Add garlic, oregano, and crushed red pepper; sauté 1 minute until aromatic. Stir in undrained tomatoes, olives, and capers. Bring to boiling; reduce heat. Simmer, uncovered, until liquid begins to thicken. Return meat and any accumulated juices to the skillet. Simmer, uncovered, for 5 to 10 minutes or until meat reaches desired doneness (135°F for medium-rare or 140°F for medium).

4. To serve, remove meat from tomato mixture; cut into thin slices. Stir parsley into tomato mixture in skillet; serve over meat.

Variations

- Replace flank steak with sirloin steak.
- Replace flank steak with pork tenderloin.
- Replace flank steak with chicken breasts; cook to 145°F.

CULINARY NOTE

After returning the meat to the skillet, do not boil the mixture. Cook over medium low heat. If the meat boils in the sauce, it will become tough and dry.

WINE SUGGESTION: *Zinfandel*

Nutrition Facts per Serving: 257 calories, 26 g protein, 15.5 g total fat (3.5 g saturated fat), 7 g carbohydrate, 2 g fiber, 37 mg cholesterol, 800 mg sodium, 29 weighted glycemic index

Slow-Braised Pot Roast
with Molasses and Mustard

This slow-cooked roast develops the rich flavor of the molasses and cinnamon to perfectly pair with beef.
Using a slow cooker makes it a great meal to come home to.

Start to Finish: 4 hours, plus 1 to 24 hours for marinating   Yield: 8 servings

CULINARY NOTES

- If the spice rub starts to stick and burn to the bottom of the pan, add a little stock to deglaze the pan.

- The amount of time needed to cook the meat will depend on the thickness of the meat. A 1-inch-thick, long piece of meat will cook faster than a 2-inch-thick, shorter piece of meat.

- The meat is lean, so cook it until it is just tender.

- To determine doneness of the meat, insert a fork into the center of the meat. It should be easy to remove the fork and the meat should lightly flake when pulled apart. If there is a lot of resistance, the meat needs to cook longer.

1	tablespoon garlic, chopped fine
1	tablespoon paprika
2	teaspoons dry mustard
1	teaspoon ground cinnamon
2	teaspoons rosemary, chopped
1	teaspoon oregano, dried
½	teaspoon ground black pepper
2	pounds top round or top sirloin roast
2	tablespoons extra-virgin olive oil
2	cups onions, diced
1	teaspoon garlic, chopped
2	tablespoons molasses
1	tablespoon Dijon mustard
1	tablespoon reduced-sodium soy sauce
1	cup low-sodium chicken stock
	Salt and pepper to taste

1. Combine garlic, paprika, mustard, cinnamon, rosemary, oregano, and pepper. Season meat with salt and pepper; rub with spice mixture. Marinate in the refrigerator up to 24 hours.

2. Heat a sauté pan over medium heat. Add olive oil and meat; brown lightly on all sides. Remove meat from pan and place in a crockpot. Add onions to the sauté pan and cook until translucent. Add garlic; cook until aromatic. Add molasses, mustard, soy sauce, and chicken stock; bring to a simmer. Pour into crockpot with meat. Cook on low for 3 to 4 hours or until the meat is tender when poked with a fork. Remove meat from crockpot; let rest in a warm spot.

3. Degrease the liquid and puree until smooth in a blender. Adjust seasoning.

4. Slice the meat ¼ inch thick; serve with the sauce.

Variation

- Use this spice mixture for grilled chicken, beef, or pork.

WINE SUGGESTION: *Merlot*

Nutrition Facts per Serving: 320 calories, 27 g protein, 12 g total fat (3 g saturated fat), 12 g carbohydrate, 1.5 g fiber, 60 mg cholesterol, 300 mg sodium, 31 weighted glycemic index

Grilled Wine Country Sirloin Steaks

with Cherry Tomato and Arugula Salad

Although this marinade contains several distinctly flavored ingredients, they fuse harmoniously. Start marinating up to a day in advance to allow the flavors to blend and save you time.

Start to Finish: 30 minutes, plus 1 to 24 hours for marinating   Yield: 4 servings

4 6-ounce boneless beef sirloin steaks, cut 1 inch thick	2 tablespoons lemon juice
Kosher salt	1 tablespoon red wine vinegar
Freshly ground black pepper	6 cups torn arugula leaves
¼ cup extra-virgin olive oil	1 cup celery, thinly sliced
2 tablespoons fresh mint, chopped	1 cup cherry tomatoes, halved
1 tablespoon fresh rosemary, chopped	2 tablespoons shredded parmesan or Asiago cheese
½ to 1 teaspoon crushed red pepper	

1. Trim fat from steaks. Season steaks with kosher salt and black pepper. Place steaks in a large self-sealing plastic bag set in a shallow dish.

2. For marinade, in a small bowl combine 2 tablespoons olive oil, 1 tablespoon mint, rosemary, and crushed red pepper. Pour over steaks. Seal bag; turn to coat steaks. Marinate in the refrigerator for 1 to 24 hours, turning bag occasionally.

3. For dressing, in a screw-top jar combine lemon juice, red wine vinegar, and remaining 2 tablespoons olive oil. Cover and shake well. Season to taste with additional kosher salt and black pepper. Set aside.

4. Drain steaks, discarding marinade. For a charcoal grill, place steaks on the rack of an uncovered grill directly over medium coals. Grill for 14 to 18 minutes for medium-rare doneness (145°F) or 18 to 22 minutes for

Nutrition Facts per Serving: 520 calories, 52 g protein, 31 g total fat (8.5 g saturated fat), 4.5 g carbohydrate, 1.5 g fiber, mg 125 cholesterol, 173 mg sodium, 20 weighted glycemic index

medium doneness (160°F), turning once halfway through grilling. For a gas grill, preheat grill. Reduce heat to medium. Place steaks on grill rack over heat. Cover and grill as above.

5. Remove steaks from grill. Cover with foil and let stand for 5 to 10 minutes. Slice meat across the grain.

6. In a large bowl, combine arugula, celery, tomatoes, and the remaining 1 tablespoon mint. Drizzle with the dressing; toss to coat.

7. To serve, divide arugula mixture among four dinner plates; top with meat slices. Sprinkle with cheese.

Variations

- Replace red wine vinegar with balsamic vinegar and add 2 tablespoon feta cheese.
- Add 1 cup blanched green beans cut in 2-inch pieces and ½ cup sliced radishes.
- Replace arugula with 4 cups shredded romaine leaves and 2 cups watercress.

WINE SUGGESTION: *Sangiovese*

Skirt Steak Sandwich

with Peperonata, Arugula, and Fresh Mozzarella

Peperonata, a typical Italian recipe, tastes even better the next day.
Try this recipe in the summer months when peppers are at their peak
for flavor and color. A great sandwich for an afternoon picnic.

Start to Finish: 20 minutes, plus up to 24 hours for marinating   Yield: 4 servings

4   whole-wheat buns, thin sliced
8   slices fresh mozzarella cheese, ¼ inch thick
1   pound grilled skirt steak (Grilled Skirt Steak with Peperonata, page 98)

2   cups peperonata (Grilled Skirt Steak with Peperonata, page 98)
2   cups arugula, washed
1   tablespoon balsamic vinegar
    Salt and pepper to taste

1. Split whole-wheat buns in half. Lightly toast in broiler or toaster.

2. Place 2 pieces of mozzarella on each bun.

3. Thinly slice skirt steak against the grain. Divide evenly between the buns. Sprinkle with salt and pepper. Top with peperonata.

4. Toss arugula with salt, pepper, and balsamic vinegar; place on top of peperonata. Position top of bun on top.

CULINARY NOTE

COOK 1X · EAT 2X   for the leftover Grilled Skirt Steak with Peperonata (page 98)

Variation

- Replace skirt steak with leftover roast chicken or pork tenderloin.

Nutrition Facts per Serving: calories, g protein, g total fat (g saturated fat), g carbohydrate, g fiber, mg cholesterol, mg sodium, 58 weighted glycemic index

Flank Steak
with Sun-Dried Tomato Pesto en Papillote

Cooking en papillote is a French cooking method that delicately seals the flavors in a steam packet made from either foil or parchment paper. The sun-dried tomatoes and basil infuse a wonderful aroma and flavor as the meat essentially steams in the oven in its own juices.

Start to Finish: 40 minutes   Yield: 4 servings

1	pound flank steak, fat removed	4	tablespoons Sun-Dried Tomato Pesto (page 392)
1	tablespoon extra-virgin olive oil	1	tablespoon basil, chopped
1	pound zucchini, bias sliced ¼ inch thick		Salt and pepper to taste
8	ounces tomatoes, about 8 slices	4	pieces parchment paper, 15 inches x 36 inches

1. Preheat oven to 400°F. Place 2 baking sheets in the oven on separate shelves.

2. Cut meat in half lengthwise. Cut each lengthwise piece in half across the middle. Season meat with salt and pepper.

3. Heat a sauté pan over high heat. When the pan is smoking hot, add olive oil and meat. Sear meat on both sides and remove from pan. The meat should still be raw but browned on the outside.

4. Fold each piece of parchment paper in half like a book. Cut into a large heart shape, with the fold at the center of the heart.

5. For each packet: Place the zucchini slices just off center of the fold. Season with salt and pepper. Lay 2 tomato slices on top of zucchini. Place flank steak on top of tomatoes. Spread pesto on top of flank steak. Sprinkle with basil.

6. Fold the other side of the paper over meat. Starting at the top of heart shape, fold up both edges of the parchment, overlapping folds as you move along the edge of the paper. When you reach the end, twist the end several times to secure.

7. Place packets on preheated baking sheets in preheated oven. Bake for 12 to 15 minutes. Remove from oven and serve immediately. The meat should be medium rare and will need to be sliced across the grain.

Nutrition Facts per Serving: 250 calories, 28 g protein, 12 g total fat (3.5 g saturated fat), 8.5 g carbohydrate, 2.5 g fiber, 38 mg cholesterol, 120 mg sodium, 25 weighted glycemic index

Seared Beef Tenderloin
with Orange and Olives

Searing beef is a convenient cooking method that takes only minutes and seals in the meat's juices to ensure a tender steak. This recipe has a distinct citrus twist from the inclusion of oranges and lemon juice.

Start to Finish: 35 minutes   *Yield: 4 servings*

12	ounces beef tenderloin, cut into 4 steaks (each about ¾ inch thick)	¼	cup pitted kalamata olives, quartered
4	large oranges	¼	cup fresh flat-leaf parsley, chopped
2	teaspoons fennel seeds, crushed	2	tablespoons lemon juice
2	teaspoons black peppercorns, crushed	1	clove garlic, minced (½ teaspoon minced)
¼	teaspoon kosher salt	½	teaspoon paprika
3	tablespoon extra-virgin olive oil	4	cups torn arugula leaves
½	cup red onion, finely chopped		Salt and pepper to taste

1. Season the beef with salt and pepper. Let sit for 15 minutes.

2. Finely shred enough of the orange peel to make 2 teaspoons. In a small bowl, combine orange peel, fennel seeds, peppercorns, and kosher salt. Sprinkle mixture evenly over beef.

2. In a large skillet, heat 1 tablespoon olive oil over medium-high heat; add the meat. Reduce heat to medium. Cook for 7 to 9 minutes or until desired doneness (135°F for medium-rare or 145°F for medium), turning once. Slice meat across the grain into thin slices.

3. Meanwhile, peel oranges, removing all of the white pith. Section oranges. In a large bowl, combine orange sections, red onion, olives, parsley, lemon juice, the 2 remaining tablespoons olive oil, garlic, and paprika.
Stir gently to combine.

4. Add arugula to orange mixture; toss to combine. Divide arugula mixture among four dinner plates. Serve with sliced meat.

CULINARY NOTES

- Season the meat ahead of time so that the salt and pepper have time to be absorbed into the meat.

- Be gentle when mixing the oranges; they are delicate and will fall apart if overmixed.

Variations
- Replace beef with lamb.
- Replace arugula with spinach.

WINE SUGGESTION: *Sparkling semisweet or rosé*

Nutrition Facts per Serving: 280 calories, 19 g protein, 15 g total fat (2.5 g saturated fat), 20 g carbohydrate, 5 g fiber, 45 mg cholesterol, 245 mg sodium, 35 weighted glycemic index

South American Hanger Steak

Latin American seasonings originated from a combination of Spanish and Portuguese ingredients with the culinary traditions of the American Indians and, later, African slaves. This delicious, simple recipe combines the flavors of fiery hot chipotle in adobo sauce with sweet citrus and the rich, spicy flavors of cumin and coriander.

Start to Finish: 30 minutes, plus 2 to 24 hours for marinating   Yield: 4 servings

CULINARY NOTES

- Scoring the meat first allows excess fat to drain during cooking and allows the marinade to penetrate more rapidly, increasing flavor absorption and tenderization.

- For less heat in the marinade, use a couple of teaspoons of the adobo sauce and leave out the chipotle peppers.

- Flank steak can be substituted for hanger steak.

* Because hot chile peppers contain oils that can burn your skin and eyes, wear rubber or plastic gloves when handling them. If your bare hands do touch the chile peppers, wash your hands well with soap and water.

1	pound beef hanger steak
1	cup lightly packed fresh cilantro
⅓	cup orange juice
4	teaspoons red wine vinegar
1	tablespoon extra-virgin olive oil
4	cloves garlic, minced
2	teaspoons ground cumin
2	teaspoons ground coriander
1½–2	teaspoons canned chipotle in adobo sauce,* finely chopped
¼	teaspoon kosher salt
¼	teaspoon freshly ground black pepper

1. Trim fat from steak. Score both sides in a diamond pattern by making shallow cuts at 1-inch intervals. Place steak in a self-sealing plastic bag set in a shallow dish.

2. In a blender combine cilantro, orange juice, vinegar, olive oil, garlic, cumin, coriander, chipotle, kosher salt, and black pepper. Cover and blend until smooth. Pour orange juice mixture over steak. Seal bag; turn to coat steak. Marinate in the refrigerator for 2 to 24 hours, turning bag occasionally.

3. Drain steak, discarding marinade. For a charcoal grill, place steak on the rack of an uncovered grill directly over medium coals. Grill for 17 to 21 minutes or until medium doneness (160°F), turning steak once halfway through grilling. For a gas grill, preheat grill. Reduce heat to medium. Place steak on grill rack over heat. Cover and grill as above.

4. To serve, thinly slice steak across the grain.

Variations

- Replace hanger steak with skirt steak.
- Replace hanger steak with chicken breasts, pork tenderloin, or pork chops.

WINE SUGGESTION: *Zinfandel*

Nutrition Facts per Serving: 212 calories, 25 g protein, 10 g total fat (3 g saturated fat), 3.8 g carbohydrate, 1 g fiber, 37 mg cholesterol, 190 mg sodium, 49 weighted glycemic index

POULTRY DINNERS

Ginger, pepper, cilantro, garlic, mint, whole-grain mustard, and curry . . . here is a start to the most delicious and easy ways to enjoy wholesome recipes featuring chicken and turkey.

Bistro Chicken and Garlic

Garlic is a powerful herb with a celebrated culinary and medicinal history. Ancient Egyptians ate garlic for strength, and medieval healers suggested its use to ward off vampires. Today it's commended for its cancer-fighting antioxidant, allicin. In this recipe, garlic is roasted to mellow and sweeten its flavor.

Start to Finish: 45 minutes   Yield: 4 servings

1	bulb garlic	¼	teaspoon dried rosemary, crushed
1	tablespoon extra-virgin olive oil	¼	teaspoon kosher salt
4	skinless, boneles s chicken breast halves (1 to 1¼ pounds total)	⅛	teaspoon freshly ground black pepper
¼	teaspoon dried basil, crushed	¼	cup dry vermouth or dry white wine
¼	teaspoon dried thyme, crushed		

1. Preheat oven to 400°F. Separate cloves of garlic, discarding small papery cloves in the center. Trim off stem end of each garlic clove but do not peel. (This will facilitate squeezing garlic from peel after it is cooked.)

2. In a large ovenproof skillet, heat olive oil over medium-high heat. Add garlic cloves and chicken. Cook about 4 minutes or until chicken is lightly browned, turning chicken and stirring garlic cloves once. Sprinkle chicken with basil, thyme, rosemary, kosher salt, and pepper; transfer skillet to the oven. Bake, covered, for 12 to 15 minutes or until chicken is tender and no longer pink (170°F) and garlic is tender.

3. Using a slotted spatula, transfer chicken to a serving platter, reserving juices in skillet; cover and keep warm. Transfer garlic cloves to a small bowl; set aside for 1 to 2 minutes to cool slightly.

CULINARY NOTE

When the garlic is cooked, it should be completely soft and golden brown. The sautéing and roasting makes the garlic sweet and mild.

4. Add vermouth or white wine to skillet. Squeeze softened garlic from skins into skillet; discard skins. On range top, bring garlic mixture to boiling over medium heat; reduce heat. Simmer gently, uncovered, about 6 minutes or until sauce thickens slightly, stirring frequently. Pour garlic sauce over chicken. If desired, garnish with sprigs of fresh herbs.

Variations

- Replace the chicken with beef tenderloin.
- Replace the chicken with pork tenderloin.
- Replace dried herbs with fresh herbs.

WINE SUGGESTION: *Syrah or merlot*

Nutrition Facts per Serving: 190 calories, 25 g protein, 6.5 g total fat (1 g saturated fat), 3.5 g carbohydrate, 0 g fiber, 75 mg cholesterol, 250 mg sodium, 13 weighted glycemic index

Braised Chicken

with Artichokes and Peppers

A slow-cooked dish that is ready for you when you return from a busy day is a treat. This is a great recipe for early fall as it still includes light flavors. Tender chicken cooked in its own stock with spices, mushrooms, artichokes, peppers, and wine and served over quinoa makes for a sumptuous meal.

Start to Finish: 2 hours   Yield: 8 servings

1 whole chicken, cut into 8 pieces, bone-in, skinless, fat removed	1 teaspoon thyme, chopped
1 tablespoon chile powder	1½ cups red peppers, cut in strips
1 teaspoon ground cumin	1 cup white wine
2 tablespoons garlic, chopped	1½ cups artichoke hearts, cooked
1 tablespoon extra-virgin olive oil	1 bay leaf
1¼ cup low-sodium chicken stock	1 tablespoon basil, chopped
3 cups onions, chopped	1 teaspoon lemon zest
1½ cups crimini brown mushrooms, cut in quarters	4 cups Toasted Quinoa Pilaf (page 120)
	Salt and pepper to taste

1. Season chicken with salt and pepper. Combine chile powder, cumin, and 1 tablespoon garlic in a bowl. Sprinkle on seasoned chicken. Let sit for 30 minutes to overnight.

2. Heat a large nonstick sauté pan over medium heat. Add olive oil and half of the chicken pieces. Lightly brown the chicken, being careful not to burn the spices. Remove from pan; repeat with remaining pieces. Place chicken in a crockpot on low heat, legs and thighs on the bottom, breast meat on top.

3. Deglaze the sauté pan with ¼ cup chicken stock. Add onions and mushrooms to the pan; cook over medium heat until translucent. Add remaining garlic, thyme, and peppers; cook until aromatic. Add white wine and reduce by three-fourths. Add artichokes,

Nutrition Facts per Serving: 315 calories, 25 g protein, 6.5 g total fat (1 g saturated fat), 34 g carbohydrate, 7.5 g fiber, 57 mg cholesterol, 115 mg sodium, 39 weighted glycemic index

bay leaf, and remaining 1 cup chicken stock; bring to a simmer. Season with salt and pepper. Pour over the chicken in the crockpot, placing the artichokes on top. Cook on low heat. Remove the chicken breasts after 1 hour if they are cooked, and let the legs continue to cook until fork-tender, about another hour.

4. When the chicken is tender, degrease the sauce. Stir in basil and lemon. Serve over Toasted Quinoa Pilaf.

CULINARY NOTE

To thicken the sauce after the chicken is cooked, place it in a saucepan and reduce until flavorful and desired consistency.

Variations

- You can prepare this recipe using chicken thighs only.
- Replace artichokes with raw fennel.

Toasted Quinoa Pilaf

Start to Finish: 30 minutes   Yield: 4 cups

2	tablespoons olive oil	2	teaspoons thyme, chopped
2	cups quinoa, rinsed, drained well	2 ½	cups water or stock
1	cup onion, diced		Salt and pepper to taste
1	tablespoon garlic, chopped		

1. Heat a small saucepan over medium heat. Add olive oil and quinoa. Stir over medium heat to toast the quinoa. It will start to pop like popcorn and have a slightly nutty aroma.

2. Add onion, garlic, and thyme; stir until aromatic. Add water; bring to a simmer. Season with salt and pepper. Reduce heat to low, cover tightly, and cook for 15 minutes.

3. Remove from heat, let sit for 4 minutes, and fluff with a fork.

Variations

- Add 1 cup diced roasted red peppers and 1 cup roasted corn; serve as a side vegetable.

- Add 1 cup roasted butternut squash and 1 tablespoon parsley.

- Add 1 tablespoon chopped chipotle in adobo sauce (less if you do not like spicy foods), 1 cup diced canned green chiles, and 1 cup roasted corn.

- Add 2 cups mushrooms sautéed with garlic.

- Add ¼ cup chopped sun-dried tomatoes and 1 tablespoon basil.

CULINARY NOTES

- Quinoa has a natural coating called saposin. It is bitter, so it is important to rinse the quinoa in water and then let it drain for a few minutes before toasting. If the grain is wet, it is more difficult to toast.

- Quinoa can also be toasted by spreading it on a sheet pan and placing in a 350°F oven for 5 to 10 minutes, stirring periodically.

- It is important to let the grain sit for a few minutes once it is removed from the heat. This allows the grain to settle and slightly firm up. If you stir it immediately after it has finished cooking, it will mush up and become gummy.

- This recipe can be the base for COOK 1X · EAT 2X salads and wraps.

Nutrition Facts per Serving: 100 calories, 4 g protein, 3 g fat (1 g saturated fat), 16 g carbohydrate, 2 g fiber, 0 mg cholesterol, 10 mg sodium, 33 weighted glycemic index

Vietnamese Chicken Curry

Inspired by the traditional Vietnamese style of curry dishes, this recipe is milder and lighter than Indian or Thai curries. You can make this recipe with chicken stock, but the coconut milk adds body and enhances the overall flavor. Serve it with steamed brown rice or rice noodles. Like other curries, it's delicious the next day.

Start to Finish: 50 minutes   Yield: 4 servings

4 chicken breasts, boneless, skinless	1 cup carrots, sliced
1 tablespoon curry powder	1 15.5-ounce can low-sodium chicken stock
1 tablespoon canola oil	1 cup broccoli florets, blanched
1 cup onion, chopped	1 cup light coconut milk
1 tablespoon garlic, chopped	Lime juice to taste
1 tablespoon ginger, chopped	1 tablespoon cilantro, chopped
1 tablespoon lemon grass or lemon verbena leaves, chopped	2 cups brown rice, cooked
¼ teaspoon chile flakes or sambal oelek chile paste	Salt and pepper to taste

1. Cut chicken into 2-inch pieces. Season with salt, pepper, and curry powder.

2. Heat a large Dutch oven or deep sauté pan over medium heat. Add oil and chicken. Cook until chicken is slightly browned on all sides but still raw. Remove chicken from pan and reserve on a plate.

3. Add onion to the sauté pan and cook until just soft (deglaze with water if necessary).

Add garlic, ginger, lemon grass, and chile flakes; cook until aromatic.

4. Add carrots and chicken stock. Bring to a simmer; cook until the carrots are tender. Add broccoli and coconut milk, and return chicken to the pan. Bring to a simmer and cook for 5 minutes until the chicken is cooked through. Season with lime juice; stir in cilantro.

5. Serve with brown rice.

Nutrition Facts per Serving: 450 calories, 30 g protein, 20 g total fat (12 g saturated fat), 35 g carbohydrate, 5 g fiber, 72 mg cholesterol, 200 mg sodium, 44 weighted glycemic index

CULINARY NOTES

* Because hot chili peppers contain oils that can burn your skin and eyes, wear rubber or plastic gloves when handling them. If your bare hands do touch the chile peppers, wash your hands well with soap and water.

■ Grilling directions: For a charcoal grill, place chicken on the lightly greased rack of an uncovered grill directly over medium coals. Grill for 12 to 15 minutes or until chicken is tender and no longer pink (170°F). For a gas grill, preheat grill. Reduce heat to medium. Place chicken on lightly greased grill rack over heat. Cover and grill as above.

■ The chicken can also be sautéed. Heat a sauté pan, add one tablespoon of olive oil, and immediately lay the chicken breasts flat in the pan. Cook until golden brown, then flip and cook on the other side.

Chicken with Salsa de Piña

These juicy chicken breasts are paired with a sweet and fiery pineapple salsa that explodes with flavor. Chipotle peppers give the salsa a spicy kick, so if you like it hot, use the high end of the range.

Start to Finish: 60 minutes   Yield: 4 servings

1½ cups chopped fresh pineapple	2 teaspoons lime juice or lemon juice
1 to 2 canned chipotle in adobo sauce, drained, seeded, and finely chopped*	4 skinless, boneless chicken breast halves (1 to 1¼ pounds total)
2 tablespoons chopped fresh chives	1 teaspoon extra-virgin olive oil
1 tablespoon honey	1 teaspoon dried thyme, crushed
1 teaspoon finely shredded lime peel or lemon peel	¼ teaspoon kosher salt
	¼ teaspoon freshly ground black pepper

1. In a medium bowl, stir together pineapple, chipotle peppers, chives, honey, lime peel, and lime juice. Let salsa stand at room temperature for 30 minutes.

2. Meanwhile, preheat broiler. Lightly brush chicken with olive oil. In a small bowl, stir together thyme, kosher salt, and black pepper. Sprinkle evenly over chicken; rub in with your fingers.

3. Place chicken on the unheated rack of a broiler pan. Broil 4 to 5 inches from heat for 12 to 15 minutes or until chicken is tender and no longer pink (170°F), turning once.

4. Slice chicken and serve with salsa.

Variations

- Replace the chicken with pork loin cut into 1-inch-thick steaks.
- Grill the pineapple in slices: Heat a grill or grill pan over high heat. Place pineapple slices on the grill, establish some grill marks, then turn 45 degrees, flip, and cook on the other side.

WINE SUGGESTION:
Sparkling semisweet

Nutrition Facts per Serving: 195 calories, 25 g protein, 4.5 g total fat (1 g saturated fat), 13 g carbohydrate, 1.5 g fiber, 75 mg cholesterol, 350 mg sodium, 55 weighted glycemic index

Braised Chicken
with White Beans and Spanish Chorizo

This is the Spanish version of an Italian cacciatore meal.
Rich and hearty, this is a perfect winter stew. The Spanish chorizo
gives a sweet paprika and garlic flavor to this dish.

Start to Finish: 1 hour   Yield: 4 servings

4 chicken legs	2 tablespoon garlic, chopped
1 tablespoon Spanish paprika	1 15-ounce can tomatoes, chopped
½ teaspoon ground cumin	2 15.5-ounce cans white beans, drained
1 teaspoon extra-virgin olive oil	2 cups low-sodium chicken stock
2 cups mushrooms, quartered	1 tablespoon oregano, chopped
2 ounces Spanish chorizo, quartered lengthwise, then cut into ¼-inch pieces	1 bay leaf
	2 cups baby spinach
2 cups onions, chopped	Salt and pepper to taste

CULINARY NOTES

- Chorizo is a pork sausage that comes in many different varieties. Make sure you use Spanish chorizo, not Mexican chorizo, for this recipe. They are different products. Mexican chorizo is seasoned with chili peppers and vinegar. Spanish chorizo is flavored with paprika (sweet or spicy), which gives the sausage its characteristic color.

- This dish will freeze well. Wrap tightly to prevent freezer burn.

1. Season chicken with salt, pepper, 2 teaspoons paprika, and cumin. Let sit for 10 minutes.

2. Heat the olive oil in a sauté pan. Add the chicken, skin side down. Cook over medium heat until the skin is golden brown. Turn over and cook for 5 minutes on the other side. Remove from the pan.

3. Pour off the excess grease from the pan. Add the mushrooms and sauté over medium heat until slightly browned. Add chorizo, onions, and garlic. Cook for 10 minutes or until onions are translucent. Add the tomatoes, white beans, chicken stock, oregano, and bay leaf. Bring to a simmer. Adjust seasoning with salt and pepper. Place the chicken on top, skin side up. Place in a 375°F oven and bake until the chicken is cooked through, about 25 minutes. Remove from oven. Stir in spinach. Adjust seasoning.

Variations

- Substitute kale or chard cut in 1-inch strips for the baby spinach.
- Substitute chickpeas for the white beans.

Nutrition Facts per Serving: 550 calories, 50 g protein, 13 g total fat (4 g saturated fat), 65 g carbohydrate, 14 g fiber, 115 mg cholesterol, 600 mg sodium, 32 weighted glycemic index

Braised Chicken

with Whole-Grain Mustard and Apples

Preparing meals in a crockpot is the way to go when you have a busy day and want to come home to a prepared meal. The flavor combination of the whole-grain mustard and apples makes for a delicious sweet and savory sauce.

Start to Finish: 2 hours   *Yield: 8 servings*

1 whole chicken, cut into 8 pieces, bone-in, skinless, fat removed	2 tablespoons whole-grain mustard
2 tablespoons extra-virgin olive oil	1 tablespoon parsley, chopped
2 cups apple juice	2 tablespoons lemon juice
4 Granny Smith apples, peeled, cored, cut into 8 pieces	1 teaspoon lemon zest
½ cup low-sodium chicken stock or water	4 cups brown rice pilaf, cooked
	Salt and pepper to taste

1. Season chicken with salt and pepper. Let sit for 30 minutes to overnight.

2. Heat a large nonstick sauté pan over medium heat. Add 1 tablespoon olive oil and half the chicken pieces; lightly brown the chicken. Remove from pan; repeat with remaining pieces. Place chicken in crockpot on low heat, legs and thighs on the bottom, breast meat on top.

3. Deglaze sauté pan with apple juice and reduce by half. Pour reduction over chicken in crockpot.

4. Add remaining olive oil to sauté pan and sauté apples until golden brown.

5. Deglaze the pan with ¼ cup chicken stock or water. Stir in whole-grain mustard. Bring to a simmer. Season with salt and pepper. Pour over the chicken in the crockpot. Cook on low heat. Remove the chicken breasts after 1 hour if they are cooked, and let the legs continue to cook until fork-tender, about another hour.

6. When the chicken is tender, degrease the sauce; stir in parsley, lemon juice, and lemon zest.

7. Serve over brown rice pilaf with sautéed chard.

Nutrition Facts per Serving: 340 calories, 21 g protein, 7 g total fat (1 g saturated fat), 48 g carbohydrate, 4.5 g fiber, 55 mg cholesterol, 100 mg sodium, 46 weighted glycemic index

Crispy Chicken
with Braised Cauliflower

A perfect alternative to fried chicken, this recipes has lots of appeal and crunch. Try seasoning the bread crumbs with a favorite spice mix for a flavorful variation.

Start to Finish: 1 hour, 10 minutes   Yield: 4 servings

4	chicken thighs, skinless	1	cup onions, diced
1	egg	1	tablespoon garlic, chopped
2	tablespoons Dijon mustard	2	cups chard or kale, cut in 1-inch pieces
2	tablespoons tarragon, chopped	½	cup low-sodium chicken stock
2	tablespoons extra-virgin olive oil		Salt and pepper to taste
1	cup whole-wheat bread crumbs		
4	cups cauliflower florets		

1. Preheat oven 350°F.

2. Season chicken with salt and pepper. Let sit while you prepare the remaining ingredients.

3. Combine egg, mustard, 1 tablespoon tarragon, salt, and pepper in a large bowl. Set aside.

4. Combine bread crumbs, 1 tablespoon tarragon, and 1 tablespoon olive oil; toss to coat bread crumbs with oil. Pour onto a flat pan. Set aside.

5. Heat a Dutch oven or large deep sauté pan over medium-high heat. Add 1 tablespoon olive oil and chicken. Brown the chicken on both sides. Remove from pan. Pour off any excess grease. Add cauliflower to pan; sauté 5 minutes until golden brown. Add onions and garlic; cook until aromatic. Add greens and chicken stock; bring to a simmer. Season with salt and pepper.

6. Toss the chicken in the bowl with the egg mixture. Stir to coat each piece. Place 1 side of each piece of chicken in the bread crumbs to coat. Place chicken with crumb side up on top of the cauliflower in the Dutch oven.

7. Bake in oven for 45 minutes or until the chicken is cooked through and the bread crumbs have browned. Remove from the oven; let rest for 5 minutes before serving.

Nutrition Facts per Serving: 280 calories, 21 g protein, 12 g total fat (2 g saturated fat), 24 g carbohydrate, 4 g fiber, 110 mg cholesterol, 340 mg sodium, 50 weighted glycemic index

Chicken Breast Stuffed
with Spinach and Feta Cheese

This entrée, which is relatively easy to make, makes a special meal for the family. Serve with brown rice, roasted vegetables, and crusty whole-grain rolls. The mushroom variation is perfect for entertaining.

Start to Finish: 1 hour 30 minutes   Yield: 4 servings

4	chicken breasts, 4 to 5 ounces each	¼	cup feta cheese
2	tablespoons olive oil	1	teaspoon thyme, chopped
½	cup onion, chopped	½	cup white wine
4	teaspoons garlic, chopped	2	cups low-sodium chicken stock
1	teaspoon oregano, chopped		Salt and pepper to taste
4	cups baby spinach		Toothpicks
1	scallion, chopped		

1. Season chicken breasts with salt and pepper. Let sit for 15 minutes.

2. While the meat rests, heat a sauté pan over medium heat. Add 1 tablespoon olive oil and onions; cook until onions are slightly browned. Add 3 teaspoons garlic and oregano; cook until aromatic. Stir in the spinach and scallion and cook until spinach is wilted. Place in a baking dish and cool in the refrigerator for 15 minutes. Once the filling is cool, fold in the feta cheese and season with salt and pepper.

3. To make a pocket in each chicken breast, lay the chicken breast flat on a cutting board. Hold the paring knife flat, parallel to the cutting board. Make an incision in the middle of the thickest part of the chicken breast. Insert the knife almost all the way into the chicken breast, leaving a ¼-inch-thick border. Keeping the knife flat, move it forward to form a pocket in the breast, trying to keep the opening to 1 inch in size, with a ¼-inch-thick border.

CULINARY NOTE

To speed up the cooling of the filling, spread it in a thin layer on a pan and place in the freezer.

4. Gently fill the pocket with ½ cup of the cool filling. Using toothpicks, close the opening of the pocket.

5. Heat a sauté pan over medium heat. Add the remaining oil. Lay the chicken breasts flat in the pan and cook until golden brown. Turn and cook on the other side until golden brown. By this time, the chicken should be cooked all the way through and the filling should be warm. If the chicken is still undercooked, place in a 350°F oven and cook for a few more minutes. Remove chicken from sauté pan and let rest in a warm place.

6. Return pan to medium heat. Add remaining teaspoon garlic and thyme. Cook 1 minute; add white wine and reduce to 1 tablespoon. Add chicken stock, bring to a simmer, and reduce by one half. Adjust seasoning and serve with warm chicken.

Variations

- Serve with tomato sauce.
- Replace spinach with chard.
- Replace feta cheese with goat cheese.

Nutrition Facts per Serving: 285 calories, 30 g protein, 12 g total fat (3 g saturated fat), 8.5 g carbohydrate, 2 g fiber, 80 mg cholesterol, 250 mg sodium, 12 weighted glycemic index

Mushroom Filling

Heat a sauté pan over medium heat. Add 1 tablespoon oil, 2 cups sliced brown mushrooms, and ¼ cup white wine. Cook until the wine evaporates and the mushrooms start to brown in the pan, about 10 minutes. Add ½ cup chopped onions, 1 tablespoon chopped garlic, and 1 teaspoon chopped thyme, oregano, chives, or tarragon. Cook until the onions are slightly browned and the garlic is aromatic. Place in a baking dish and cool in the refrigerator for 15 minutes. Once the filling is cool, fold in 2 tablespoons feta cheese and season with salt and pepper.

Nutrition Facts per Serving: 270 calories, 30 g protein, 12 g total fat (2.5 g saturated fat), 6.5 g carbohydrate, 1 g fiber, 78 mg cholesterol, 200 mg sodium, 11 weighted glycemic index

CULINARY NOTE

The water may be unnecessary if tomatoes are juicy and contain enough moisture.

Chicken with Red and Yellow Cherry Tomatoes

A simple topping of delightfully tangy red and yellow cherry tomatoes makes this meal perfect weeknight fare. Cooking the tomatoes boosts their antioxidant availability and gives them a richer flavor.

Start to Finish: 25 minutes   Yield: 4 servings

4 skinless, boneless chicken breast halves (1 to 1¼ pounds total)	4 cups red and/or yellow cherry tomatoes, halved
½ teaspoon kosher salt	2 tablespoons water
¼ teaspoon freshly ground black pepper	¼ cup chopped fresh flat-leaf parsley or basil or 2 tablespoons chopped fresh tarragon
1 tablespoon extra-virgin olive oil	2 tablespoons white wine vinegar

1. Sprinkle chicken with ¼ teaspoon kosher salt and ⅛ teaspoon pepper. In a large nonstick skillet, heat olive oil over medium-high heat. Add chicken; cook for 10 to 12 minutes or until chicken is no longer pink (170°F), turning once. Transfer chicken to a serving platter; cover and keep warm.

2. Drain fat from skillet. Add tomatoes, water, parsley, vinegar, the remaining ¼ teaspoon salt, and the remaining ⅛ teaspoon pepper to skillet. Bring to boiling; reduce heat. Simmer, uncovered, for 3 to 4 minutes or until tomatoes begin to soften, stirring occasionally. Serve the tomato mixture over chicken.

WINE SUGGESTION: *White zinfandel or pinot noir*

Nutrition Facts per Serving: 190 calories, 26 g protein, 6.5 g total fat (1 g saturated fat), 6 g carbohydrate, 2 g fiber, 75 mg cholesterol, 380 mg sodium, 23 weighted glycemic index

Chipotle Albondigas
with Garbanzo Beans and Chard Soup

Albondigas soup is a traditional Mexican meatball soup (*albondigas* means "meatballs" in Spanish). It is the Mexican version of comfort food. What makes the flavor of albondigas soup distinctive is the herbs in the meatballs. Traditionally, mint was included in these herbs. You can add ½ teaspoon chopped fresh mint or ¼ teaspoon dried mint along with the oregano. You can also vary the vegetables, depending on what you have on hand and what's in season.

Start to Finish: 80 minutes   Yield: 8 servings, 2 albondigas and 1½ cups broth each

For the broth

1	tablespoon extra-virgin olive oil
2	cups onions, chopped
2	cups mushrooms, chopped
1	tablespoon garlic, chopped
½	teaspoon ground cumin
1½	teaspoons chipotle in adobo sauce, chopped
2	15-ounce cans tomatoes, chopped
2½	15-ounce cans low-sodium chicken stock
1	15-ounce can garbanzo beans, drained
2	cups chard, cut into 1-inch slices
2	tablespoons cilantro, chopped
8	lime wedges
	Salt and pepper

For the meatballs

1	tablespoon extra-virgin olive oil
½	cup celery, chopped
½	cup onion, chopped
1	tablespoon garlic
½	teaspoon Mexican oregano
2	tablespoons nonfat milk
¼	cup fresh whole-wheat bread crumbs
1	egg, slightly beaten
1½	teaspoons chipotle in adobo sauce, chopped
1	pound ground turkey
	Salt and pepper to taste

1. For the broth: Heat a soup pot over low heat. Add olive oil, onions, mushrooms, and a pinch of salt and pepper. Cook for 5 minutes until translucent. Add garlic and cumin; cook 1 minute until aromatic. Add chipotle, tomatoes, and chicken stock. Bring to a simmer. Add chickpeas; bring to a simmer. Cook for 15 minutes or until the flavors have melded.

2. While the broth is simmering, prepare the meatballs. Heat a sauté pan over medium heat; add olive oil, celery, and onion. Season with salt and pepper; cook until translucent. Add garlic and oregano; sauté 1 minute until aromatic. Set aside to cool. In a large bowl, combine milk and bread crumbs. Stir in egg, chipotle, cooled vegetables, ground turkey, salt, and pepper. Adjust seasoning. Form into 16 meatballs.

3. Bring broth to a simmer, stir in chard, add meatballs, and simmer gently until cooked through, about 15 minutes.

4. Serve a bowlful of broth with 2 meatballs. Garnish with chopped cilantro and a wedge of lime.

Variations

- Replace turkey with ground chicken or lean ground pork.
- Replace chipotles with chile powder.
- Replace mushrooms with zucchini or corn.
- Replace garbanzo beans with white beans or black beans.

Nutrition Facts per Serving: 265 calories, 24 g protein, 8 g total fat (2 g saturated fat), 27 g carbohydrate, 4.5 g fiber, 52 mg cholesterol, 750 mg sodium, 35 weighted glycemic index

Coq au Vin Stew
with Whole-Wheat Egg Noodles

Coq au vin is a classic French dish of chicken slowly braised in red wine,
a surprisingly easy way to make delectable chicken that is an all-time favorite
anywhere in the world. This recipe has a mild flavor of dark chocolate to
complement the rich flavors of the wine.

Start to Finish: 45 minutes   Yield: 4 servings

2 tablespoons extra-virgin olive oil	½ cup dry red wine
4 chicken legs, bone-in, skinless, fat removed	¾ cup low-sodium chicken stock
½ cup onion, chopped	2 cups brown button mushrooms, trimmed and quartered
½ cup celery, chopped	1 tablespoon unsweetened baker's chocolate
1 cup carrot, chopped	1 tablespoon Italian parsley, chopped
1 tablespoon garlic, chopped	½ pound whole-wheat egg noodles, cooked according to package directions
1 tablespoon tomato paste	
1 tablespoon flour	Salt and freshly ground black pepper to taste
½ cup canned tomatoes, diced	
1 bay leaf	
¼ teaspoon dried thyme	

1. Heat a large Dutch oven or deep sauté pan over medium heat. Add 1 tablespoon oil and chicken; lightly brown chicken evenly on all sides. Remove from pan and reserve. Deglaze pan with water; add onion, celery, and carrots. Cook until onions are slightly browned. Add garlic; cook until aromatic.

Add tomato paste and cook for 2 minutes. Periodically deglaze the pan with 1 to 2 tablespoons of water if the bottom starts to get too brown. Add flour and cook for 2 minutes; then add tomatoes, bay leaf, thyme, red wine, and chicken stock. Bring to a simmer. Return chicken and any residual juices to the pan. Gently simmer until the chicken is tender, about 20 minutes.

2. Heat a separate sauté pan over medium high heat. Add 1 tablespoon oil and mushrooms. Sauté until they are golden brown and have released their juices. Add the mushrooms to the chicken. Add the chocolate. Bring to a simmer. Cook for 5 minutes. Adjust seasoning with salt and pepper. Stir in parsley.

3. Serve with cooked whole-wheat egg noodles.

Variations

- Add 1 cup peeled pearl onions. To peel pearl onions, trim the root end of the onion. Blanch in boiling water for 30 seconds; shock in ice water. Remove from the water and peel. Blanching makes it easier to remove the skin of the onions.

- Add 1 cup parsnips, peeled and cut in ½-inch pieces, with the carrots.

Nutrition Facts per Serving: 480 calories, 38 g protein, 15 g total fat (3.5 g saturated fat), 52 g carbohydrate, 12 g fiber, 60 mg cholesterol, 220 mg sodium, 40 weighted glycemic index

Indian-Style Curried Chicken

Indian dishes commonly feature many aromatic spices—ginger, cumin, turmeric, coriander. These spices combine to give a slightly exotic flavor to this saucy chicken.

Start to Finish: 45 minutes   Yield: 4 servings

1 pound skinless, boneless chicken breast halves, cut into 1-inch pieces	2 tablespoons extra-virgin olive oil
1 tablespoon lemon juice	2 cups finely chopped onion
½ teaspoon kosher salt	2 teaspoons ground coriander
¼ teaspoon freshly ground black pepper	½ teaspoon ground cumin
3 medium tomatoes, cored and quartered	¼ teaspoon cayenne pepper
3 tablespoons coarsely chopped garlic	¼ teaspoon ground turmeric
1 tablespoon coarsely chopped fresh ginger	¼ cup chopped fresh cilantro
	½ teaspoon garam masala spice blend
	2 cups hot cooked brown basmati or long-grain brown rice

1. Place chicken in a medium bowl. Add lemon juice, kosher salt, and black pepper; toss to coat. Set aside to marinate for at least 15 minutes.

2. In a blender or food processor, combine tomatoes, garlic, and ginger. Cover and blend or process until smooth, stopping and scraping side as necessary; set aside.

3. In a large skillet, heat olive oil over medium heat. Add onion; cook and stir about 8 minutes or until golden brown. Add tomato mixture, coriander, cumin, cayenne pepper, and turmeric. Bring to boiling; reduce heat. Simmer, uncovered, for 10 minutes, stirring occasionally.

CULINARY NOTE

After covering the skillet, check periodically to make sure that the liquid is not boiling hard. The meat will become tough if boiled over high heat.

4. Add chicken to the skillet; stir to coat with the tomato mixture. Return to boiling; reduce heat. Cover and simmer about 15 minutes or until chicken is tender and no longer pink. Remove from the heat; stir in cilantro and garam masala.

5. Serve with brown rice.

Variation

- Use 1 cup chopped canned tomatoes in place of fresh tomatoes.

WINE SUGGESTION: *Sparkling semisweet*

Nutrition Facts per Serving: 365 calories, 29 g protein, 11 g total fat (1.5 g saturated fat), 37 g carbohydrate, 5 g fiber, 72 mg cholesterol, 380 mg sodium, 42 weighted glycemic index

Moroccan-Style Chicken
with Sweet Spices

The flavors of this dish are inspired by North African cooking.
If you have time, marinate the chicken in the spices overnight, which will
enhance the flavor. You can also add golden raisins or dates.
Serve this dish with couscous or brown rice.

Start to Finish: 2 hours   Yield: 8 servings

1 whole chicken, cut into 8 pieces, bone-in, skinless, fat removed	1 tablespoon garlic, chopped
1 teaspoon ground ginger	1 cup low-sodium chicken stock
2 teaspoons ground cumin	1 15.5-ounce can chickpeas with liquid
1 tablespoon paprika	1 tablespoon Italian parsley, chopped
1 teaspoon ground coriander	1 teaspoon lemon zest
1 teaspoon turmeric	4 cups whole-wheat couscous, prepared according to package directions
1 pinch chile flakes	Salt and pepper to taste
1 pinch dried mint	
1 tablespoon olive oil	
3 cups onions, chopped	

CULINARY NOTE

If the sauce is diluted after the chicken is cooked, place it in a saucepan and reduce until flavorful.

1. Season chicken with salt and pepper. Combine all spices in a bowl. Sprinkle 1 teaspoon on seasoned chicken.

2. Heat a large nonstick sauté pan over medium heat. Add olive oil and half the chicken pieces; lightly brown the chicken, being careful not to burn the spices. Remove from pan; repeat with remaining pieces. Place chicken in crockpot on low heat, legs and thighs on the bottom, breast meat on top.

3. Add onions to the sauté pan and cook over medium heat until translucent. Add garlic and the rest of the combined spices; cook until aromatic. Add chicken stock and chickpeas with their liquid. Bring to a simmer. Season with salt and pepper. Pour over the chicken in the crockpot. Cook on low heat. Remove the chicken breasts after 1 hour if they are cooked, and let the legs continue to cook until fork-tender, about another hour.

4. When the chicken is tender, degrease the sauce; stir in parsley and lemon zest.

5. Serve over whole-wheat couscous.

Variations

- You can prepare this recipe using chicken thighs only.

- When the chicken is tender, add 1 cup chicken stock and 1 cup coarse bulgur. Cook for 20 to 30 minutes or until the bulgur is cooked.

- Add ¼ cup golden raisins or dried apricots.

Nutrition Facts per Serving: 260 calories, 25 g protein, 4 g total fat (1 g saturated fat), 33 g carbohydrate, 6 g fiber, 57 mg cholesterol, 245 mg sodium, 33 weighted glycemic index

CULINARY NOTES

- Season the meat well before grilling. Combine all ingredients to prepare the burger meat, but cook a teaspoon-size patty in a sauté pan to check the seasoning first before forming all the patties. This way you can adjust the seasoning if necessary before shaping.

- Sprinkle the burgers with salt and pepper before grilling.

* Note: The internal color of a burger is not a reliable doneness indicator. A turkey patty cooked to 165°F is safe, regardless of color. To measure the doneness of a patty, insert an instant-read thermometer through the side of the patty to a depth of 2 to 3 inches.

Grilled Mushroom Turkey Burgers

Italian flat-leaf parsley is no garnish in these juicy burgers;
it's a key ingredient that adds color, flavor, and vitamins A and C. Top your
burger with any of the suggested condiments for a more filling meal.

Start to Finish: 50 minutes   Yield: 4 servings

2 tablespoons dried porcini or shiitake mushrooms	2 teaspoons chopped fresh sage
1 cup boiling water	¼ teaspoon kosher salt
12 ounces ground turkey breast	⅛ teaspoon freshly ground black pepper
½ cup bottled salsa	4 whole-wheat hamburger buns, split and toasted (optional)
½ cup finely chopped onion	Lettuce leaves, bottled salsa, sliced red onion, sliced avocado, and/or sliced tomato (optional)
2 tablespoons chopped fresh flat-leaf parsley	
6 cloves garlic, minced (1 tablespoon minced)	

1. Rinse dried mushrooms well. Place mushrooms in a small bowl; add boiling water. Let stand about 20 minutes or until soft. Drain the mushrooms well; finely chop mushrooms.

2. In a medium bowl, combine the mushrooms, turkey, ½ cup salsa, onion, parsley, garlic, sage, kosher salt, and pepper. Shape mixture into four ¾-inch-thick patties.

3. For a charcoal grill, place patties on the greased rack of an uncovered grill directly over medium coals. Grill for 14 to 18 minutes or until no longer pink (165°F),* turning once halfway through grilling. For a gas grill, preheat grill. Reduce heat to medium. Place burgers on the greased grill rack over heat. Cover and grill as above.

4. If desired, serve burgers on whole-wheat buns with lettuce, additional salsa, sliced red onion, sliced avocado, and/or sliced tomato.

WINE SUGGESTION:
Sparkling pinot noir

Nutrition Facts per Serving: 280 calories, 29 g protein, 3 g total fat (.5 g saturated fat), 35 g carbohydrate, 7 g fiber, 33 mg cholesterol, 450 mg sodium, 57 weighted glycemic index

Roast Chicken
with Roasted Vegetables

Who doesn't love a home-cooked, oven-roasted chicken?
Enjoy these flavorful variations of this all-time-favorite meal with different
flavors inspired by global cuisines. These are great recipes to include in many
other Sonoma meals as COOK 1X · EAT 2X variations.

Start to Finish: 1½ hours   Yield: 4–6 servings (about 4 ounces of chicken and 1 cup vegetables)

2 ounces olive oil	2 cups turnips, peeled, cut in ¾-inch pieces
1 ounce white wine	2 cups carrots, peeled, cut in ¾-inch pieces
1 tablespoon Dijon mustard	2 cups cauliflower, cut in 1½-inch florets
2 tablespoons rosemary, chopped	1 ounce olive oil
1 tablespoon garlic, chopped	Salt and pepper to taste
1 whole chicken, giblets and fat removed	

CULINARY NOTES

- Placing the chicken on a rack allows the hot air in the oven to circulate around the chicken so it cooks evenly.

- Basting the chicken while it cooks will give the chicken an even color and keep the skin moist.

- Never cover or tightly wrap a chicken while it is roasting. If steam is trapped by a foil cover, the chicken will steam rather than roast.

1. Place a shallow roasting pan with a rack in the oven. Preheat oven to 375°F.

2. Combine 1 ounce olive oil, wine, mustard, rosemary, and garlic. Season with salt and pepper.

3. Gently loosen the skin from the breast and legs of the chicken, being careful not to tear the skin. Rub ¾ of rosemary mixture underneath the skin of the chicken. Rub the remaining ¼ all over the skin. Season the chicken well with salt and pepper.

4. Place the chicken on the rack in the roasting pan in the oven. Cook for 10 minutes.

5. Toss the vegetables with 1 ounce olive oil. Place around the chicken in the bottom of the pan. Every 10 to 15 minutes, baste the chicken with the juices and fat that have accumulated in the bottom of the pan, and turn the vegetables. Roast another 45 to 50 minutes until the juice runs clear or until the chicken is 165°F at the thigh or about 160°F at the breast.

6. Let rest in a warm place for 15 minutes before carving.

Nutrition Facts per Serving: 320 calories, 38 g protein, 12 g fat (2 g saturated fat), 15 g carbohydrate, 4 g fiber, 115 mg cholesterol, 300 mg sodium, 49 weighted glycemic index

Variations

- You can replace the turnips and carrots with onions, fennel, squash, beets, celery root, parsnips, or rutabagas, peeled and cut in ¾-inch pieces.

Mediterranean Variation

Replace rosemary with		*Replace vegetables for roasting with*	
¾	tablespoon each of oregano, thyme, and marjoram, chopped	1	cup carrots, peeled, cut in ¾-inch cubes
		2	cups fennel, cut into ¾-inch cubes
		2	cups celery root, peeled, cut in ¾-inch cubes

Serve chicken and vegetables with ½ cup quinoa or whole-grain rice.

Nutrition Facts per Serving: 286 calories, 38 g protein, 9 g fat (1.7 g saturated fat), 13 g carbohydrate, 3.7 g fiber, 115 mg cholesterol, 240 mg sodium, 45 weighted glycemic index

Asian Variation

Replace oil, white wine, mustard, rosemary, and garlic mixture with

2 tablespoons soy sauce

2 teaspoons ginger, chopped

1 scallion, chopped

½ tablespoon sugar

½ tablespoon rice vinegar

1 teaspoon sesame oil

Replace vegetables for roasting with

2 cups mushrooms, cut in quarters

1 cup carrots, peeled, cut in ¾-inch cubes

1 cup sweet potatoes, peeled, cut in ¾-inch cubes

2 cups daikon, peeled, cut in ¾-inch cubes

Serve chicken and vegetables with ½ cup brown rice.

Nutrition Facts per Serving: 340 calories, 38 g protein, 13 g fat (2.4 g saturated fat), 16 g carbohydrate, 3.7 g fiber, 115 mg cholesterol, 480 mg sodium, 40 weighted glycemic index

Southeast Asian Variation

Replace oil, white wine, mustard, garlic, and rosemary mixture with

2 tablespoons fish sauce

½ tablespoon sugar

2 teaspoons garlic

2 teaspoons ginger

1 tablespoon lime juice

Replace vegetables for roasting with

2 cups mushrooms, cut in quarters

1 cup carrots, peeled, cut in ¾-inch cubes

2 cups daikon, peeled, cut in ¾-inch cubes

Serve chicken and vegetables with ½ cup brown rice.

Nutrition Facts per Serving: 275 calories, 38 g protein, 9.5 g fat (1.8 g saturated fat), 8 g carbohydrate, 1.5 g fiber, 115 mg cholesterol, 500 mg sodium, 40 weighted glycemic index

Latin Variation

Replace oil, white wine, mustard, rosemary, and garlic mixture with

1 tablespoon garlic, chopped

½ teaspoon ground cumin

1 teaspoon chipotle in adobo sauce, chopped

1 teaspoon Mexican oregano

2 lime juice

Replace vegetables for roasting with

2 cups carrots, peeled, cut in ¾-inch cubes

2 cups chayote, peeled, seed removed, cut in ¾-inch cubes

2 cups summer squash, cut in ¾-inch cubes

Serve chicken and vegetables with 1 corn tortilla and red or green salsa.

Nutrition Facts per Serving: 275 calories, 38 g protein, 10 g fat (1.3 g saturated fat), 8 g carbohydrate, 6 g fiber, 118 mg cholesterol, 600 mg sodium, 32 weighted glycemic index

Indian Variation

Replace oil, white wine, mustard, rosemary, and garlic mixture with

¼ cup yogurt

1 tablespoon curry powder

¼ teaspoon cayenne pepper

1 tablespoon ginger, chopped

Replace vegetables for roasting with

1 cup mushrooms, cut in quarters

2 cups carrots, peeled, cut in ¾-inch cubes

2 cups summer squash, cut in ¾-inch cubes

1 cup sweet potatoes, peeled, cut in ¾-inch cubes

Serve chicken and vegetables with ½ cup brown basmati rice.

Nutrition Facts per Serving: 307 calories, 38 g protein, 9 g fat (1.9 g saturated fat), 17 g carbohydrate, 4 g fiber, 115 mg cholesterol, 200 mg sodium, 32 weighted glycemic index

Mughlai Chicken
with Almonds and Golden Raisins

This is a meal for special occasions—it is so rich in flavor! Evolving from the royal kitchens of the Mughal dynasty, the recipe contains a strong touch of Persian and Turkish cuisines—generally spicy and cooked using fresh ground and whole spices.

Start to Finish: 3 hours   Yield: 8 servings

1 whole chicken, cut into 8 pieces, bone in, skinless, fat removed	1 cup low-sodium chicken stock
1 pinch chile flakes	½ cup plain nonfat yogurt
2 teaspoons ground cumin	4 tablespoons almonds, chopped
2 teaspoons ground coriander	2 tablespoons golden raisins
¾ teaspoon turmeric	2 tablespoons cilantro, chopped
¼ teaspoon cinnamon	4 cups brown basmati rice, cooked according to package directions
¼ teaspoon cardamom	8 cups roasted cauliflower or sautéed greens
1 tablespoon canola oil	Salt, pepper, and lemon juice to taste
1 tablespoon ginger, chopped	
1 tablespoon garlic, chopped	

1. Season chicken with salt and pepper. Combine spices and sprinkle 1 teaspoon on seasoned chicken.

2. Heat a large nonstick sauté pan over medium. Add oil and half the chicken pieces; lightly brown the chicken, being careful not to burn the spices. Remove from pan; repeat with remaining pieces. Place chicken in crockpot on low heat, legs and thighs on the bottom, breast meat on top.

3. Add ginger, garlic, and remaining spices to sauté pan; cook until aromatic, about 30 seconds. Add ½ cup chicken stock to deglaze the pan. Bring to a simmer. Add remaining chicken stock and stir in yogurt until smooth. Season with salt and pepper.

Nutrition Facts per Serving: 285 calories, 23 g protein, 8 g total fat (1 g saturated fat), 30 g carbohydrate, 3 g fiber, 58 mg cholesterol, 255 mg sodium, 48 weighted glycemic index

Add almonds and raisins, and pour over the chicken in the crockpot. Cook on low heat. Remove the chicken breasts after 1 hour if they are cooked, and let the legs continue to cook until fork-tender, about 1 hour more.

4. When the chicken is tender, degrease the sauce, stir in cilantro and lemon juice to taste.

5. Serve over brown basmati rice and cauliflower or greens.

Variations

- You can prepare this recipe using chicken thighs only.
- Add ¼ cup dried apricots.

Summer Vegetable Chicken Sauté

In summer you can enjoy some of the best tomatoes of the season, such as the Early Girl variety. This light and flavorful dish features many bright colors and appetizing textures.

Start to Finish: 40 minutes   *Yield: 4 servings*

2 cups fresh green beans, cut into 2-inch pieces

1 tablespoon extra-virgin olive oil

1 pound skinless, boneless chicken breast halves, cut into 1-inch pieces

1 tablespoon chopped fresh oregano or thyme

2 cups sliced yellow summer squash and/or zucchini

1 15-ounce can cannellini beans (white kidney beans), rinsed and drained

¼ cup reduced-sodium chicken broth

6 cloves garlic, minced (1 tablespoon minced)

1 cup cherry tomatoes, halved

1 tablespoon chopped fresh basil or flat-leaf parsley

¼ teaspoon kosher salt

¼ teaspoon freshly ground black pepper

1. In a covered medium saucepan, cook green beans in a small amount of salted boiling water for 8 to 10 minutes or until crisp-tender. Drain; submerse beans in enough ice water to cover and let stand until cool. Drain again; set aside.

2. Meanwhile, in a very large skillet, heat olive oil over medium heat. In a large bowl, toss chicken with oregano, salt, and pepper. Add chicken to hot oil in skillet; cook for 5 to 6 minutes or until no longer pink, stirring frequently. Do not overcrowd the pan or the chicken will not brown. Cook the chicken in batches if necessary. Remove chicken from skillet and set aside.

3. Add squash to the skillet; cook and stir over medium-high heat for 3 minutes. Stir in chicken, green beans, cannellini beans, chicken broth, and garlic. Bring to boiling. Add tomatoes, basil, kosher salt, and pepper. Cook about 1 minute or until heated through.

Variations

- Replace chicken with pork tenderloin.
- Replace chicken with firm tofu. To remove moisture, cut the tofu into 2 slabs 1 inch thick. Line a baking sheet with paper towels; place tofu slabs, cut side down, on towels. Top with more paper towels and another baking sheet. Let sit for 10 minutes or longer. Cut tofu into 1-inch pieces. When sautéing tofu, make sure it browns on all sides.

WINE SUGGESTION: *Sauvignon blanc*

Nutrition Facts per Serving: 290 calories, 33 g protein, 6.5 g total fat (1 g saturated fat), 25 g carbohydrate, 7.5 g fiber, 72 mg cholesterol, 525 mg sodium, 32 weighted glycemic index

Spicy Chicken
with Garlic Chile Sauce

This is a zesty, spicy chicken dish that has wonderful flavors. Serve with brown rice for a complete meal that is ready in minutes.

Start to Finish: 30 minutes   Yield: 4 servings

1 tablespoon cornstarch	2 tablespoons canola oil
1 tablespoon dry sherry or shaoxing rice wine	1 tablespoon ginger, chopped
12 ounces chicken breast, sliced ⅛ inch thick by 1 inch long	1 tablespoon garlic, chopped
	½ cup onion, sliced
1 pound Japanese eggplant, slice in half lengthwise, then in ¼-inch pieces	1 cup red bell peppers, seeded, julienne
2 tablespoons soy sauce	1 teaspoon cornstarch
1 tablespoon chile sauce (sambal oelek or Asian chile sauce)	1 tablespoon water
	2 tablespoons basil leaves, sliced in half
2 teaspoons sugar	1 tablespoon cilantro leaves, chopped
¼ cup chicken stock	3 cups brown rice, cooked
	Salt and pepper to taste

CULINARY NOTES

- The cornstarch and sherry mixture helps the chicken meat stay plump and tender. Simmering the chicken in hot water also helps plump it.

- Salting the eggplant draws some of its bitterness and helps it cook more quickly with less oil.

1. Combine 1 tablespoon cornstarch and sherry. Add chicken; season with a pinch of salt. Let sit for 15 minutes.

2. Season eggplant with salt. Let sit for 15 minutes.

3. Combine soy sauce, chile sauce, sugar, and chicken stock. Set aside.

4. Bring a small pot of water to a simmer.

Add the chicken and cook for 5 minutes. The chicken should still be raw, but slightly white.

5. Heat a large sauté pan or wok over medium-high heat. Add oil and eggplant and sauté until slightly browned all over. Add ginger, garlic, onions, and peppers; sauté 3 minutes. Add chicken and stir; add soy sauce mixture. Cover the pan and cook until eggplant is tender, about 15 minutes.

6. Mix 1 teaspoon cornstarch with water; add to pan and bring to a simmer. Once the sauce thickens, adjust seasoning with salt and pepper. Add basil and cilantro and serve with rice.

Variations

- Replace chicken with pork tenderloin.
- Replace chicken with beef tri tip cut or sirloin.
- Sauté 1 cup sliced mushrooms with the eggplant.
- Replace eggplant with snow peas.

Nutrition Facts per Serving: 400 calories, 25 g protein, 10 g total fat (1.5 g saturated fat), 52 g carbohydrate, 7.5 g fiber, 55 mg cholesterol, 650 mg sodium, 49 weighted glycemic index

Zucchini and Red Peppers Stuffed

with Turkey Picadillo

Chiles Rellenos con Picadillo is a traditional Oaxacan entrée. Picadillo, generally a minced meat filling, often includes sweet and salty ingredients such as raisins, almonds, and green olives. This Sonoma-inspired version features the rich Latin flavors in combination with zucchini.

Start to Finish: 45 minutes   *Yield: 4 servings*

2 zucchini or yellow squash, cut in half lengthwise	1 ounce parmesan cheese, grated
2 red bell peppers, cut in half	1 cup red salsa, purchased
1 pound Ground Turkey Picadillo with Golden Raisins and Olives (recipe below)	Salt and pepper to taste

1. Preheat oven to 375°F.

2. Using a small spoon, remove the seeds and flesh from the inside of the zucchini, leaving a ¼-inch thick shell. Be careful not to pierce the skin.

3. Remove the seeds and core from the red peppers.

4. Season the inside of the vegetables with salt and pepper. Fill the zucchini and red peppers with the picadillo. Sprinkle with parmesan cheese. Place vegetables in an oven-proof baking dish. Pour salsa over the vegetables.

5. Bake in preheated oven uncovered until the vegetables are tender and beginning to brown, about 45 minutes. Transfer the stuffed vegetables to a platter and serve.

Nutrition Facts per Serving: 215 calories, 21 g protein, 5 g total fat (1.5 g saturated fat), 25 g carbohydrate, 5 g fiber, 28 mg cholesterol, 430 mg sodium, 44 weighted glycemic index

Ground Turkey Picadillo
with Golden Raisins and Olives

This is a traditional recipe used in many Latin dishes as a stuffing for tacos, peppers, and pastries. The sweet, salty, and savory flavor combinations give this recipe a unique character.

Start to Finish: 45 minutes   Yield: 8 servings

1	tablespoon extra-virgin olive oil	1	pinch chile flakes
1	cup onions, diced	1	pound lean ground turkey
½	cup carrots, chopped	1	cup zucchini, chopped
½	cup celery, chopped	1	15.5-ounce can tomatoes, diced
2	cups mushrooms, chopped	½	cup golden raisins
2	tablespoons garlic, chopped	¼	cup green olives, chopped
1	pinch cumin	2	tablespoons cilantro, chopped
2	tablespoons chile powder		Salt and pepper to taste

1. Heat olive oil in a Dutch oven or deep sauté pan over medium heat. Add onions, carrots, celery, and mushrooms; season with salt and pepper. Sauté until tender, about 5 minutes. Add garlic, cumin, chile powder, and chile flakes; cook until aromatic, about 20 seconds.

2. Add turkey and zucchini; cook 5 minutes. Add tomatoes and raisins. Bring to a simmer; cook for 10 minutes or until the vegetables are tender. Stir in olives and cilantro. Adjust seasonings with salt and pepper.

CULINARY NOTE

Use picadillo as a filling for roasted chiles or tacos.

Variations

- Replace chopped zucchini with cauliflower or sweet potato.
- Replace chile powder with 1 teaspoon chipotle in adobo sauce.

Nutrition Facts per Serving: 140 calories, 16 g protein, 2 g total fat (0 g saturated fat), 16 g carbohydrate, 2.5 g fiber, 22 mg cholesterol, 305 mg sodium, 44 weighted glycemic index

Turkey and Soba Noodle Stir-Fry

Japanese buckwheat noodles are amazingly versatile and becoming increasingly popular as Western cooks learn to appreciate the nutty flavor and nutritional value. As the foundation of this vitamin C–rich stir-fry, buckwheat noodles add additional protein and fiber.

Start to Finish: 25 minutes   Yield: 4 servings

6	ounces dried soba (buckwheat) noodles or multigrain spaghetti	4	green onions, bias-sliced into 1-inch pieces
2	teaspoons extra-virgin olive oil	12	ounces turkey breast tenderloin, cut into bite-size strips
2	cups fresh sugar snap peas	1	teaspoon toasted sesame oil
2	medium red bell peppers, cut into thin strips	½	cup bottled plum sauce
2	teaspoons minced fresh ginger	¼	teaspoon crushed red pepper
4	cloves garlic, minced (2 teaspoons minced)		

1. Cook soba noodles according to package directions; drain. Return to hot saucepan; cover and keep warm.

2. Meanwhile, pour olive oil into a wok or large skillet. (Add more oil as necessary during cooking.) Heat over medium-high heat. Add sugar snap peas, bell peppers, ginger, and garlic and stir-fry for 2 minutes. Add green onions. Stir-fry for 1 to 2 minutes more or until vegetables are crisp-tender. Remove vegetables from wok.

3. Add turkey and sesame oil to the hot wok. Stir-fry for 3 to 4 minutes or until turkey is tender and no longer pink. Add plum sauce and crushed red pepper. Return cooked vegetables to wok; stir to coat all ingredients with sauce. Heat through. Serve immediately over soba noodles.

WINE SUGGESTION:
Sparkling semisweet

Nutrition Facts per Serving: 390 calories, 30 g protein, 6 g total fat (1 g saturated fat), 60 g carbohydrate, 8 g fiber, 33 mg cholesterol, 250 mg sodium, 31 weighted glycemic index

CULINARY NOTE

Soba noodles are prepared from buckwheat flour, yielding a more delicate noodle than Italian noodles or dry pasta. Soba noodles are also cooked differently. When cooking soba, heat a large pot of water to a simmer, add the noodles, and bring back to a simmer. Add 1 cup of ice water and bring the liquid back to a simmer. Repeat until the noodles are just cooked through. Drain and rinse well if preparing in advance.

Chicken and Dumplings

This is the ultimate all-American comfort food,
without excess fat and calories, but with all the flavor we love.

Start to Finish: 40 minutes   Yield: 4 servings

4 teaspoons extra-virgin olive oil	*For the dumplings*
2 tablespoons whole-wheat all-purpose flour	¼ cup whole-wheat all-purpose flour
3 cups low-sodium chicken stock	¼ cup unbleached all-purpose flour
½ pound chicken, cooked, cut in ½-inch x 1-inch pieces	1 teaspoon baking powder
3 cups roasted vegetables	1 pinch salt
¼ cup peas, frozen	1 teaspoon butter
1 tablespoon Italian parsley, chopped (optional)	¼ cup low-fat milk
Salt and pepper to taste	

CULINARY NOTES

Once the chicken stock has been added to the flour and oil, it should simmer for 15 to 20 minutes to prevent a floury taste. Do not boil or simmer hard or the liquid will over-reduce.

1. Preheat oven 400°F.

2. For the dumplings: Combine the flours, baking powder, and salt in a food processor. Pulse in the butter until it becomes small pieces. Move to a bowl. Stir in the milk until just combined.

Nutrition Facts per Serving: 340 calories, 26 g protein, 11 g total fat (2.5 g saturated fat), 33 g carbohydrate, 3.5 g fiber, 52 mg cholesterol, 350 mg sodium, 57 weighted glycemic index

3. For the chicken mixture: Place the olive oil in a saucepan or Dutch oven 9 inches by 3 to 4 inches deep. Heat over medium heat, add flour, and stir and cook for 3 minutes. Pour in the chicken stock in a gradual stream, stirring constantly with a whisk to remove all lumps. Bring to a simmer; then reduce to a bare simmer. Cook for 15 minutes. Add the chicken, vegetables, peas, and parsley. Bring to a simmer and adjust seasonings. Drop dumpling mixture by teaspoons on top of stew. Cover and place in preheated oven. Bake for 15 minutes or until dumplings are cooked through.

Variations

- Add ½ cup cooked white beans.
- Add assorted frozen vegetables in place of the roasted vegetables.
- Add chopped herbs and 1 tablespoon grated parmesan cheese to the dumplings.
- For a Southwest version, add ½ teaspoon cumin and 1 teaspoon chili powder to the chicken stock. Add 1 pinch of cayenne pepper to the dumplings.

PORK DINNERS

Pork is a favorite meat in the Sonoma region. Try the amazing flavor combinations of figs, olives, cranberries, toasted almonds, port, and white wine, which are sure to enhance your collection of favorite menus with pork. These great recipes feature the leanest cuts of pork with a burst of taste and appeal.

Barbecue Pork Sandwiches

Whether you use your favorite home-style secret barbecue sauce or a Sonoma-inspired barbecue sauce, this is an easy meal with great southern flavors.

Start to Finish: 20 minutes   Yield: 4 servings

1 pound Barbecue Pulled Pork (page 161)	2 tablespoons barbecue sauce (your favorite or Red Wine Barbecue Sauce, page 389)
½ cup Barbecue Pulled Pork cooking liquid	4 thin whole-grain buns
1 teaspoon cider vinegar	2 cups Asian Cabbage Slaw (page 242)

1. Slice the pork into thin slices or chop coarsely. Mix with cooking liquid, vinegar, and barbecue sauce. Bring to a simmer to warm.

2. Toast the buns. Top with 4 ounces pork and sauce. Place ½ cup cabbage slaw on top.

CULINARY NOTE

This is a COOK 1X · EAT 2X recipe for Barbecue Pulled Pork (page 161).

Nutrition Facts per Serving: 350 calories, 30 g protein, 15 g total fat (4 g saturated fat), 32 g carbohydrate, 7 g fiber, 50 mg cholesterol, 80 mg sodium, 45 weighted glycemic index

Barbecue Pulled Pork

The key to this tender, mouth-watering meal is the slow cooking time and sweet barbecue flavors. Get your crockpot and taste buds ready for this delicious southern barbecue pulled pork dinner.

Start to Finish: 15 minutes plus marinating overnight
plus 5 hours cooking in a crockpot   Yield: 8 servings

2 pounds pork sirloin, fat removed, cut into 2-inch pieces	2 tablespoons molasses
2 tablespoons barbecue spice rub	½ teaspoon cider vinegar
¼ cup ketchup	¼ cup chicken stock
	Salt and pepper to taste

1. Season the meat with salt and pepper. Sprinkle all over with spice rub. Let sit overnight in the refrigerator.

2. Combine the ketchup, molasses, cider vinegar, and chicken stock. Place in crockpot. Add pork. Cook over low heat for 4 to 5 hours until the meat is tender, but not falling apart.

3. Remove from sauce. Degrease sauce and return meat to sauce to store.

4. To serve: cut meat across the grain in thin pieces. Toss with some of the sauce.

Variation

- Replace ketchup, molasses, and vinegar with ¼ cup of your favorite barbecue sauce mixed with ¼ cup chicken stock.

CULINARY NOTE

Cook the pork in large batches and freeze in 1-pound portions.

Nutrition Facts per Serving: 170 calories, 24 g protein, 4.5 g total fat (1.5 g saturated fat), 5.5 g carbohydrate, 0 g fiber, 71 mg cholesterol, 145 mg sodium, 69 weighted glycemic index

Grilled Balsamic Pork Chops
with Tomatoes and Feta Cheese

Balsamic vinegar is aromatic, so a tablespoon is all you need for these chops.
The combination of balsamic vinegar, tomatoes, and feta cheese
creates a simple but exquisite topping.

Start to Finish: 30 minutes   Yield: 4 servings

½ cup tomato, seeded and chopped

1 tablespoon chopped parsley

1 tablespoon bottled balsamic vinaigrette salad dressing (such as Newman's Own brand)

4 boneless pork loin chops, cut ¾ inch thick (about 1¼ pounds total)

1 teaspoon lemon-pepper seasoning

¼ cup crumbled feta cheese with garlic and herbs (1 ounce)

Fresh oregano (optional)

1. In a small bowl, combine tomato, parsley, and salad dressing; set aside.

2. Trim fat from chops. Sprinkle lemon-pepper seasoning evenly over both sides of each chop. For a charcoal grill, place chops on the rack of an uncovered grill directly over medium coals. Grill for 12 to 15 minutes or until done (160°F) and juices run clear, turning once halfway through grilling. For a gas grill, preheat grill. Reduce heat to medium. Place chops on grill rack over heat. Cover and grill as above.

3. Slice pork chops. Transfer pork to four dinner plates. Top chops with feta cheese and tomato mixture. If desired, garnish with oregano.

Variations

- Replace lemon-pepper seasoning with 1 teaspoon fresh lemon zest, ¼ teaspoon freshly ground black pepper, and salt.

- Replace lemon-pepper seasoning with 1 teaspoon lemon zest, 1 teaspoon chopped oregano or rosemary, and 1 teaspoon freshly ground black pepper.

WINE SUGGESTION: *Cabernet sauvignon*

Nutrition Facts per Serving: 265 calories, 43 g protein, 8 g total fat (3 g saturated fat), 2 g carbohydrate, 0 g fiber, 71 mg cholesterol, 145 mg sodium, 15 weighted glycemic index

Indian-Spiced Pork Loin
with Yogurt Marinade

The combination of cumin's warm and earthy flavors with the bright and citrusy flavors of coriander adds depth to this marinade. Coriander is the seed of the cilantro plant. These fragrant spices complement the mint and yogurt in this easy-to-prepare marinade.

Start to Finish: 20 minutes, plus 15 minutes to overnight for marinating   Yield: 4 servings

1 pound pork loin, fat removed	½ teaspoon ground cumin
¼ cup plain probiotic yogurt	½ teaspoon ground coriander
¼ teaspoon turmeric	¼ teaspoon dried mint
¼ teaspoon paprika	Salt and pepper to taste

1. Season pork with salt and pepper.

2. Combine remaining ingredients and stir to mix. Place in a leakproof container or resealable bag such as a Ziploc bag; add pork. Force out all the air so that the meat is in contact with the marinade. Let sit for 15 minutes to overnight.

3. Grill or sauté the meat.

Variation

• Replace pork with 1 pound chicken breast.

CULINARY NOTE

COOK 1X · EAT 2X for Spiced Pork Salad with Chickpeas and Radishes (page 169). If you plan on making this dish as a COOK 1X · EAT 2X recipe, increase the pork to two pounds and double the ingredients in this recipe.

Nutrition Facts per Serving: 155 calories, 25 g protein, 4 g total fat (1.2 g saturated fat), 1.5 g carbohydrate, 0 g fiber, 79 mg cholesterol, 78 mg sodium, 7 weighted glycemic index

Korean-Style Pork Tenderloin
with Asian Cabbage Slaw

This barbecue style, known as *gogi gui*, is often used for meat cooked at the table on a built-in gas or charcoal grill. The spicy, salty flavors and the combination of the textures and temperatures of crisp Asian slaw or lettuce greens with succulent grilled pork are amazing.

Start to Finish: 30 minutes plus overnight for marinating   Yield: 4 servings

2 tablespoons soy sauce	¼ cup Asian pear or green apple, peeled and cored
1 tablespoon agave syrup	1 teaspoon chile paste, sambal oelek, or Korean chile paste
1 teaspoon sesame oil	
1 tablespoon garlic, chopped	1 pound pork tenderloin, fat removed
1 teaspoon ginger, chopped	6 cups Asian Cabbage Slaw (page 242)
1 teaspoon orange zest	
1 scallion, chopped	

1. Combine all ingredients except pork tenderloin and cabbage slaw in blender. Blend until smooth. Place pork in marinade and let sit overnight in the refrigerator.

2. Preheat grill over medium-high heat. Grill pork until it reaches an internal temperature of 145°F. Allow meat to rest for 10 minutes. Slice pork tenderloin thin across the grain. Serve with Asian Cabbage Slaw or wrapped in red lettuce leaves or butter leaf lettuce.

variations

- Replace pork with chicken.
- Replace pork with beef flank steak or skirt steak.

Nutrition Facts per Serving: 165 calories, 25 g protein, 4 g total fat (1 g saturated fat), 7.5 g carbohydrate, 1g fiber, 74 mg cholesterol, 330 mg sodium, 18 weighted glycemic index

Grilled Pork Chops

with Smoky Black Bean Relish

These grilled chops have a distinct southwestern taste.
Black beans have a rich, slightly sweet flavor and contain
molybdenum, folate, and fiber; they are also rich in antioxidants.
When combined with corn, lime, tomatoes, and chile peppers,
the result is a truly authentic-tasting meal.

Start to Finish: 30 minutes   Yield: 6 servings

6 boneless pork top loin chops, cut ½ inch thick (about 1¾ pounds total)	6 cloves garlic, minced (1 tablespoon minced)
Kosher salt	2 cups cherry tomatoes, quartered
Freshly ground black pepper	1 15-ounce can black beans, rinsed and drained
3 tablespoons lime juice	½ cup sliced scallions
2 tablespoons fresh cilantro, chopped	¼ cup fresh cilantro, chopped
1 tablespoon extra-virgin olive oil	1–2 teaspoons canned chipotle in adobo sauce, finely chopped
1 cup frozen whole-kernel corn, thawed	

1. Trim fat from chops. Season chops with kosher salt and pepper. In a small bowl, combine 2 tablespoons of the lime juice and cilantro; brush over chops.

2. For a charcoal grill, place chops on the rack of an uncovered grill directly over medium coals. Grill for 7 to 9 minutes or until chops are done (160°F) and juices run clear. For a gas grill, preheat grill. Reduce heat to medium. Place chops on grill rack over heat. Cover and grill as above.

3. Meanwhile, in a large skillet, heat oil over medium-high heat. Add corn; cook and stir about 3 minutes or until lightly browned. Clear a spot in the center of the pan, reduce the heat, and add garlic; cook for 30 seconds.

4. In a large bowl, combine the corn mixture, tomatoes, black beans, scallions, ¼ cup cilantro, chipotle peppers, and the remaining 1 tablespoon lime juice. Season to taste with kosher salt and pepper.

5. Serve chops with corn mixture.

Variations

- Grill the corn instead of sautéing if desired.
- Use leftover grilled corn.
- Replace black beans with pinto beans.
- Use Southwestern Rub (page 391) in place of lime and cilantro marinade.
- Combine 1 15-ounce can white cannellini beans, drained, 1 tablespoon sautéed chopped garlic, 2 cups quartered cherry tomatoes, 1 tablespoon chopped basil, 1 cup sautéed zucchini, and 1 pinch of chile flakes.

CULINARY NOTE

Toast the corn in a pan over medium heat for richer flavor.

WINE SUGGESTION: *Zinfandel*

Nutrition Facts per Serving: 550 calories, 36 g protein, 18 g total fat, (5 g saturated fat), 59 g carbohydrate, 10 g fiber, 85 mg cholesterol, 375 mg sodium, 29 weighted glycemic index

Spiced Pork Salad
with Chickpeas and Radishes

The wonderfully seasoned pork flavors are a perfect match for the tart yogurt and mint dressing, served on a crunchy salad of romaine and spinach.

Start to Finish: 20 minutes   Yield: 4 servings

½ cup Yogurt Mint Sauce (page 393)	¼ cup radishes, sliced thin
¼ teaspoon cumin, toasted and ground	1 tablespoon lemon juice
2 heads hearts of romaine lettuce	1 pound Indian-Spiced Pork Loin with Yogurt Marinade, sliced thin (page 164)
2 cups spinach cut in 1-inch pieces or baby spinach	2 tablespoons toasted slivered almonds
1 cup chickpeas, drained (canned garbanzo beans)	Salt and pepper to taste

1. Combine the yogurt mint dressing with the toasted cumin. Mix well.

2. Combine the lettuce, spinach, chickpeas, and radishes in a large bowl. Add lemon juice and season with salt and pepper.

3. Add the yogurt mint dressing and mix well.

4. Mound the salad on 4 plates and top with the sliced pork. Sprinkle with almonds.

Variations

- Omit toasted cumin.
- Use arugula in place of spinach. Use marinated chicken in place of the pork.
- Add 1 cup roasted corn.

CULINARY NOTE

Use leftover meat from Indian-Spiced Pork Loin with Yogurt Marinade (page 164).

Nutrition Facts per Serving: 245 calories, 30 g protein, 8 g total fat (2 g saturated fat), 15 g carbohydrate, 4 g fiber, 68 mg cholesterol, 400 mg sodium, 29 weighted glycemic index

Sonoma Plum and Rosemary Pork Roast

With the many varieties of plums available, you can experiment with the flavor of this recipe every time you make it. No matter which plum variety you choose, its flavor will enhance the pork roast.

Start to Finish: 1 hour and 30 minutes   *Yield: 6 servings*

1	2-pound boneless pork top loin roast (single loin)	2	tablespoons fresh rosemary, chopped
	Kosher salt	2	cloves garlic, minced (1 teaspoon minced)
	Freshly ground black pepper	1 ½	cups port
1	tablespoon extra-virgin olive oil	¼	cup reduced-sodium chicken broth
1	medium onion, chopped	6	fresh plums, pitted and quartered
1	medium carrot, chopped		Fresh rosemary sprigs (optional)

1. Preheat oven to 300°F. Season pork with kosher salt and pepper. In a 4- to 5-quart oven-going Dutch oven, heat oil over medium heat. Add pork; cook for 5 to 8 minutes or until browned, turning roast to brown evenly on all sides. Remove pork from pan; set aside.

2. Add onion and carrot to Dutch oven. Cook about 5 minutes or until the onion is golden brown, stirring frequently. Stir in the rosemary and garlic; cook and stir for 1 minute more. Add port and broth. Return the pork to the pan. Heat just until boiling.

3. Cover Dutch oven and bake for 20 minutes. Add plums. Bake, covered, for 20 to 25 minutes more or until an instant-read thermometer inserted into center of pork registers 145°F.

4. Transfer the pork to a cutting board; cover with foil and let stand for 15 minutes before slicing. The temperature of the pork after standing should be 150°F. Meanwhile, using a slotted spoon, transfer plums to a serving platter. Remove any grease from the sauce. Place Dutch oven over medium-high heat on the stove. Reduce heat; boil gently, uncovered, about 10 minutes or until sauce is reduced to about ¾ cup.

5. To serve, thinly slice pork. Arrange pork slices on platter with plums. Serve with sauce. If desired, garnish with fresh rosemary.

Variation
- Replace fresh plums with figs, dried figs, or dried plums.

WINE SUGGESTION: *Pinot noir*

Nutrition Facts per Serving: 360 calories, 35 g protein, 8.5 g total fat (2 g saturated fat), 21 g carbohydrate, 1.7 g fiber, 95 mg cholesterol, 90 mg sodium, 44 weighted glycemic index

Mandarin Stir-Fried Pork Tenderloin
and Broccoli

An all-time-favorite ingredient for stir-fry, broccoli pairs nicely
with ginger, garlic, and the sweet and spicy mandarin flavors of hoisin sauce.
Wonderful when served with a bowl of steaming, fluffy brown rice.

Start to Finish: 20 minutes, plus 30 minutes to overnight for marinating   Yield: 4 servings

1 tablespoon Chinese rice wine (shaoxing)	1 teaspoon extra-virgin olive oil or canola oil
1 teaspoon cornstarch	1 tablespoon garlic, chopped
1 egg white, slightly beaten	1 tablespoon ginger, chopped
12 ounces pork tenderloin, sliced ⅛ inch thick x 1inch wide	3 cups broccoli cut in florets, stems peeled and sliced
1 tablespoon hoisin sauce	2 teaspoons cornstarch mixed with 1 tablespoon water
1 tablespoon oyster sauce	2 tablespoons scallion, chopped
3 tablespoons low-sodium chicken stock	2 cups brown rice, cooked
1 teaspoon sesame oil	Salt and pepper to taste

1. Combine rice wine, cornstarch, and egg white. Mix in 1 pinch salt and pepper. Add pork. Let sit for 30 minutes or overnight.

2. Combine hoisin sauce, oyster sauce, chicken stock, and sesame oil; set aside.

3. Heat a wok or large sauté pan over medium heat. Add olive oil, garlic, and ginger. Stir until aromatic. Add pork and turn up heat. Sauté 1 to 2 minutes. Add broccoli and toss. Add sauce mixture and bring to a simmer; cover and cook until the broccoli is al dente. Stir in cornstarch mixture. Bring to a simmer and stir in scallions.

4. Serve with brown rice.

Variations

- Replace broccoli with sugar snap peas.
- Replace broccoli with baby bok choy.
- Add 2 teaspoons chile paste for extra-spicy pork.

Nutrition Facts per Serving: 265 calories, 23 g protein, 4 g total fat (1.5 g saturated fat), 30 g carbohydrate, 3.5 g fiber, 55 mg cholesterol, 275 mg sodium, 47 weighted glycemic index

Stir-Fried Pork
and Sugar Snap Peas with Oyster Sauce

This quick and easy stir-fry packs a tremendous amount of umami flavor. Ginger, garlic, and soy sauce complement the rich savory flavors of oyster sauce. It is wonderful served over a bowl of steaming, fluffy brown rice.

Start to Finish: 30 minutes   Yield: 4 servings

1 tablespoon cornstarch	1 tablespoon ginger, chopped
1 tablespoon dry sherry or shaoxing rice wine	1 tablespoon garlic, chopped
12 ounces pork tenderloin, sliced ⅛ inch thick x 1 inch long	½ cup onion, sliced
2 tablespoons oyster sauce	1 pound sugar snap peas
1 tablespoon soy sauce	1 teaspoon cornstarch mixed with 1 tablespoon water
1 teaspoon sugar	1 tablespoon cilantro leaves
¼ cup low-sodium chicken stock	¼ cup scallion, sliced
2 tablespoons canola oil	3 cups brown rice, cooked
	Salt

1. Combine cornstarch and dry sherry. Add pork; season with a pinch of salt. Let sit for 15 minutes.

2. Combine oyster sauce, soy sauce, sugar, and chicken stock. Set aside.

3. Bring a small pot of water to a simmer. Add pork, stir, and drain immediately. The pork should still be raw, but slightly white.

4. Heat a large sauté pan or wok over medium-high heat. Add oil, ginger, garlic, and onion; sauté 3 minutes. Add pork and snap peas; sauté 2 minutes. Stir in oyster sauce mixture. Cover the pan and cook until snap peas are tender.

5. Stir cornstarch mixture; stir in to sauce and bring to a simmer. Once the sauce thickens, adjust seasoning with salt and pepper. Stir in cilantro and scallion. Serve with brown rice.

Variations

- Replace pork with chicken breast.
- Replace snap peas with snow peas or broccoli.
- Replace snap peas with corn and spinach.

Nutrition Facts per Serving: 420 calories, 25 g protein, 10 g total fat (1.5 g saturated fat), 49 g carbohydrate, 6 g fiber, 52 mg cholesterol, 500 mg sodium, 49 weighted glycemic index

Spiced Pork Tenderloin
with Grilled Vegetables and Salsa Verde

This fabulous pork tenderloin marinade has a medley of flavors,
bright and citrusy coriander, sweet essence of orange zest,
mild sweet anise flavors of fennel, and a touch of heat from cayenne.
A perfect pairing for rustic Italian salsa verde and grilled vegetables.

Start to Finish: 30 minutes   Yield: 4 servings

1 pound pork tenderloin, fat removed	1 teaspoon orange zest
1 tablespoon oregano, chopped	Nonstick cooking spray
1 teaspoon garlic, chopped fine	1 recipe Grilled Vegetables (page 250)
1 teaspoon fennel seeds, ground	
1 teaspoon black peppercorns, ground	1 recipe Salsa Verde for Meat or Vegetables (page 390)
1 teaspoon ground coriander	
1 pinch cayenne pepper	Salt and pepper to taste

1. Season meat with salt and pepper. Let sit for 15 minutes.

2. Combine oregano, garlic, spices, and orange zest in a small bowl. Rub generously over meat.

3. Preheat grill to medium-high.

4. Lightly spray pork with nonstick cooking spray. Place on grill and cook 4 minutes per side, turning to establish grill marks on all sides evenly. Cook to an internal temperature of 143°F for medium doneness. Let rest for 10 minutes.

5. Grill vegetables and arrange on a large platter.

6. Prepare salsa verde.

7. Slice meat on a bias ¼ inch thick. Place on the platter with the grilled vegetables; top with salsa verde.

Variations
- Replace pork with chicken breast.
- Replace pork with flank steak.

Nutrition Facts per Serving: 275 calories, 25 g protein, 13 g total fat (2.5 g saturated fat), 2.5 g carbohydrate, 1 g fiber, 75 mg cholesterol, 150 mg sodium, 14 weighted glycemic index

Spicy Southwestern Pork Stew

This is a great meal to come home to. Cooking long slow hours in the crockpot brings these rich, earthy flavors of the Southwest together into a fabulous home-style meal.

Start to Finish: 3 hours in a crockpot, plus marinating overnight   Yield: 8 servings

2 pounds pork cushion, fat trimmed, cut into 1-inch pieces	1 14-15 ounce can tomatoes, diced, with liquid
2 tablespoons Southwestern Rub (page 391)	2 cups corn kernels
2 tablespoons extra-virgin olive oil	1 cup roasted red peppers, julienned
1 cup low-sodium chicken stock	¼ cup cilantro, chopped
2 cups onions, diced	1 lime, juiced
2 tablespoons garlic, chopped	Kosher salt and pepper to taste

CULINARY NOTES

- If the spice rub starts to burn in the pan while you are browning the meat, add some chicken stock to deglaze the pan and loosen the pan drippings or fond.

- Pork cushion is a lean cut of meat; it is best to cook it until it is almost tender, not fork-tender. Fork-tender may make the meat seem dry.

- Serve with corn tortillas.

1. Season pork cubes with salt and pepper. Sprinkle generously with rub. Let sit up to overnight.

2. Heat a sauté pan over medium heat. Add pork and extra-virgin olive oil; brown meat. Deglaze pan with ¼ cup of the chicken stock; if the meat starts to stick, add a small amount of water. Remove meat from pan.

3. Add onions and garlic to the pan; cook until slightly caramelized. Add tomatoes and the rest of the stock. Pour into crockpot; add pork. Cook on low heat for 2½ hours or until the meat is tender, but not shredding. Add corn and red peppers; cook for 30 minutes. Adjust seasoning with salt and pepper. Stir in cilantro and lime juice.

Variations

- Add 4 cups chopped chard or spinach leaves.
- Add 1 15-ounce can white beans.
- Use for filling in tacos.
- Use for filling in enchiladas.
- Use for filling in a torta.

Nutrition Facts per Serving: 230 calories, 27 g protein, 6.5 g total fat (1.5 g saturated fat), 1.5 g carbohydrate, 2 g fiber, 73 mg cholesterol, 300 mg sodium, 37 weighted glycemic index

SEAFOOD

Culinary delights from the sea are abundant in these simple recipes. Inspired by the coastal California way of eating, these delicious fish and seafood recipes will become regulars at your table. Cedar Plank Roasted Salmon, Spicy Crab Cakes with Whole-Grain Mustard Vinaigrette, and grilled tuna served with white bean salad are sure to become favorites.

Cabbage Slaw for Fish Tacos or Pork Sandwiches

The bright citrus flavors in this crunchy slaw are a perfect filling for soft tacos.

Start to Finish: 15 minutes   Yield: 2 cups

2 cups green cabbage, shredded	2 tablespoons lime juice
4 tablespoons red onions, fine julienned, rinsed, drained well	2 tablespoons orange juice
1 Roma tomato, seeded, julienned	2 tablespoons cilantro, chopped
1 teaspoon cider vinegar	1 teaspoon jalapeño, chopped
	Salt and pepper to taste

1. Place cabbage in a colander; season with salt. Let sit for 10 minutes until the cabbage starts to release water. Gently press to remove excess liquid.

2. Add red onions, tomato, vinegar, juices, cilantro, and jalapeño. Season well with salt and pepper.

CULINARY NOTE

This cabbage slaw should be salty, peppery, and spicy. Use as an accompaniment for barbecued pork sandwiches or fish tacos.

Variations

- Use a combination of red and green cabbage.
- Add julienned green apple.

Nutrition Facts per Serving: 20 calories, .5 g protein, 1 g total fat (0 g saturated fat), 5 g carbohydrate, 1 g fiber, 0 mg cholesterol, 7 mg sodium, 23 weighted glycemic index

Grilled Fish Tacos

Tacos are the perfect party food—have a *taquisa* party and be sure to include a roasted tomatillo green salsa or roasted tomato habanero salsa. The bright citrus flavors of the crunchy cabbage slaw are perfect in these soft tortilla tacos.

Start to Finish: 15 minutes   Yield: 4 servings, 2 tacos each

1 pound salmon or halibut fillets, skinless, boneless	Nonstick cooking spray
2 tablespoons lime juice	1 tablespoon lime juice
2 tablespoons orange juice	8 corn tortillas
1 teaspoon jalapeño, chopped (optional)	2 cups Cabbage Slaw for Fish Tacos or Pork Sandwiches (page 180)
2 tablespoons cilantro, chopped	Salt and pepper to taste

1. Season fish with salt and pepper; let sit for 10 minutes.

2. Combine lime juice, orange juice, jalapeño, 1 tablespoon cilantro, salt, and pepper. Add fish and let sit for 15 minutes.

3. Preheat a grill.

4. Remove the fish from the marinade. Spray with nonstick cooking spray. Place on grill. Grill until the fish is cooked halfway, 5 to 15 minutes depending on thickness of fish. Flip and cook on other side. Let rest for 5 minutes. Flake the fish into ½-inch-thick pieces in a bowl. Toss with 1 tablespoon cilantro and lime juice; season with salt and pepper.

5. Heat tortillas on a dry griddle; top with seasoned fish and Cabbage Slaw.

CULINARY NOTE

You can use any leftover grilled or sautéed fish for tacos. Just season with orange and lime juice.

Variation

- Use fresh store-bought salsa and 1 ounce shredded lettuce in place of cabbage slaw.

Nutrition Facts per Serving: 290 calories, 26 g protein, 8 g total fat (1.3 g saturated fat), 28 g carbohydrate, 4 g fiber, 62 mg cholesterol, 80 mg sodium, 46 weighted glycemic index

Cedar Plank Roasted Salmon

Using a cedar plank to roast salmon is a technique that was
originally used by Native Americans. The fish would be tacked to
a cedar plank and held next to the fire to roast.
The unique flavors that the cedar plank imparts to the fish are delicious!

Start to Finish: 30 minutes plus 2 hours to soak plank   Yield: 4 servings

1	wine barrel stave or cedar plank for roasting salmon	1	tablespoon molasses
1	pound salmon fillet, boneless, skinless, cut in 4-ounce portions	1	tablespoon lemon juice
1	tablespoon soy sauce	1	tablespoon lemon zest
1	tablespoon Dijon mustard		Salt and pepper to taste
			Nonstick cooking spray

1. Soak plank in cold water for 2 hours. Drain.

2. Season salmon with salt and pepper. Let sit for 15 minutes

3. Combine soy sauce, mustard, molasses, lemon juice, and lemon zest. Brush on fish.

4. Preheat oven to 450°F.

5. Place plank in the oven for 5 minutes to heat through. Spray with nonstick cooking spray. Lay seasoned fish on top of plank, return to oven, and bake for 15 minutes or until just cooked through.

6. Serve with Salsa Verde (page 390).

Variations

- Use lemon and your favorite herb marinade.

- Replace salmon with halibut, sea bass, or cod.

WINE SUGGESTION: *Sauvignon blanc*

Nutrition Facts per Serving: 185 calories, 23 g protein, 7 g total fat (1 g saturated fat), 5 g carbohydrate, 0 g fiber, 60 mg cholesterol, 350 mg sodium, 57 weighted glycemic index

Sonoma Salmon Burgers

A rich source of iron and vitamins A and C, arugula can now be found in many American supermarkets. Because it is highly perishable, arugula should be used quickly and refrigerated for no more than two days.

Start to Finish: 30 minutes   Yield: 4 servings

1 pound fresh or frozen salmon fillets, skinless, boneless	1 ½ cups arugula leaves, lightly packed
¾ cup pitted ripe olives, sliced	¼ cup celery, thinly sliced
¼ cup scallions, chopped	1 medium shallot, thinly sliced
1 tablespoon fresh dill, chopped	2 tablespoons lemon juice
2 teaspoons lemon zest	2 large whole-wheat pita bread rounds, halved crosswise
½ teaspoon kosher salt	Lemon wedges (optional)
1 tablespoon extra-virgin olive oil	

CULINARY NOTES

- Do not overwork the salmon in the food processor or the patties will be rubbery and chewy.

- Grill a tablespoon-size salmon patty first to see if the seasoning is correct.

1. Thaw salmon, if frozen. Rinse; pat dry with paper towels. Cut salmon into pieces and place in food processor. Cover and pulse with several on-off turns until salmon is coarsely ground. Transfer salmon to a large bowl.

2. Add olives, scallions, dill, lemon zest, and kosher salt to salmon; mix well. Shape salmon mixture into four ½-inch-thick patties. Brush both sides of each salmon patty with olive oil.

3. For a charcoal grill, place salmon patties on the rack of an uncovered grill directly over medium-hot coals. Grill for 8 to 12 minutes or until golden brown, carefully turning once halfway through grilling. For a gas grill, preheat grill. Reduce heat to medium-high. Place salmon patties on grill rack over heat. Cover and grill as above.

4. Meanwhile, in a small bowl, combine arugula, celery, shallot, and lemon juice.

5. Open each pita half to form a pocket. Place one salmon burger and one-fourth of the arugula mixture in each pita half. If desired, serve with lemon wedges.

Variation

- Replace olives, dill, and lemon zest with 1 tablespoon chopped jalapeño, 1 teaspoon ground cumin, 1 tablespoon chopped cilantro, and 1 teaspoon lime juice.

WINE SUGGESTION: *Zinfandel*

Nutrition Facts per Serving: 350 calories, 26.5 g protein, 18 g total fat (4.5 g saturated fat), 21 g carbohydrate, 3.5 g fiber, 56 mg cholesterol, 650 mg sodium, 49 weighted glycemic index

Saffron Seafood Stew

In this Provençal-style dish, saffron and fennel make for a delicious, aromatic broth that can also be used for poaching other favorite seafood. One of my favorites, especially when served with a slice of crunchy country bread and green salad.

Start to Finish: 1 hour   Yield: 8 servings

1	pound manila clams, rinsed well		1	tablespoon garlic
1	pound shrimp (21 to 25 shrimp), peeled and deveined		1	tablespoon fennel seeds, crushed or ground
2	pounds sea bass or monkfish, boneless, skinless, cut in 1-inch cubes		1	pinch chile flakes
			2	15.5-ounce can tomatoes chopped
2	tablespoons extra-virgin olive oil		2	cups zucchini, cut in quarters lengthwise, then in ¼-inch pieces
2	cups onions, chopped		½	cup low-sodium chicken stock
1	cup celery, chopped		2	tablespoons basil, chopped
1	cup fennel, chopped			Salt and pepper to taste
1	pinch saffron			

CULINARY NOTE

Clean the exterior of the clams before adding them to the stew.

1. Place clams in a bowl of salted cold water. Let sit for 30 minutes in the refrigerator. Drain and rinse well.

2. Season shrimp with salt and pepper. Let sit for 15 minutes.

3. Season the fish with salt and pepper. Let sit for 15 minutes.

4. Heat Dutch oven or deep sauté pan over medium heat. Add 1 tablespoon oil, onions, celery, and fennel. Cook 8 minutes or until the onions are tender. Add saffron, garlic, fennel seeds, and chile flakes; cook until aromatic. Add tomatoes. Bring to a simmer and cook for 20 minutes on low heat until the flavors blend.

5. Heat a sauté pan over high heat. Add 1 tablespoon oil and zucchini; sauté for 2 minutes until just cooked, but still crunchy. Add zucchini, clams, shrimp, and chicken stock to Dutch oven. Bring to a simmer and cover. After the first few clams open, add basil and bury the fish in the liquid. Cook until the fish pieces are cooked through, about 20 minutes. Serve in a large wide bowl.

Variations

- Add scallops or more shrimp in place of some of the fish.
- Use mussels instead of clams.
- Add 1 teaspoon lemon zest.
- Add a 15.5-ounce can of cannellini beans with the tomatoes.
- You can use this liquid to poach 4-ounce portions of fish or chicken for a Provençal-style meal.

Nutrition Facts per Serving: 300 calories, 42 g protein, 7 g total fat (1.3 g saturated fat), 13.5 g carbohydrate, 3 g fiber, 150 mg cholesterol, 450 mg sodium, 20 weighted glycemic index

Scallops with Tropical Salsa

Sweet-tart bursts of papaya enliven this dish. Scallops are low in fat and an excellent source of tryptophan, but because of their delicacy, be cautious not to overcook them or they will toughen and lose their subtle texture.

Start to Finish: 25 minutes   Yield: 4 servings

1 cup papaya or mango, finely chopped	1 fresh jalapeño chile pepper, seeded and finely chopped
½ cup red bell pepper, seeded and chopped	4 teaspoons lime juice
½ cup cucumber, seeded and finely chopped	3 teaspoons extra-virgin olive oil
2 tablespoons fresh cilantro, chopped	12 ounces fresh or frozen scallops
	Kosher salt
	Freshly ground black pepper
	Lime wedges (optional)

1. For salsa, in a small bowl, stir together papaya, bell pepper, cucumber, cilantro, chile pepper, lime juice, and 1 teaspoon olive oil. Season with salt and pepper. Let stand at room temperature for at least 15 minutes to allow flavors to blend.

2. Meanwhile, thaw scallops, if frozen. Rinse scallops; pat dry with paper towels. Cut any large scallops in half. Season scallops lightly with kosher salt and black pepper.

3. Heat a large nonstick skillet over medium-high heat. Add the remaining 2 teaspoons of olive oil and scallops. Cook and stir for 2 to 3 minutes or until scallops are opaque. Use a slotted spoon to remove scallops; drain on paper towels. Serve the scallops with the salsa. If desired, serve with lime wedges.

CULINARY NOTE

The scallops must be cooked in a hot pan. Heat the empty pan first; then add the oil and scallops. The pan should be smoking hot so the scallops brown immediately.

WINE SUGGESTION:
Sparkling semisweet

Nutrition Facts per Serving: 130 calories, 15 g protein, 4 g total fat (.5 g saturated fat), 7.5 g carbohydrate, 1 g fiber, 28 mg cholesterol, 163 mg sodium, 27 weighted glycemic index

Sautéed Halibut

with White Wine Braised Cabbage and Cannellini Beans

White wine in this recipe is used to make a light and flavorful sauce. Choose a dry white wine such as sauvignon blanc to make the sauce.

Start to Finish: 40 minutes   Yield: 4 servings

1 pound halibut fillet, cut into 4 portions	1 15.5-ounce can cannellini beans, drained
2 tablespoons extra-virgin olive oil	½ cup low-sodium vegetable or chicken stock
3 cups green cabbage, julienned	½ cup scallions, chopped
1 tablespoon garlic, chopped	2 tablespoons Italian parsley leaves
1 tablespoon sage, chopped	Salt, pepper, and lemon juice to taste
1 pinch chile flakes	
½ cup dry white wine	

1. Season halibut with salt and pepper. Set aside.

2. Heat a large sauté pan over medium heat. Add 1 tablespoon olive oil and cabbage. Sprinkle with salt and pepper. Sauté for 5 minutes or until the cabbage is slightly wilted. Add garlic, sage, and chile flakes; cook until aromatic. Add white wine; reduce by 75%. Add beans and vegetable or chicken stock. Bring to a simmer. Cook for 15 minutes over medium-low heat until the flavors blend. Stir in ¼ cup scallions and 1 tablespoon chopped parsley. Season with salt, pepper, and lemon juice.

3. Heat another large sauté pan over medium heat. Add 1 tablespoon olive oil and the halibut and brown both sides. When the juices start to accumulate on top, flip and finish cooking on other side. The fish should be golden brown on the exterior and just cooked through.

4. Combine remaining scallions and parsley leaves in a bowl. Season with lemon juice, salt, and pepper.

5. Divide cabbage and cannellini mixture between 4 soup plates or plates with rims. Place fish on top. Drizzle with a little of the broth from the beans; sprinkle with scallion and parsley leaf mixture.

Variations

- Replace halibut with salmon or sea bass fillets.
- Poach fish in cabbage mixture instead of sautéing. After seasoning fish, make a well in the center of the cabbage mixture and bury the fish in the mixture. Bring to a simmer; reduce heat so there are barely any bubbles. Cover; baste periodically until the fish is just cooked, about 10 minutes.

WINE SUGGESTION: *Sauvignon blanc*

Nutrition Facts per Serving: 330 calories, 32 g protein, 10 g total fat (1.5 g saturated fat), 22 g carbohydrate, 6.5 g fiber, 36 mg cholesterol, 380 mg sodium, 31 weighted glycemic index

Pan-Seared Salmon

with Asparagus and Mushrooms

Very few foods naturally contain vitamin D, but you'll get a double dose with the salmon and mushrooms in this recipe.

Start to Finish: 45 minutes   Yield: 4 servings

4	fresh or frozen skinless salmon fillets, about 1 inch thick (about 1 pound total)	1	tablespoon fresh thyme, chopped
	Kosher salt	1	cup dry white wine
	Freshly ground black pepper	1	cup clam juice, fish stock, chicken stock, or chicken broth
2	tablespoons extra-virgin olive oil	2	cups asparagus cut into 1 ½-inch-long pieces
2	cups sliced assorted fresh mushrooms (such as button, cremini, and/or stemmed shiitake)	1	cup cherry tomatoes, halved
		1	tablespoon fresh flat-leaf parsley, chopped
1	cup onion, chopped	1	teaspoon lemon juice
6	cloves garlic, minced (1 tablespoon minced)		Fresh thyme sprigs (optional)

1. Thaw fish, if frozen. Rinse fish; pat dry with paper towels. Measure thickness of fish fillets. Season with kosher salt and pepper. Set aside.

2. In a large skillet, heat 1 tablespoon of the olive oil over medium heat. Add mushrooms; cook about 5 minutes or until golden brown. Add onion, garlic, and thyme; cook until mushrooms are tender, stirring occasionally. Add wine. Bring to boiling; reduce heat. Simmer, uncovered, about 15 minutes or until liquid is reduced to ¼ cup.

3. Add clam juice. Return to boiling; reduce heat. Simmer, uncovered, about 15 minutes more or until liquid is reduced to ¾ cup. Add the asparagus. Cover and cook about 3 minutes or until asparagus is crisp-tender. Stir in tomatoes, parsley, and lemon juice. Season to taste with kosher salt and pepper. Transfer to a serving platter and keep warm.

4. In the same skillet, heat the remaining olive oil over medium heat. Add salmon; cook for 4 to 6 minutes per ½-inch thickness or until salmon flakes easily when tested with a fork, turning once. Serve salmon over vegetable mixture. If desired, garnish with fresh thyme.

CULINARY NOTES

- After adding the wine to the mushrooms, reduce it by at least three-quarters to cook off the alcohol.

- Add the lemon juice just before serving because the lemon will discolor the asparagus.

WINE SUGGESTION: *Sauvignon blanc*

Nutrition Facts per Serving: 360 calories, 27 g protein, 19 g total fat (4.5 g saturated fat), 12 g carbohydrate, 3 g fiber, 55 mg cholesterol, 170 mg sodium, 14 weighted glycemic index

Sautéed Shrimp

with Tomato and Basil

A bed of nutrient-packed spinach sets the stage for America's favorite shellfish. Shrimp may be small, but they have huge appeal, especially when combined with cooked tomatoes, onions, and basil.

Start to Finish: 25 minutes   Yield: 4 servings

1 pound fresh or frozen medium shrimp	¼ cup fresh basil, chopped
1 tablespoon extra-virgin olive oil	3 tablespoons balsamic vinegar
½ cup red onion, thinly sliced	Kosher salt
3 cups cherry tomatoes, halved	Freshly ground black pepper
	4 cups fresh baby spinach

1. Thaw shrimp, if frozen. Peel and devein shrimp. Rinse shrimp; pat dry with paper towels. Season with salt and pepper. In a large skillet, heat olive oil over medium-high heat. Add shrimp; cook about 3 minutes or until shrimp are opaque, turning occasionally. Remove shrimp from skillet; set aside.

2. Add red onion to skillet; cook about 3 minutes or until crisp-tender, stirring occasionally. Add tomatoes; cook for 1 minute more. Return shrimp to skillet. Add basil and vinegar; heat through. Season to taste with kosher salt and pepper.

3. Divide spinach among 4 dinner plates. Top with shrimp mixture.

Variations

- Add 2 ounces feta cheese or goat cheese to the skillet with the tomatoes.

- Toss the spinach with the tomatoes to just wilt it.

- Replace shrimp with scallops. Sear the scallops in a hot sauté pan over high heat. Remove from pan. Continue with recipe; then add scallops back to pan just to warm through.

WINE SUGGESTION: *Zinfandel or sangiovese*

Nutrition Facts per Serving: 200 calories, 25 g protein, 5.5 g total fat (1 g saturated fat), 11.5 g carbohydrate, 3 g fiber, 170 mg cholesterol, 215 mg sodium, 16 weighted glycemic index

Grilled Salmon
with Citrus Herb Crust

Succulent salmon fillets are a good source of vitamin A, B vitamins, protein, and omega-3 fatty acids. These fillets are crusted with cilantro and scallions for brilliant color.

Start to Finish: 25 minutes   Yield: 4 servings

12 ounces fresh or frozen skinless salmon fillet, about ¾ inch thick	1 clove garlic
⅓ cup coarsely chopped fresh oregano	1 tablespoon lemon juice
⅓ cup coarsely chopped fresh cilantro	1 tablespoon lemon and orange zest
¼ cup sliced scallions	2 teaspoons extra-virgin olive oil
	Salt and pepper to taste

1. Thaw salmon, if frozen. Rinse; pat dry with paper towels. Season with salt and pepper. Cut fish into 4 pieces (about 3 ounces). Set aside.

2. In a food processor or a mini chopper, combine oregano, cilantro, scalions, garlic, lemon juice, zest, oil, salt, and pepper. Cover and process until chopped. (Or use a knife to finely chop the oregano, cilantro, scallions, and garlic. Transfer to a shallow bowl. Stir in lemon juice, zest, oil, salt, and pepper.) Generously coat both sides of the salmon with the herb mixture. Allow the fish to marinate 15 minutes to 1 hour for maximum flavor.

3. For a charcoal grill, place salmon on the rack of an uncovered grill directly over medium-hot coals. Grill for 6 to 8 minutes or just until the salmon flakes easily when tested with a fork. For a gas grill, preheat grill. Reduce heat to medium-high. Place salmon on grill rack over heat. Cover and grill as above.

Variations
- Replace oregano and cilantro with parsley and basil.
- Replace salmon with halibut or sea bass.
- Replace salmon with shrimp or scallops.

WINE SUGGESTION:
Sauvignon blanc

Nutrition Facts per Serving: 180 calories, 17 g protein, 11 g total fat (3 g saturated fat), 2 g carbohydrate, 5 g fiber, 42 mg cholesterol, 160 mg sodium, 17 weighted glycemic index

CULINARY NOTE

To cook the fish to medium rare: Grill over high heat on one side until grill marks are visible, about 5 minutes; flip and cook the other side for another 5 minutes, or until the fish is cooked to the desired level of doneness.

Grilled Tuna and Cannellini Bean Salad

A no-fuss spinach and cannellini bean salad perfectly accompanies grilled tuna steaks to become a nutritious meal.

Start to Finish: 30 minutes   Yield: 4 servings

2	5- to 6-ounce fresh or frozen tuna steaks, cut 1 inch thick
2	tablespoons lemon juice
2	tablespoons extra-virgin olive oil
1	tablespoon balsamic vinegar
1	tablespoon Dijon mustard
4	cups fresh baby spinach leaves
2	15-ounce cans cannellini beans, rinsed and drained
1	cup thinly sliced red onion, rinsed and drained
1	cup thinly sliced celery
¼	cup oil-packed sun-dried tomatoes, drained and chopped
2	tablespoons chopped fresh flat-leaf parsley
	Salt and pepper to taste

1. Thaw fish, if frozen. Rinse fish; pat dry with paper towels. Season with salt and pepper. Let sit for 10 minutes. For a charcoal grill, place fish on the greased rack of an uncovered grill directly over medium coals. Grill for 8 to 10 minutes or until fish flakes easily when tested with a fork, gently turning once halfway through grilling. For a gas grill, preheat grill. Reduce heat to medium. Place fish on greased grill rack over heat. Cover and grill as above.

2. Meanwhile, for dressing, in a screw-top jar combine lemon juice, olive oil, balsamic vinegar, and Dijon mustard. Cover and shake well. Set aside 1 tablespoon of the dressing to drizzle over grilled fish.

3. In a large bowl, combine spinach, beans, red onion, celery, tomatoes, and parsley. Drizzle with remaining dressing; toss gently.

4. To serve, arrange spinach mixture on a serving platter. Slice tuna; place on top. Drizzle fish with reserved dressing.

WINE SUGGESTION:
Sauvignon blanc

Nutrition Facts per Serving: 360 calories, 32 g protein, 8.5 g total fat (1.5 g saturated fat), 42 g carbohydrate, 12 g fiber, 36 mg cholesterol, 515 mg sodium, 33 weighted glycemic index

Grilled Shrimp

with White Beans, Rosemary, and Arugula

To devein the shrimp, make a shallow slit along the center of the back and remove the vein by simply washing it out under cold water. These skewered shrimp are grilled in mere minutes with no hassle.

Start to Finish: 40 minutes   Yield: 4 servings

16 fresh or frozen extra-large shrimp in shells (about 1 pound total)	2 tablespoons oil-packed dried tomatoes, drained and finely chopped
3 tablespoons extra-virgin olive oil	2 tablespoons chopped fresh flat-leaf parsley
4 cloves garlic, minced (2 teaspoons minced)	8 cups lightly packed arugula leaves, fresh spinach, and/or watercress, tough stems removed
4 teaspoons chopped fresh rosemary	1 15-ounce can cannellini beans (white kidney beans), rinsed and drained
6 cloves garlic, thinly sliced	
¼ teaspoon crushed red pepper	
¼ teaspoon kosher salt	½ cup thinly sliced red onion
¼ teaspoon freshly ground black pepper	8 long sprigs fresh rosemary (optional)
1 teaspoon lemon zest	4 skewers
¼ cup lemon juice	

1. Thaw shrimp, if frozen. Peel and devein shrimp, leaving tails intact. Thread shrimp onto four 8-inch skewers,* leaving a ¼-inch space between pieces. In a small bowl, combine 1 tablespoon olive oil, minced garlic, and 1 teaspoon rosemary. Brush the oil mixture over the shrimp.

2. For a charcoal grill, place skewers on the rack of an uncovered grill directly over medium coals. Grill about 8 minutes or until shrimp are opaque, turning once halfway through grilling. For a gas grill, preheat grill. Reduce heat to medium. Place skewers on grill rack over heat. Cover and grill as above.

3. Meanwhile, in a very large skillet, combine the remaining 2 tablespoons oil, the remaining 3 teaspoons rosemary, sliced garlic, crushed red pepper, kosher salt, and black pepper. Cook over medium-low heat about 8 minutes or until garlic is lightly browned, stirring occasionally. Stir in lemon zest, lemon juice, tomatoes, and parsley.

4. Add half of the arugula, beans, and onion to the skillet. Cook, tossing constantly, just until arugula begins to wilt. Add the remaining arugula; cook, tossing constantly, about 1 minute more or just until arugula is wilted.

5. Divide arugula mixture among four dinner plates. If desired, remove shrimp from wooden skewers and skewer two shrimp on each rosemary sprig. Serve shrimp with arugula mixture.

Variations

- Use scallops in place of the shrimp.
- Use halibut or salmon in place of shrimp.
- Use a grill pan in place of a wood-fired grill.

CULINARY NOTES

* If using wooden skewers, soak in enough water to cover for at least 1 hour before grilling.

▪ For a fine lemon zest, use a microplane. Use the yellow exterior of the lemon only. The white portion of the lemon will be bitter. Zest the lemons before juicing them.

WINE SUGGESTION: *Sauvignon blanc*

Nutrition Facts per Serving: 250 calories, 14 g protein, 11 g total fat (1.5 g saturated fat), 25 g carbohydrate, 7 g fiber, 40 mg cholesterol, 450 mg sodium, 30 weighted glycemic index

Seared Halibut

with Shaved Zucchini and Almond Salad

This refreshing change-of-pace salad is all health and colorful combinations of paper-thin sliced vegetables.

Start to Finish: 45 minutes   *Yield: 4 servings*

1 pound halibut fillet, cut in 4 portions	1 tablespoon basil, julienne
1 tablespoon lemon zest	1 tablespoon mint, chopped
1 tablespoon chives, chopped	2 tablespoons lemon juice
1 pound zucchini, medium size	3 tablespoons extra-virgin olive oil
¼ cup red onion, sliced paper-thin, rinsed, and drained	2 tablespoons almonds, toasted and slivered
	Salt and pepper to taste

1. Season the halibut with salt and pepper. Combine lemon zest and chives. Sprinkle over halibut. Set aside.

2. Trim the ends off the zucchini. Slice into paper-thin ribbons (¹⁄₁₆ inch thick) lengthwise on a Japanese mandolin. Place ribbons in a large bowl. Combine with red onions, basil, and mint. Toss with lemon juice and 1 tablespoon of the olive oil. Season with salt and pepper.

3. Divide zucchini salad among 4 dinner plates. Reserve vinaigrette liquid in the bottom of the bowl.

4. Heat a nonstick sauté pan over medium-high heat. Add the remaining 2 tablespoons olive oil to coat pan. Place halibut in pan. Cook until golden brown; flip and cook on other side until translucent inside.

5. Place halibut on top of zucchini; drizzle with the remaining vinaigrette from the zucchini salad. Sprinkle with toasted almonds. Add more lemon juice if necessary.

CULINARY NOTE

A Japanese mandolin or vegetable slicer is a great tool for slicing vegetables evenly and thin. If you do not have a slicer, use a peeler to slice zucchini ¹⁄₁₆ inch thick.

Nutrition Facts per Serving: 265 calories, 26 g protein, 15 g total fat (2 g saturated fat), 6 g carbohydrate, 2 g fiber, 36 mg cholesterol, 71 mg sodium, 15 weighted glycemic index

Spicy Crab Cakes
with Whole-Grain Mustard Vinaigrette

In northern California, Dungeness crab is the choice for delicious crab cakes. Serve these with tangy Whole-Grain Mustard Vinaigrette and a squeeze of lemon. Perfect for entertaining!

Start to Finish: 45 minutes   Yield: 4 servings, two 2-ounce crab cakes per serving

1 tablespoon extra-virgin olive oil	½ tablespoon Dijon mustard
¼ cup celery, chopped fine	½ teaspoon sambal oelek or Tabasco
1 cup red and yellow peppers, chopped fine	Salt and pepper to taste
1 teaspoon garlic, chopped fine	½ teaspoon lemon juice
1 pound crab meat, cleaned, shells removed	1 cup corn flakes or multigrain flake cereal, crushed
1 tablespoon whole-wheat bread crumbs	Nonstick cooking spray or olive oil in a mister
2 tablespoons scallion, chopped	1 pound salad greens
1 tablespoon parsley, chopped	½ cup Whole-Grain Mustard Vinaigrette (recipe below)
2 tablespoons low-fat mayonnaise	

1. Preheat oven to 450°F. Spray a baking sheet with nonstick cooking spray.

2. Heat a sauté pan over medium heat. Add olive oil, celery, and peppers. Season with salt and pepper. Sauté until celery is tender. Add garlic; cook until aromatic. Remove from sauté pan and cool on a plate in the refrigerator.

3. Combine the crab meat, celery mixture, bread crumbs, scallion, parsley, mayonnaise, mustard, and hot sauce in a bowl. Gently mix. Adjust seasonings with salt, pepper, and lemon juice.

4. Divide the mixture into eight 2-ounce balls. Lightly dredge in corn flakes. Place crab cakes on prepared baking sheet. Spray tops with nonstick cooking spray or olive oil.

Nutrition Facts per Serving: 220 calories, 15 g protein, 10 g total fat (1.5 g saturated fat), 19.5 g carbohydrate, 5 g fiber, 40 mg cholesterol, 440 mg sodium, 40 weighted glycemic index

Bake 8 to 10 minutes until heated through and slightly golden. If the cakes are warm, but not browned, place under broiler for 1 to 2 minutes.

5. Toss the salad greens with half the mustard vinaigrette. Season with salt and pepper.

6. Divide the salad greens evenly among 4 plates. Place 2 crab cakes on each salad and drizzle with the remaining mustard vinaigrette.

CULINARY NOTES

- Be careful when mixing the crab cakes. Try to keep the crab meat in large pieces by gently folding the mixture together.

- To crush the corn flakes, place the corn flakes in a sealed plastic bag and roll with a rolling pin to make crumbs.

WINE SUGGESTION: *Sauvignon blanc*

Whole-Grain Mustard Vinaigrette

Start to Finish: 15 minutes   *Yield: ½ cup, 8 servings, 1 tablespoon each*

1 tablespoon shallots, minced	3 tablespoons extra-virgin olive oil
1 tablespoon lemon juice	1 tablespoon chives, chopped
2 tablespoons champagne vinegar	Salt and pepper to taste
1 tablespoon whole-grain mustard	

Place the shallots in a bowl with a pinch of salt, lemon juice, and vinegar. Allow to sit for 10 minutes. Add the mustard and whisk in the extra-virgin olive oil. Adjust the seasonings with salt and pepper. Stir in the chives.

Variations

- Replace red and yellow peppers with roasted peppers.

- Add 2 tablespoons dried fruits or nuts to the salad.

- Add ¼ cup julienne carrots or cucumbers to the salad.

Nutrition Facts per Serving: 50 calories, 0 g protein, 6 g total fat (.5 g saturated fat), 1.5 g carbohydrate, 0 g fiber, 0 mg cholesterol, 15 mg sodium, 33 weighted glycemic index

Grilled Halibut
with Corn and Pepper Relish

You'll find it helpful to have your *mise en place* before starting this recipe. *Mise en place* is a French term referring to having all your ingredients measured and ready to combine.

Start to Finish: 45 minutes   *Yield: 4 servings (plus leftover relish)*

4 5- to 6-ounce fresh or frozen halibut steaks, cut 1 inch thick	1 cup finely chopped green bell pepper
Kosher salt	2 cloves garlic, minced (1 teaspoon minced)
Freshly ground black pepper	⅛ teaspoon cayenne pepper
3 tablespoons extra-virgin olive oil	½ cup seeded and chopped tomato
4 tablespoons chopped fresh flat-leaf parsley	¼ cup finely chopped red onion
1 tablespoon chopped fresh oregano	1 tablespoon white wine vinegar
1½ cups fresh or frozen corn kernels	Fresh oregano (optional)
1 cup finely chopped red bell pepper	

1. Thaw fish, if frozen. Rinse fish; pat dry with paper towels. Season both sides of each halibut steak with kosher salt and black pepper. In a small bowl, combine 1 tablespoon olive oil, 1 tablespoon parsley, and oregano. Rub over both sides of each halibut steak; set aside for 10 minutes.

2. In a large skillet, heat 1 tablespoon of the remaining olive oil over medium-high heat. Add corn; cook about 4 minutes or until corn starts to brown, stirring occasionally.

Add bell peppers; cook and stir for 2 minutes more. Stir in the garlic, ¼ teaspoon kosher salt, and cayenne pepper. Cook and stir for 1 minute more. Remove from heat and let cool slightly.

CULINARY NOTE

If using fresh corn, remove husks and silk, place on grill, and grill until slightly brown.

3. For a charcoal grill, place fish on the rack of an uncovered grill directly over medium coals. Grill for 8 to 12 minutes or until fish flakes easily when tested with a fork, gently turning once halfway through grilling. For a gas grill, preheat grill. Reduce heat to medium. Place fish on grill rack over heat. Cover and grill as above.

4. Meanwhile, in a medium bowl combine cooled corn mixture, tomato, red onion, 3 tablespoons parsley, white wine vinegar, and the remaining 1 tablespoon oil; toss well. Serve each halibut steak with ½ cup of the relish. Cover and chill remaining relish for another use. If desired, garnish with fresh oregano.

Variations

- Replace halibut with salmon or tuna steaks.

- Fish can also be broiled. Place fish on the unheated rack of a broiler pan. Broil 4 inches from the heat for 8 to 12 minutes or until fish flakes easily when tested with a fork, turning once halfway through broiling.

WINE SUGGESTION: *Chardonnay*

Nutrition Facts per Serving: 340 calories, 35 g protein, 15 g total fat (2 g saturated fat), 15 g carbohydrate, 3 g fiber, 50 mg cholesterol, 315 mg sodium, 47 weighted glycemic index

Broiled Barbeque-Spiced Rubbed Salmon

The cooking time for this highly seasoned salmon dish depends on the thickness of the fish, but rest assured, this recipe is simple and speedy.

Start to Finish: 25 minutes   Yield: 6 servings

6	4-ounce fresh or frozen skinless, boneless salmon fillets, about 1 inch thick	1	teaspoon kosher salt
1	tablespoon sweet paprika	1	teaspoon garlic powder
1	tablespoon smoked paprika or ground ancho chile pepper	1	teaspoon freshly ground black pepper
1	tablespoon chili powder	½	teaspoon ground cumin
		½	teaspoon dried oregano, crushed
		3	tablespoons extra-virgin olive oil

1. Thaw fish, if frozen. Rinse fish; pat dry with paper towels. Measure thickness of fish. Set aside.

2. In a small bowl combine sweet paprika, smoked paprika, chili powder, kosher salt, garlic powder, black pepper, cumin, and oregano. Transfer spice mixture to a piece of waxed paper. Gently roll fish fillets in spice mixture to coat.

3. Brush about half of the olive oil on the bottom of a broiler pan or 15- by 10-inch baking pan. Place fish fillets in prepared pan; turn any thin portions under to make uniform thickness. Drizzle tops of fillets with remaining olive oil.

4. Broil fish 4 inches from the heat for 4 to 6 minutes per ½-inch thickness of fish or until fish flakes easily when tested with a fork, carefully turning once halfway through broiling.

Variation

- Cook fish on a cedar plank. Soak prepared plank in water for 30 minutes to 1 hour. Place plank in a 400°F oven for 5 minutes. Place fish on plank and roast until cooked through.

WINE SUGGESTION: *Sparkling semisweet*

Nutrition Facts per Serving: 257 calories, 23 g protein, 19 g total fat, (4.5 g saturated fat), 25 g carbohydrate, 1.5 g fiber, 56 mg cholesterol, 385 mg sodium, 19 weighted glycemic index

Grilled Scallops on Orange and Fennel Slaw

Champagne vinegar is a very light and mild vinegar, ideal for delicate dressings. If you cannot find champagne vinegar, you can substitute white wine or rice vinegar, but neither will be quite as mild.

Start to Finish: 25 minutes   *Yield: 4 servings*

12	fresh or frozen sea scallops (1 to 1½ pounds total)	2	tablespoons extra-virgin olive oil
2	medium fennel bulbs	1	tablespoon champagne vinegar
3	medium oranges, peeled and sectioned	½	teaspoon kosher salt
¾	cup pitted ripe olives, quartered	½	teaspoon freshly ground black pepper
2	tablespoons chopped tarragon	¼	cup sliced almonds, toasted
3	tablespoons lemon juice		Fresh tarragon (optional)
			Skewers

1. Thaw scallops, if frozen. Rinse scallops; pat dry with paper towels. Set aside. If desired, reserve some of the feathery tops from fennel for garnish. Cut off and discard upper stalks from fennel bulbs. Remove any wilted outer layers and cut and discard a thin slice from each fennel base. Cut fennel bulbs into very thin slices.

2. In a large bowl, combine fennel, oranges, olives, tarragon, lemon juice, 1 tablespoon of the olive oil, and the champagne vinegar. Stir in ¼ teaspoon of the kosher salt and ¼ teaspoon of the pepper. Cover and let stand for 15 minutes.

3. Meanwhile, in a large bowl, toss scallops with remaining 1 tablespoon olive oil, remaining ¼ teaspoon kosher salt, and remaining ¼ teaspoon pepper. Thread scallops onto long skewers,* leaving a ¼-inch space between scallops.

4. For a charcoal grill, place skewers on the rack of an uncovered grill directly over medium coals. Grill for 5 to 8 minutes or until scallops are opaque, turning once halfway

through grilling. For a gas grill, preheat grill. Reduce heat to medium. Place skewers on grill rack over heat. Cover and grill as above.

5. Divide fennel mixture among four dinner plates. Top with scallops; sprinkle with almonds. If desired, garnish with tarragon and/or reserved feathery tops from fennel.

Broiling directions: Preheat broiler. Place skewers on the unheated rack of a broiler pan. Broil 4 inches from the heat about 8 minutes or until scallops are opaque, turning once halfway through broiling.

WINE SUGGESTION: *Sauvignon blanc*

CULINARY NOTES

- Remove the white muscle attached to the scallop. Not all scallops will have this, but if you see it, remove it.

* Soak wooden skewers in water for 1 hour before using.

Nutrition Facts per Serving: 250 calories, 12 g protein, 13 g total fat (1.6 g saturated fat), 25 g carbohydrate, 7.5 g fiber, 14 mg cholesterol, 590 mg sodium, 27 weighted glycemic index

MEATLESS MEALS

There is no skimping on the protein for these nutrient-rich, satisfying meals. Your entire family will enjoy delicious tarts made with flaky phyllo dough, multigrain penne pasta with cherry tomatoes and fresh mozzarella, and seasonal variations of an all-time Sonoma favorite—risotto!

Zucchini and Tomato Torta

These are great for brunch and perfect for entertaining.
Tortas are similar to frittatas but have a denser vegetable filling. You can use
this recipe as a template to include other vegetables, such as artichoke hearts,
Swiss chard, or roasted peppers. The tortas refrigerate well and are
delicious warm or at room temperature.

Start to Finish: 45 minutes   Yield: 24 tortas, 8 servings, 3 tortas per serving

4 eggs	*Filling*
2 tablespoons low-fat milk	½ tablespoon extra-virgin olive oil
¼ teaspoon black pepper	½ cup onion, sliced
2 teaspoons parsley, chopped	1 teaspoon garlic, chopped
	1 cup zucchini, sliced in quarters lengthwise, then sliced ⅛ inch thick
	½ cup canned diced tomatoes, drained well
	1 tablespoon parmesan cheese
	Salt and pepper to taste
	Nonstick cooking spray

CULINARY NOTE

The basic ratio of these torta is 1 cup cooked vegetable to four eggs. Use any leftover cooked vegetables or canned beans to make delicious variations.

1. Preheat oven to 350°F.

2. Spray a mini muffin tin generously with nonstick cooking spray.

3. In a medium bowl, whisk together eggs, milk, pepper, and parsley.

Nutrition Facts per Serving: 65 calories, 4 g protein, 5 g total fat (1 g saturated fat), 3 g carbohydrate, .5 g fiber, 100 mg cholesterol, 85 mg sodium, 50 weighted glycemic index

4. Heat a large nonstick skillet over medium heat. Add extra-virgin olive oil and onion; sauté for 1 minute. Add garlic and sauté 10 seconds. Add zucchini and sauté for 2 minutes; add tomatoes and toss to warm. Add to eggs; mix well. Season with salt and pepper.

5. Spoon mixture into the mini muffin pan. Sprinkle tops with parmesan cheese. Place muffin tin on sheet pan and bake for 10 minutes or until the center is just set.

Variations

- Use cooked chicken or bay shrimp with fresh herbs in place of the zucchini to create a delicious appetizer.

- Use eggplant or summer squash in place of zucchini.

- Use chicken, shrimp, or pork to replace half the zucchini.

Barley Risotto

In this hearty recipe, made according to the traditional Italian risotto technique, pearl barley replaces arborio rice. Pearl barley is a nutrient-rich whole grain that gives this recipe a creamy texture and a wonderful, wholesome flavor.

Start to Finish: 1 hour   Yield: 4 servings

1 cup onion, chopped	1–2 cups cooked vegetables (see *Variations* on the next page)
1 tablespoon extra-virgin olive oil	
1 tablespoon garlic, minced	2 cups greens, cut in ½-inch pieces (see *Variations* on the next page)
¾ cups pearl barley	
½ cup white wine (optional)	¼ cup parmesan cheese, grated (optional)
5 cups hot vegetable stock or chicken stock	1 teaspoon lemon zest
1 bay leaf	Salt, pepper, and lemon juice to taste

1. In a large skillet, sauté the onions in the olive oil until golden. Add garlic and cook until aromatic. Add barley and stir to coat. Add wine and reduce until dry.

2. Add about 1 cup of hot stock and the bay leaf to the barley, just enough to come to the top of the grain. Cook over medium heat until liquid is absorbed, stirring occasionally. (This should take about 5 minutes. If the liquid absorbs too quickly, reduce the heat.) Repeat with 4 more cups of hot stock, adding 1 cup at a time and cooking until all the liquid is absorbed before adding more, stirring occasionally. (This should take about 35 minutes).

3. Stir in the vegetables; cook until the barley is slightly creamy and just tender. (This should take about 15 minutes. Increase heat slightly if the mixture is too wet.) Just before serving, remove the bay leaf; stir in the greens and allow to wilt. Stir in cheese and zest. Adjust seasoning with salt, pepper, and lemon juice.

Nutrition Facts per Serving: 315 calories, 14 g protein, 7 g total fat (2 g saturated fat), 46 g carbohydrate, 8.5 g fiber, 5 mg cholesterol, 185 mg sodium, 19 weighted glycemic index

Barley, Corn, and Spinach Risotto
(pictured on previous spread)

Use 1 cup corn, cut from the cob or frozen, and 2 cups baby spinach or spinach cut in 1-inch pieces.

Seasonal Variations

Fall/Winter

- 1 cup roasted butternut squash and 2 cups chopped spinach, kale, or chard, cut in ½-inch pieces
- 2 cups broccoli and ¼ cup sun-dried tomatoes
- 1½ cups roasted sweet potatoes and 1 cup frozen peas
- 2 cups sautéed julienne Brussels sprouts
- 2 cups sautéed mushrooms, sliced

Spring

- 1½ cup cooked asparagus and 1½ cup peas. Add the asparagus and peas at the very end so they do not discolor and overcook.
- 1½ cup blanched green beans, cut in 1-inch pieces, and 1 cup roasted red pepper, diced
- 2 cups sautéed artichokes hearts, cut in ½-inch pieces, and ½ cup roasted red pepper, diced
- 1½ cup sautéed fennel, diced, and 1 cup roasted red peppers, diced

Summer

- 1 cup sautéed zucchini and 1 cup roasted red pepper strips. Add at the very end of cooking so they do not discolor and overcook.
- 1½ cup sweet 100 tomatoes and 2 cups greens
- 1½ cups sugar snap peas cut in half and 1 cup corn

CULINARY NOTES

- Make sure the liquid is hot and add it gradually. Adding hot broth keeps the temperature of the risotto hot so the grains retain their texture while cooking. This is what gives risotto its creamy consistency.

- If you have used up all the stock and the barley is still crunchy and not cooked through, add more hot liquid. The amount of liquid you use will depend on how high the heat is and how quickly the liquid reduces.

Nutrition Facts per Serving: 310 calories, 14 g protein, 8 g total fat (2 g saturated fat), 45 g carbohydrate, 8 g fiber, 5 mg cholesterol, 190 mg sodium, 26 weighted glycemic index

Grilled Vegetable Sandwich

with Creamy Artichoke Dip, Arugula, and Oven-Dried Tomatoes

This is a great veggie sandwich that packs a lot of protein and energy from creamy white beans, whole grains, and feta cheese. The oven-dried tomatoes give this sandwich a meaty flavor and texture, with a smoky essence: you won't even notice the absence of meat in this sandwich.

Start to Finish: 15 minutes   Yield: 4 sandwiches

4 Multigrain Thin Buns (100-calorie buns by Orrowheat) or whole-wheat buns	12 ounces grilled vegetables (zucchini, eggplant, onions)
½ cup Creamy Artichoke Dip (page 275)	12 slices Oven-Dried Tomatoes (page 263)
3 tablespoons feta cheese, crumbled	2 cups arugula
	1 tablespoon balsamic vinegar
	Salt and pepper to taste

1. Toast buns in toaster.

2. Spread onto each bun 1 tablespoon creamy artichoke dip. Sprinkle with ¾ tablespoon feta cheese. Top with 3 ounces grilled vegetables and 3 slices of oven-dried tomatoes. Sprinkle with salt and pepper. Toss arugula with balsamic vinegar and divide evenly among buns. Cover with top bun.

Variations

- Use pesto in place of artichoke dip.
- Replace feta cheese with 1 slice of fresh mozzarella cheese per sandwich.

CULINARY NOTE

Use leftover grilled vegetables for this sandwich. If you do not have grilled vegetables, use bottled roasted peppers.

Nutrition Facts per Serving: 220 calories, 10 g protein, 7 g total fat (2.5 g saturated fat), 35 g carbohydrate, 10 g fiber, 11 mg cholesterol, 450 mg sodium, 53 weighted glycemic index

Zucchini, Tomato, and Ricotta Phyllo Tart

Inspired by the typical Greek phyllo pies, known as spanakopita, this tart is flavored with fragrant herbs, olive oil, and feta cheese. This recipe is perfect for an appetizer or a light meal.

Start to Finish: 60 minutes   Yield: 4 servings

1	cup low-fat ricotta cheese		3	tablespoons oat flour
2	tablespoons feta cheese, crumbled		3	tablespoons almond flour
1	tablespoon basil		8	sheets phyllo dough (9 inches x 12inches)
1½	teaspoons garlic, chopped		1	tomato, cut in half, then sliced ⅛ inch thick (about 20 slices)
1	egg, beaten			
1	zucchini, sliced ⅛ inch thick			Nonstick cooking spray
1	tablespoon extra-virgin olive oil			Salt and pepper to taste
5	cherry tomatoes, cut in quarters			

1. Preheat oven to 425°F.

2. Combine ricotta cheese, feta cheese, 2 teaspoons chopped basil, garlic, and egg. Mix well; season with salt and pepper.

3. Place sliced zucchini in a bowl. Season with salt and pepper. Let sit for 10 minutes to draw out some of the moisture. Drain and pat dry. Toss with 1 teaspoon extra-virgin olive oil. In a separate bowl, gently toss the cherry tomatoes with salt and pepper.

4. Combine oat and almond flour in a small bowl.

5. Line a sheet pan with parchment paper. Lay 1 large sheet of phyllo dough on the paper (keep the rest of the dough covered with plastic wrap). Spray with nonstick cooking spray and sprinkle lightly with the oat and almond flour mixture. Place another sheet of phyllo on top; gently press down. Spray sheet with olive oil spray and sprinkle lightly with oat and almond flour mixture. Repeat with the remaining sheets of phyllo, ending with a plain sheet of phyllo on top. Work quickly so the edges do not dry out. Spray the top sheet with nonstick cooking spray to prevent it from drying out. Roll up 1 inch of each edge toward the center, forming a rim. The final tart shell should be 7 inches x 10 inches.

6. Spread ricotta mixture over the tart shell in an even layer. Place tomato slices slightly overlapping around the edge of the tart. Lay the zucchini slightly overlapping the tomatoes and on a bias down the center of the tart. Place the cherry tomatoes down the center of the tart. Sprinkle the entire tart with the remaining 1 teaspoon thinly sliced basil.

7. Bake in preheated oven for 25 to 30 minutes, or until the crust is brown and crispy. Let cool on wire rack before serving.

Variation

- Replace feta cheese with goat cheese or parmesan cheese.

CULINARY NOTES

- Use a silpat for baking; it is a silicon baking sheet that is reusable and durable. Do not cut with a knife on it.

- Keep the phyllo dough covered with plastic wrap until ready to handle it. It dries out quickly.

- Drain zucchini well so it will brown during the cooking.

Broccoli Rabe and Penne

Broccoli rabe is one of my all-time-favorite bitter greens. Preparing it with extra-virgin olive oil, a sprinkle of crushed red pepper flakes, and a squeeze of lemon juice is a great flavor combination to mellow the bitterness of the broccoli rabe. This recipe is an easy template for cooking almost any greens, such as kale, chard, or mustard.

Start to Finish: 25 minutes   Yield: 6 servings

1 pound broccoli rabe	¼–½ teaspoon crushed red pepper
8 ounces dried multigrain penne pasta (such as Barilla Plus)	¼ cup grated Parmesan cheese
2 tablespoons extra-virgin olive oil	1 tablespoon lemon juice
6 cloves garlic, minced (1 tablespoon minced)	Kosher salt
	Freshly ground black pepper
	⅓ cup shredded parmesan cheese

1. Trim tough stems from broccoli rabe; discard stems. Coarsely chop the broccoli rabe leaves. Bring a large pot of water to a boil. Add salt and the broccoli rabe. Cook for 5 to 7 minutes or until tender. Drain; submerse broccoli rabe in a large bowl of ice water to cool quickly. When cool, drain well.

2. Meanwhile, cook pasta according to package directions. Drain pasta, reserving ¾ cup of the cooking water.

3. In a large skillet, heat olive oil over medium heat. Add garlic and crushed red pepper; cook for 1 minute. Add drained broccoli rabe; toss to coat with oil. Add the drained pasta, reserved pasta cooking water, grated parmesan cheese, and lemon juice. Cook and stir until heated through. Season to taste with kosher salt and black pepper. Sprinkle each serving with shredded parmesan cheese.

CULINARY NOTE

Broccoli rabe is a bitter green; blanching reduces the bitterness, but a balance of salt and acid is essential when seasoning.

Nutrition Facts per Serving: 250 calories, 11 g protein, 8 g total fat (2 g saturated fat), 32 g carbohydrate, 3.5 g fiber, 7 mg cholesterol, 150 mg sodium, 30 weighted glycemic index

Variations

- Replace broccoli rabe with broccoli florets.
- Add 1 cup chopped tomatoes or cherry tomatoes cut in half.
- Add 1 cup fresh mozzarella cheese and toss to warm at the end.

WINE SUGGESTION: *Sauvignon blanc*

Sonoma Pasta Salad

with Green Beans and Sun-Dried Tomatoes

This summery pasta dish comes together in no time, and with all those colorful vegetables, you know this dish is full of health and nutrition. Dried tomatoes accent the dish with bursts of sweet-tart flavor.

Start to Finish: 35 minutes   Yield: 4 servings

4 quarts water	¼ cup oil-packed sun-dried tomatoes, drained and cut into ¼-inch-thick slices
1 tablespoon kosher salt	
12 ounces fresh green beans or 3 cups frozen whole green beans	2 tablespoons fresh basil, flat-leaf parsley, and/or oregano, chopped
8 ounces dried multigrain penne (such as Barilla Plus)	3 tablespoons balsamic vinegar
	Kosher salt
1 tablespoon extra-virgin olive oil	Freshly ground black pepper
3 large red and/or yellow bell peppers, seeded and cut into bite-size strips	2 ounces fresh mozzarella cheese, cut up
1 tablespoon bottled minced garlic	Fresh basil leaves (optional)

1. If using fresh green beans: Bring 2 quarts of water to a boil in a saucepan. Add 1 tablespoon salt; then add fresh green beans. Cook for 4 to 5 minutes or until crisp-tender. Drain beans; place immediately in ice water to stop the cooking process. Once cool, drain well and set aside.

2. In a large Dutch oven, combine 2 quarts water and 1 tablespoon kosher salt; bring to boiling. Add pasta. Cook according to pasta package directions, adding frozen green beans (if using) for the last 2 minutes of cooking time. Drain, reserving 1 cup of the cooking water.

3. Meanwhile, in a large skillet heat olive oil over medium-high heat. Add pepper strips;

cook for 5 minutes, stirring occasionally. Add garlic; cook for 30 seconds more. Add dried tomatoes, basil, and the drained green beans and pasta. Cook, tossing frequently, until heated through. Stir in balsamic vinegar and enough of the reserved pasta liquid to moisten pasta to desired consistency. Season to taste with additional kosher salt and black pepper. Top with cheese. If desired, garnish with fresh basil.

Variations

- Use leftover cooked green beans or broccoli.
- Replace green beans with spinach.

WINE SUGGESTION: *Zinfandel*

Nutrition Facts per Serving: 385 calories, 13 g protein, 10 g total fat (2.5 g saturated fat), 60 g carbohydrate, 10 g fiber, 11 mg cholesterol, 290 mg sodium, 29 weighted glycemic index

Multigrain Penne Pasta Salad
with Zucchini, Cherry Tomatoes, and Fresh Mozzarella

Colorful vegetables make this pasta salad a beautiful presentation. Make this one day ahead; it will taste even better as the flavors develop and complement each other. It is also delicious as a cold salad, perfect for when you need to pack a lunch.

Start to Finish: 30 minutes   Yield: 6 servings, 1 ¼ cup per serving

6 ounces dry whole wheat or Barilla Plus penne pasta (or 2 cups cooked pasta)	1 cup cherry tomatoes, cut in half
1 tablespoon extra-virgin olive oil	1 tablespoon capers
2 tablespoons garlic, sliced thin	1 tablespoon basil, chopped
1 pinch chile flakes	1 cup fresh mozzarella cheese, cut in ½-inch cubes
2 cups zucchini, cut in quarters lengthwise, sliced ¼ inch thick	1 teaspoon lemon zest
	1 tablespoon lemon juice
	Salt and pepper to taste

1. Bring 6 quarts of water to a boil in a large pot. Add 2 tablespoons salt; bring back to a boil. Add pasta; cook for 10 minutes, or follow the directions on the pasta package. Reserve 1 cup of pasta water. Drain pasta in a colander. Spread on a baking sheet to cool.

2. While the pasta is cooking, cook oil and garlic over low heat in a large sauté pan until garlic is translucent. Add chile flakes, salt, and pepper. Transfer to a small bowl and set side.

3. Return sauté pan to high heat and add zucchini. Sauté until crisp and slightly brown. Add tomatoes, capers, basil, and garlic. Season with salt and pepper.

4. Add cooked pasta and ¼ to ½ cup pasta water to zucchini mixture; toss. Add mozzarella, lemon zest, and lemon juice, and toss to warm mozzarella through. Adjust seasoning with salt and pepper if necessary. Serve immediately.

Nutrition Facts per Serving: 190 calories, 8.5 g protein, 7.5 g total fat (3 g saturated fat), 24 g carbohydrate, 3 g fiber, 15 mg cholesterol, 71 mg sodium, 30 weighted glycemic index

Variations

- Replace zucchini with summer squash.
- Replace cherry tomatoes with ½-inch pieces of tomatoes
- COOK 1X · EAT 2X for roasted chicken: Add 8 ounces of shredded leftover roast chicken with the pasta water. Heat just to warm through; then continue with the recipe.

CULINARY NOTE

Using the pasta water when tossing the ingredients together adds flavor and a little starch and seasoning, forming a sauce to coat the pasta.

Cauliflower and Chickpea Gratin

A truly unique gratin, this dish features chickpeas, a legume used extensively in Mediterranean cooking. Don't let the labels fool you: chickpeas and garbanzo beans are actually the same thing.

Start to Finish: 45 minutes   Yield: 6 servings

3 tablespoons extra-virgin olive oil	2 tablespoons capers, rinsed and drained
2 cups chopped onion	1 tablespoon fresh oregano, chopped
2 14.5-ounce cans diced tomatoes, drained	1 tablespoon lemon juice
1 15-ounce can garbanzo beans (chickpeas), rinsed and drained	1 teaspoon fresh thyme, chopped
6 cloves garlic, minced (1 tablespoon minced)	½ teaspoon kosher salt
¼ cup fresh flat-leaf parsley, chopped	¼ teaspoon freshly ground black pepper
	1¾ pounds cauliflower, cut into florets
	4 ounces feta cheese, crumbled

1. In a large saucepan, heat olive oil over medium-high heat. Add onion; cook about 5 minutes or until tender, stirring occasionally. Add drained tomatoes, garbanzo beans, and garlic. Bring to boiling; reduce heat to low. Cover and simmer for 15 minutes. Stir in parsley, capers, oregano, lemon juice, thyme, kosher salt, and pepper.

2. Meanwhile, in a covered Dutch oven, cook cauliflower in a small amount of boiling water about 5 minutes or just until tender. Drain and keep warm.

CULINARY NOTES

- The cauliflower should be cooked until crisp-tender, and held warm. The cauliflower does not cook further; it is only topped with the tomato mixture and cheese and warmed through.

- If you are using frozen cauliflower that has been thawed and brought to room temperature, there is no need to cook the cauliflower; proceed with step 3.

3. Transfer cauliflower to a 2- to 2½-quart broiler-proof baking dish. Top with hot tomato mixture. Sprinkle with feta cheese. Broil 3 to 4 inches from the heat for 1 to 2 minutes or just until cheese begins to brown. Serve immediately.

Variations

- Add 1 tablespoon chopped kalamata olives.
- Replace chickpeas with cannellini beans.
- Replace cauliflower with fennel, tops trimmed, and cut into ½-inch wedges.

WINE SUGGESTION: *Chardonnay*

Nutrition Facts per Serving: 285 calories, 11 g protein, 12 g total fat (3.5 g saturated fat), 35 g carbohydrate, 8 g fiber, 11 mg cholesterol, 700 mg sodium, 31 weighted glycemic index

Wild Mushroom Tart
with Oven-Dried Tomatoes and Goat Cheese

A delightfully delicate tart that combines the savory flavors of wild mushrooms, smoky tomatoes, and creamy goat cheese. The phyllo dough gives it a light and flaky texture with an appealing rustic presentation. This is a great wine country recipe to serve when entertaining.

Start to Finish: 1 hour   Yield: 8 servings

3 tablespoons oat flour	2 eggs, beaten
3 tablespoons almond flour	½ cup low-fat sour cream
2 tablespoons extra-virgin olive oil	16 slices Oven-Dried Tomatoes (page 263)
8 cups mixed fresh wild mushrooms, large mushrooms cut in quarters	½ cup goat cheese
2 cups onions, diced	8 sheets phyllo dough (9 inches x 12 inches)
2 tablespoons garlic, diced	Salt and pepper to taste
2 tablespoons fresh herbs (thyme, parsley, or marjoram), chopped	Olive oil spray, as needed
1 tablespoon lemon zest	Parchment paper

1. Combine oat flour and almond flour in a small bowl. Set aside.

2. Heat a sauté pan over medium-high heat. Add oil and mushrooms. Sauté for 5 to 10 minutes or until the mushrooms release their moisture and begin to shrink (cook mushrooms in batches if necessary).

CULINARY NOTES

- If using portabello mushrooms, remove gills and cut into 1-inch wedges.
- If using crimini, button, or shiitake mushrooms, cut in ¼-inch wedges.

Continue cooking the mushrooms until all the liquid has evaporated and the mushrooms start to brown. Add onions, garlic, and half the herbs. Cook for 5 minutes or until the onions are soft. Stir in zest and adjust seasoning. Let cool. Add beaten egg and sour cream. Adjust seasoning.

3. Preheat oven to 400°F.

4. Line a sheet pan with parchment paper. Lay 1 large sheet of phyllo on the paper (keep the rest of the dough covered with plastic wrap). Spray with olive oil spray and sprinkle lightly with the oat and almond flour mixture. Place another sheet of phyllo on top; gently press down. Spray sheet with olive oil spray and sprinkle lightly with oat and almond flour mixture. Repeat with the remaining sheets of phyllo, ending with a plain sheet of phyllo on top. Work quickly so the edges do not dry out. Spray the top sheet with olive oil spray to prevent it from drying out. Roll up 1 inch of each edge toward the center, forming a rim. The final tart shell should be 7 inches x 10 inches.

5. Spread mushroom mixture evenly over the phyllo. Top with tomatoes and evenly distribute goat cheese on top. Sprinkle with remaining herbs.

6. Bake in preheated oven for 25 to 30 minutes, or until the crust is brown and crispy. Cool on wire rack before serving.

CULINARY NOTES

- Be sure to cook the mushrooms until they are golden brown and have released their moisture. If the mushrooms are too wet, they will soak through the phyllo dough.

- Make sure mushrooms will have time to chill. The egg will scramble if added to hot mushrooms. Fill the tart after the mushrooms have cooled.

- Use a silpat for baking; it is a silicon baking sheet that is reusable and durable. Do not cut with a knife on it.

Variations

- Replace goat cheese with parmesan.

Mushroom Spinach Tart

Follow recipe directions with these additions: Add 2 cups sautéed spinach (sauté 1 pound spinach with ½ cup minced onions and 1 tablespoon minced garlic; squeeze out excess liquid). Combine with 4 cups sautéed mushrooms and ½ cup roasted red pepper, chopped.

Nutrition Facts per Serving: 265 calories, 10.5 g protein, 14 g total fat (5.5 g saturated fat), 26 g carbohydrate, 4.5 g fiber, 69 mg cholesterol, 205 mg sodium, 39 weighted glycemic index

Ribollita Stew

This famous Tuscan soup is reminiscent of minestrone. Perfect on a cold winter day served with country-style bread and a salad of baby greens. There are many variations, but the main ingredients are white cannellini beans, carrots, onions, and tomatoes in a rich broth. Add a finishing touch of chopped kale and a sprinkle of parmesan cheese to make the soup even more authentic and, of course, delicious.

Start to Finish: 1 hour   Yield: 6 servings, 1½ cups per serving

2	tablespoons extra virgin olive oil		2	15-ounce cans diced tomatoes
1	cup mushrooms, chopped		4	cups low-sodium chicken stock
2	cups onions, chopped		2	16-ounce cans white cannellini beans, with liquid
1	cup carrots, chopped		2	cups water
1	cup celery, chopped		1	tablespoon parsley, chopped
2	tablespoons garlic, chopped			Salt, pepper, and lemon juice to taste
½	tablespoon thyme, chopped			
½	tablespoon oregano, chopped			

1. Heat a large soup pot over medium-high heat. Add extra-virgin olive oil and mushrooms. Cook for 5 minutes or until the mushrooms are slightly browned.

2. Add onions, carrots, and celery; sauté 4 minutes. Add garlic and herbs; sauté until aromatic. Add tomatoes and chicken stock; cook for 10 minutes. Add beans and water. Bring to a simmer and cook for 45 minutes.

3. Season with salt, pepper, and a squeeze of lemon. Stir in parsley.

Variations

- If you want to replace the canned beans with 1 pound dried white beans, rinse them and soak them in water overnight. Increase the 2 cups of water to 9 cups, adding the water and the soaked beans with the tomatoes and chicken stock. Cook the soup for 1½ hours at a low temperature.

- Try different varieties of beans and vegetables, such as kidney beans, kale, zucchini, and squash.

Nutrition Facts per Serving: 390 calories, 24 g protein, 6.5 g total fat (1 g saturated fat), 62 g carbohydrate, 14.5 g fiber, 0 mg cholesterol, 420 mg sodium, 33 weighted glycemic index

Pasta with Eggplant and Caper Tomato Sauce

A flavorful blend of capers, kalamata olives, basil, and thyme fills this dish with flavors of typical Mediterranean cuisine. The meaty flesh of the eggplant is filling but contains very few calories and little fat, making it a perfect vegetarian main-dish option.

Start to Finish: 75 minutes   *Yield: 8 servings*

1 medium eggplant, peeled and cut into 1-inch cubes (about 1 pound)	½ cup pitted kalamata olives, coarsely chopped
¼ cup extra-virgin olive oil	2 tablespoons fresh basil, chopped
1 large onion, chopped	1 tablespoon fresh oregano, chopped
6 cloves garlic, minced (1 tablespoon minced)	1 tablespoon fresh thyme, chopped
	Kosher salt
3 pounds tomatoes, cored and chopped, or four 14.5-ounce cans diced tomatoes, undrained	Freshly ground black pepper
	12 ounces dried multigrain spaghetti (such as Barilla Plus)
½ cup capers, rinsed and drained	¼ cup finely shredded parmesan cheese (2 ounces)

1. Preheat oven to 375°F. Place eggplant cubes in a 15 x 10 x 1-inch baking pan. Drizzle eggplant with 2 tablespoons of the olive oil; toss to coat. Bake for 18 to 20 minutes or until eggplant is tender but still holding its shape.

2. Meanwhile, in a large saucepan heat the remaining 2 tablespoons olive oil over medium heat. Add onion; cook for 5 minutes, stirring occasionally. Add eggplant and garlic; cook about 10 minutes more or until eggplant is very soft and starting to break apart, stirring occasionally.

3. Add tomatoes, capers, and olives to eggplant mixture. Bring to a boil; reduce heat, cover, and simmer for 10 minutes, stirring occasionally. Uncover and simmer for 15 to

20 minutes more or until desired consistency, stirring occasionally. Stir in basil, oregano, and thyme. Season to taste with kosher salt and pepper.

4. Meanwhile, cook pasta according to package directions; drain well. Return to hot pan; cover and keep warm. Serve sauce over cooked pasta; sprinkle with cheese.

Variation

- Add 2 tablespoons golden or black raisins.

CULINARY NOTES

- When roasting the eggplant, periodically stir the eggplant so it cooks evenly.
- Add a pinch of sugar if the eggplant is bitter.

WINE SUGGESTION: *Sangiovese*

Nutrition Facts per Serving: 285 calories, 10 g protein, 9.5 g total fat (1.5 g saturated fat), 45 g carbohydrate, 10 g fiber, 2 mg cholesterol, 440 mg sodium, 14 weighted glycemic index

Puttanesca Sauce

This slightly spicy Italian pasta sauce has immense flavor. The last-minute addition of thyme and marjoram lends a warm, minty accent.

Start to Finish: 45 minutes   *Yield: 6 servings*

1	tablespoon extra-virgin olive oil	¼	teaspoon freshly ground black pepper
6	cloves garlic, minced (1 tablespoon minced)	1	tablespoon fresh thyme, chopped
3	14.5-ounce cans crushed tomatoes	2	teaspoons fresh marjoram, chopped
¼	teaspoon crushed red pepper	10	ounces dried multigrain pasta, such as lasagna noodles, spaghetti, or fettuccine (such as Barilla Plus)
¼	cup pitted kalamata olives, chopped		
¼	cup capers, rinsed and drained	¼	cup finely shredded parmesan cheese (1 ounce)
2	tablespoons balsamic vinegar		
¼	teaspoon kosher salt		

1. In a medium saucepan, heat olive oil over medium heat. Add garlic; cook for 30 seconds. Stir in tomatoes and crushed red pepper; bring to a simmer.

2. Stir in olives, capers, vinegar, kosher salt, and black pepper. Return to boiling; reduce heat to low. Simmer, uncovered, about 30 minutes or until desired consistency. Stir in thyme and marjoram.

3. Meanwhile, cook pasta according to package directions. Drain. Serve sauce over hot cooked pasta. Sprinkle with parmesan cheese.

Variations

Use the sauce with a chicken entrée. Season 4 chicken breasts with salt and pepper. Heat a sauté pan and sear the chicken until golden brown on both sides, but still undercooked. Add 2 cups of sauce. Bring to a simmer and cook until the chicken is cooked through and the juices run clear. Remove chicken from pan and allow to rest for 5 minutes. Add 2 cups spinach to sauce; toss to wilt. Slice chicken on a bias in ¼-inch slices. Place sauce on plate, top with sliced chicken. Garnish with grated parmesan cheese.

CULINARY NOTES

- Cook the pasta in a large pot of boiling water. Once the water is at a full boil, add salt and then add pasta. Cook until al dente, slightly chewy, but cooked through. Drain the water; toss the pasta with the sauce. Do not rinse the pasta because the starch that adheres to the pasta will thicken the sauce slightly.

- If cooking the pasta in advance, follow the above directions, but slightly undercook the pasta. Drain well and place on a sheet pan. Toss with a little extra-virgin olive oil and let cool.

Nutrition Facts per Serving: 245 calories, 10 g protein, 4.5 g total fat (1 g saturated fat), 44 g carbohydrate, 7 g fiber, 3 mg cholesterol, 700 mg sodium, 31 weighted glycemic index

Pan-Grilled
Asian Marinated Tofu

The nutritional powerhouse benefits of tofu are well known. What may be a surprise is just how easy it is to prepare and how versatile it is when it comes to flavors. Tofu's mild flavor profile picks up any tasty flavors you prepare it with. This recipe is all about mild Asian flavor with a hint of savory—otherwise known as umami flavor—from the shiitake mushrooms.

Start to Finish: 60 minutes   Yield: 4 servings

1 16-ounce package water-packed firm tofu (fresh bean curd), well drained	1 tablespoon red wine vinegar
	1 tablespoon water
2 tablespoons fresh shiitake mushrooms, stemmed and chopped, or 1 tablespoon dried shiitake or porcini mushrooms	6 cloves garlic, minced (1 tablespoon minced)
	1 tablespoon fresh flat-leaf parsley, chopped
2 tablespoons extra-virgin olive oil	¼ teaspoon kosher salt
2 tablespoons soy sauce	¼ teaspoon freshly ground black pepper

1. Cut tofu into 1-inch-thick slices. Line a 3-quart rectangular baking dish with a clean towel. Arrange tofu slices on top. Place another clean towel on top. Set aside.

2. If using dried mushrooms, combine dried mushrooms and enough hot water to cover in a small bowl; let stand for 5 minutes. Drain and rinse mushrooms; chop mushrooms.

3. For marinade, in a blender combine the mushrooms, 1 tablespoon of the olive oil, soy sauce, vinegar, water, garlic, parsley, kosher salt, and pepper. Cover and blend until nearly smooth.

4. Remove towels from baking dish. Spoon marinade over tofu in dish. Turn tofu slices to coat with marinade. Cover and marinate at room temperature for 30 minutes, carefully turning tofu slices occasionally.

5. In a large skillet, heat remaining 1 tablespoon olive oil over medium heat. Remove tofu slices from marinade, allowing excess to drip off; discard marinade. Add tofu to skillet. Cook for 6 to 8 minutes or until browned and heated through, turning once.

Latin-Style Marinated Tofu

Prepare as directed, except add 2 to 3 canned chipotle peppers in adobo sauce and 1 teaspoon fresh oregano leaves to the blender with the other marinade ingredients.

Asian-Style Marinated Tofu

Prepare as directed, except substitute rice vinegar for the red wine vinegar and add 1 teaspoon grated fresh ginger and 1 teaspoon toasted sesame oil to the blender with the other marinade ingredients.

WINE SUGGESTION: *Chardonnay*

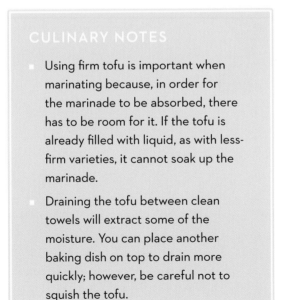

CULINARY NOTES

- Using firm tofu is important when marinating because, in order for the marinade to be absorbed, there has to be room for it. If the tofu is already filled with liquid, as with less-firm varieties, it cannot soak up the marinade.

- Draining the tofu between clean towels will extract some of the moisture. You can place another baking dish on top to drain more quickly; however, be careful not to squish the tofu.

Nutrition Facts per Serving: 240 calories, 19 g protein, 17 g total fat (2.5 g saturated fat), 7 g carbohydrate, 3 g fiber, 0 mg cholesterol, 400 mg sodium, 15 weighted glycemic index

SIDES

Your Sonoma Smart Plate deserves only the best when it comes to sides. A wholesome basil and quinoa salad, grilled artichokes with balsamic vinaigrette, and savory roasted tomatoes with a crispy bread topping are just a few of the delicious recipes you will find here to complement your meals.

Confetti Summer Salad

Fresh, crisp, and colorful is just what you're looking for in a summer salad. The fresh veggies in this dish are most abundant during summer months but are available yearlong, so the salad never goes out of season.

Start to Finish: 30 minutes   Chill: 4 to 24 hours   Yield: 8 side-dish servings

4   medium ears fresh corn or 2 cups frozen whole-kernel corn, thawed

4   baby zucchini, thinly sliced, or ½ of a small zucchini, halved lengthwise and thinly sliced (½ cup)

2   medium tomatoes, seeded and chopped

2   scallions, sliced

1   medium yellow bell pepper, seeded and chopped

1   medium red bell pepper, seeded and chopped

½   cup bottled Italian salad dressing made with olive oil

¼   teaspoon cayenne pepper (optional)

Fresh thyme (optional)

1. If using fresh corn, cook ears of corn in a small amount of boiling water in a covered large saucepan for 4 minutes. Drain; rinse with cold water to cool. When cool enough to handle, cut corn from cobs (you should have about 2 cups corn kernels).

2. In a large bowl, combine fresh cooked corn or thawed corn, zucchini, tomatoes, scallions, bell peppers, salad dressing, and, if desired, cayenne pepper. Cover and chill for 4 to 24 hours, stirring occasionally. If desired, garnish with fresh thyme.

Variations

- Replace the zucchini with summer squash or yellow crookneck squash.
- Add thinly sliced carrots.

CULINARY NOTE

Roast or grill the corn for a richer flavor.

Nutrition Facts per Serving: 67 calories, 3 g protein, 1.5 g total fat (.5 g saturated fat), 15 g carbohydrate, 2 g fiber, 0 mg cholesterol, 185 mg sodium, 38 weighted glycemic index

Asian Cabbage Slaw

Delicious bright flavors, a crunchy texture, and a light finish are some of the reasons you will love this versatile Asian slaw. Asian chile paste gives this slaw its unique fiery characteristic that complements just about any dish you serve it with.

Start to Finish: 30 minutes   Yield: 6 cups, serves 12

6   cups Napa cabbage, sliced ¼ inch thick

1   cup red peppers, julienned

2   tablespoons cilantro, chopped

1   tablespoon ginger, chopped

¼   cup scallion, chopped

1   cup Asian pear or green apple, peeled, cored, and julienned

1   teaspoon chile paste, sambal oelek, or Korean chile paste

½   cup Soy Sesame Vinaigrette (page 391)

1   tablespoon sesame seeds, toasted

¼   cup almonds, toasted and slivered

Salt and pepper to taste

1. Combine all ingredients except almonds in a large bowl.

2. Garnish with toasted, slivered almonds.

Variations

- Replace Napa cabbage with green cabbage.
- Add 1 tablespoon roughly chopped mint.

CULINARY NOTE

Do not mix too far in advance or the cabbage will become soggy.

Nutrition Facts per Serving: 65 calories, 2 g protein, 4 g total fat (.5 g saturated fat), 3 g carbohydrate, 1.5 g fiber, 0 mg cholesterol, 80 mg sodium, 25 weighted glycemic index

Basil Quinoa Salad
with Red Bell Pepper

With quinoa playing the starring role, nutrients abound in this full-flavored grain side dish. A great addition to any dinner, this dish goes especially well with a crisp salad.

Start to Finish: 25 minutes   Yield: 8 servings

1 cup lightly packed fresh basil leaves	2 cups cooked quinoa (according to package directions)
2 tablespoons freshly grated parmesan cheese	1 cup chopped red bell pepper
2 tablespoons lemon juice	½ cup scallions, sliced
2 tablespoons extra-virgin olive oil	Kosher salt
4 cloves garlic, minced (2 teaspoons minced)	Freshly ground black pepper
	¼ cup shelled sunflower seeds

1. In a small saucepan, bring 2 cups water to boiling. In a small bowl, combine cold water and ice cubes to make an ice bath. Add the basil to the boiling water; stir once and drain immediately. Place basil in the ice bath to cool quickly. Drain and gently squeeze out any excess water.

2. Place basil in a food processor. Add parmesan cheese, lemon juice, olive oil, and garlic. Cover and process until nearly smooth.

3. In a medium bowl, stir together cooked quinoa, bell pepper, and scallions. Add basil mixture. Season to taste with kosher salt and black pepper. Sprinkle with sunflower seeds.

Variations

- Add ½ cup cherry tomato halves.
- Add ½ cup diced fresh mozzarella cheese.
- Replace red peppers with roasted red peppers.

CULINARY NOTE

Toast the quinoa prior to cooking to add a nutty flavor. Place on a sheet pan and toast for 5 to 8 minutes at 325°F, stirring periodically until golden brown.

Nutrition Facts per Serving: 125 calories, 4 g protein, 7 g total fat (1 g saturated fat), 13 g carbohydrate, 2.5 g fiber, 1 mg cholesterol, 25 mg sodium, 46 weighted glycemic index

CULINARY NOTES

- Prepare this dish in the summer when these vegetables are at their peak for flavor and color.

- Select small squashes, 1 inch in diameter by 6 inches in length.

- Be sure to slice the squashes and tomatoes as evenly as possible for even cooking.

Tomato, Squash, and Feta Gratin

This is a beautiful dish and a great way to use the many different seasonal varieties of tomatoes and squash. Shop at your local farmers' market for inspirational ideas and choices of these wonderful vegetables. This recipe tastes even better the next day.

Start to Finish: 1 hour   Yield: 4 servings, 1 cup each

6 ounces zucchini, sliced ¼ inch thick on a long bias	2 scallions, chopped
6 ounces yellow squash, sliced ⅛ inch thick on a long bias	1½ teaspoon garlic, minced
	1½ teaspoon oregano, chopped
12 ounces tomatoes, cut in half, then sliced ¼ inch thick crosswise	2 ounces feta cheese, crumbled
	2 teaspoons extra-virgin olive oil
	Salt and pepper to taste

1. Preheat oven to 400°F. Lightly oil a 6-inch-diameter ovenproof sauté pan.

2. Toss zucchini with salt and pepper. Toss yellow squash with salt and pepper. In a bowl, mix the scallions, garlic, oregano, and cheese.

3. Lay zucchini slices in the pan, slightly overlapping them like shingles. Sprinkle with salt and pepper. Top with a layer of tomatoes, slightly overlapping like shingles. Sprinkle with ½ of the scallion mixture. Top with a layer of yellow squash, then another layer of tomatoes; sprinkle layers with salt and pepper. Top with remaining scallion mixture. Drizzle with extra-virgin olive oil.

4. Place on a sheet pan in the oven. Bake for 30 minutes or until the vegetables are tender and the top is slightly browned. Allow to sit for 10 minutes. Cut into wedges and serve.

Variations
- Add 1 tablespoon roasted diced red pepper between the layers.
- Replace oregano with basil, thyme, or rosemary.
- Replace feta cheese with goat cheese or parmesan cheese.

Nutrition Facts per Serving: 95 calories, 4.5 g protein, 5.5 g total fat (2 g saturated fat), 7.5 g carbohydrate, 2.5 g fiber, 8 mg cholesterol, 110 mg sodium, 22 weighted glycemic index

Gingered Turkey Wontons

Wonton noodles or *wantan mee* is a Cantonese noodle dish that is popular in Hong Kong, Malaysia, Thailand, and Singapore. The dish is usually served in a hot broth, garnished with leafy vegetables and wonton dumplings.

Start to Finish: 40 minutes   *Yield: 18 wontons, 6 servings, 3 wontons each*

Dipping sauce		*Wontons*	
¼	cup water	1	tablespoon ginger, finely chopped
¼	cup soy sauce	1	tablespoon garlic, finely chopped
¼	cup rice wine vinegar	1	tablespoon soy sauce
2½	teaspoons agave syrup	8	ounces ground turkey
2	teaspoons ginger, finely chopped	½	teaspoon sesame oil
½	teaspoon toasted sesame oil	1	tablespoon scallions, chopped fine
½	teaspoon Thai chili paste	1	teaspoon cilantro, chopped
			Salt and pepper to taste
		18	wonton wrappers

1. For the dipping sauce: Combine all ingredients in a bowl. Set aside.

2. For the wontons: Combine all ingredients except wonton wrappers in a large bowl. Mix well. Adjust seasoning with salt and pepper. Cook a small patty of the filling and taste for seasonings. Adjust seasonings if necessary.

CULINARY NOTE

- The wonton wrappers will dry out if left uncovered. Keep them covered with plastic wrap until you are ready to fold them.

Nutrition Facts per Serving: 40 calories, 4 g protein, 1 g total fat (0 g saturated fat), 5 g carbohydrate, 0 g fiber, 5 mg cholesterol, 80 mg sodium, 44 weighted glycemic index

3. Lay 18 wonton wrappers in a single layer on a flat surface. Place 1 tablespoon of the filling in the center of each wrapper. Brush edges of wrapper with water. Fold the wrapper in half, matching edges, and pinch edges closed. Place on a baking sheet in a single layer.

4. Bring a large pot of water to a simmer. Add wontons one at a time; bring water back to a simmer and cook for 5 minutes. Lift from water and serve with dipping sauce.

Variations

- Replace chicken with lean chopped pork.
- Replace soy sauce with Vietnamese fish sauce.

CULINARY NOTES

- You can freeze the wontons once you have shaped them. Place in a single layer on a parchment-lined baking sheet. Wrap tightly in plastic wrap. Place in the freezer until frozen. Transfer to a smaller container, laying them in a single layer with parchment paper between each layer.

Broccoli with Goat Cheese and Walnuts

Dressed up with tangy buttermilk and a topping of tart goat cheese and walnuts, this side dish runs the gamut of flavors. With broccoli as its star, this dish is loaded with such nutrients as vitamins A and C and folate.

Start to Finish: 30 minutes   *Yield: 6 servings*

1 pound broccoli, trimmed and cut into 1-inch pieces	¼ teaspoon kosher salt
½ cup buttermilk	⅛ teaspoon ground nutmeg
1 tablespoon fresh flat-leaf parsley, chopped	⅛ teaspoon freshly ground black pepper
1 tablespoon Dijon mustard	½ cup red onion, thinly slivered
2 teaspoons extra-virgin olive oil	¼ cup walnuts, toasted and coarsely chopped
1 teaspoon fresh thyme, chopped	1 ounce semisoft goat cheese or feta cheese, crumbled
1 teaspoon red wine vinegar	Salt
1 clove garlic, minced (½ teaspoon minced)	

1. Bring 2 quarts of water to a boil in a saucepan. Add 1 teaspoon salt; bring back to a boil and add broccoli. Cook for 6 to 8 minutes or until crisp-tender. Drain and set aside.

2. In a large bowl, whisk together buttermilk, parsley, mustard, olive oil, thyme, red wine vinegar, garlic, kosher salt, nutmeg, and pepper. Add the broccoli and red onion; stir gently to coat. Top with walnuts and goat cheese.

Variations

- Add 1 cup diced roasted red peppers.
- Add 1 cup cherry tomatoes, cut in half.

CULINARY NOTES

- The acid in the vinaigrette will discolor the broccoli if allowed to sit overnight. To prepare ahead of time, mix in the broccoli just before serving.

- Make-ahead directions: Prepare as directed, except do not top with walnuts and goat cheese. Cover and chill for up to 4 hours. To serve, top with walnuts and goat cheese.

Nutrition Facts per Serving: 100 calories, 5 g protein, 7 g total fat (2 g saturated fat), 7.5 g carbohydrate, 3 g fiber, 5 mg cholesterol, 205 mg sodium, 17 weighted glycemic index

Grilled Vegetables

This is a great recipe to be used in many different ways and with a wide variety of vegetables.

Start to Finish: 30 minutes   Yield: 4 servings

1 tablespoon extra-virgin olive oil	2 tablespoons herbs, chopped (choice of parsley, thyme, oregano)
1 teaspoon garlic, chopped	
1 tablespoon low-sodium soy sauce	1 teaspoon lemon zest
1 tablespoon lemon juice	2 pounds of vegetables (*see Culinary Notes*)

1. Preheat a clean grill over medium-high heat.

2. Combine olive oil, garlic, soy sauce, lemon juice, herbs, and lemon zest. Toss with sliced vegetables.

3. Grill vegetables until grill marks are visible and they start becoming tender. Turn and finish cooking on the other side (see cooking times in Culinary Notes).

Variations

- Replace soy sauce with orange juice.
- Replace soy sauce and lemon juice with balsamic vinegar.

Nutrition Facts per Serving: 95 calories, 4 g protein, 4 g total fat (.5 g saturated fat), 13.5 g carbohydrate, 4.5 g fiber, 0 mg cholesterol, 145 mg sodium, 15 weighted glycemic index

CULINARY NOTES

- **Asparagus:** trim off the ends of asparagus. Pencil-thin asparagus will cook in 5 minutes; thicker ones will take up to 10 minutes.

- **Eggplant:** slice eggplant ½ inch thick. Salt and allow to sit for 30 minutes. Rinse and pat dry; season and grill until the eggplant is soft and translucent. If the grill is hot, establish grill marks first; then finish in a 350°F oven.

- **Mushrooms (portabello):** remove gills from portabellos. Place gill side up on the grill. Then flip and cook on the other side.

- **Onions:** slice ½ inch thick. Thread a skewer through the center of the onion. Cook until well browned on each side, about 15 minutes.

- **Red, green, and yellow peppers:** cut ½ inch off top and bottom of pepper. Make a slit down one side. Open up the pepper and remove seeds, ribs, and core. Grill in a large piece for 5 minutes.

- **Zucchini and yellow squash:** cut in ¼ inch slices lengthwise; grill over high heat until just wilted. They should be slightly underdone. They will continue to cook after being removed from the heat.

Grilled Artichokes
with Concord Grape Balsamic Vinaigrette

Artichokes are the bud of a thistle plant. Widely consumed in the
Mediterranean, they have quickly become very popular in wine country
cuisine. They are easy to cook, fun to eat, and a wonderful source
of important nutrients such as vitamin C and fiber.
My family's favorite way to enjoy artichokes is to grill them.

Start to Finish: 20 minutes   Yield: 4 servings

4	cooked artichokes, directions below	¼	cup Concord Grape Balsamic Vinaigrette (page 386)
2	tablespoons extra-virgin olive oil		Salt and pepper to taste

1. Preheat grill to high heat.

2. Toss cooked artichokes with salt, pepper, and extra virgin olive oil. Cook on the hot grill until slightly charred on each side. Remove to a plate.

3. Serve with a side of Concord Grape Balsamic Vinaigrette.

Variations

- Serve with your favorite salsa or dressing.
- Serve with Caesar dressing.
- Serve on a bed of arugula and fennel drizzled with the vinaigrette.

CULINARY NOTES

Cooking Artichokes. Wash artichokes under cold running water. Cut off stems at base and remove small bottom leaves. Stand artichokes upright in a deep saucepan large enough to hold snugly. Add 1 teaspoon salt and two to three inches boiling water. (Lemon juice, herbs such as thyme and parsley, 1 chopped garlic clove, and ½ cup white wine may be added, if desired.) Cover and boil gently 35 to 45 minutes or until base can be pierced easily with fork. (Add a little more boiling water, if needed.)

Nutrition Facts per Serving: 170 calories, 7 g protein, 9 g total fat (1 g saturated fat), 21 g carbohydrate, 10 g fiber, 0 mg cholesterol, 250 mg sodium, 23 weighted glycemic index

Pickled Red Onions

Here is a recipe with minimal ingredients, but one that delivers a maximum punch of flavor! The tangy, crunchy flavors of these pickled onions are sensational. The curry powder infuses a blend of sweet, hot, and earthy spices, and the beautiful pink hues will make any dish even more appealing. Get creative and include your own favorite seasonings to vary the flavors in this recipe.

Start to Finish: 30 minutes   *Yield: Serves 6*

2 cups red onions, julienned	1 teaspoon curry powder
¼ cup apple cider vinegar	1 pinch chile flakes
½ teaspoon cracked black pepper	1 pinch sugar
1 whole clove	Salt and pepper to taste

1. Bring a pot of water to a boil. Add the onions, stir 10 seconds, and drain immediately.

2. Combine remaining ingredients in a small pot. Bring to a simmer but do not allow liquid to reduce. Add onions and just enough water to barely cover. Let sit for 15 minutes or until cool.

Variations

- **Latin:** Replace all spices with ¼ teaspoon cumin seeds, ¼ teaspoon Mexican oregano, 1 bay leaf, and 1 pinch chile flakes.

- **Winter Holiday:** Replace all spices with 1 clove, 1 pinch chile flakes, ½ of a cinnamon stick, and ¼ teaspoon ginger.

CULINARY NOTES

- The onions should become red or pink after sitting for 15 minutes.

- Use as a condiment in chicken or tuna salads.

- Curry powders vary in quality and strength. Try several varieties and brands to explore different flavors. To revive store-bought curry powder, toast it for a few minutes in a skillet over low heat while shaking the pan until it gives off a fragrant aroma.

Nutrition Facts per Serving: 40 calories, 1 g protein, 0 g total fat (0 g saturated fat), 8 g carbohydrate, 1.5 g fiber, 0 mg cholesterol, 5 mg sodium, 16 weighted glycemic index

Ranchero Beans

I grew up in South Texas eating some of the best ranch-style beans in the country. Here is a recipe from one homesick Texan (even though I now consider myself a citizen of the wine country). Enjoy these rich, earthy flavors in the spirit of a classic western menu. Perfect when served with cornbread, salad, or your favorite barbecue.

Start to Finish: 30 minutes   Yield: 5 cups, 10 servings, ½ cup each

1	tablespoon extra-virgin olive oil	1	15-ounce can pinto beans, drained well
1	cup onions, diced	1	15-ounce can black beans, drained well
1	tablespoon garlic, chopped		
¼	teaspoon cumin seeds	1	cup low-sodium chicken stock
1	tablespoon chile powder		
1	cup tomatoes, diced, canned or fresh		

1. Heat a saucepan over medium heat. Add extra-virgin olive oil, onions, and garlic; cook for 4 minutes or until onions are tender and a little brown.

2. Add cumin seeds; cook 1 minute. Add chili powder and stir. Add tomatoes. Bring to a simmer. Add beans and chicken stock. Bring back to a simmer. Cook for 15 minutes or until the flavors meld.

Variation

- Add ½ cup of green chiles or roasted poblano chiles.

CULINARY NOTES

- The beans need to simmer together for a few minutes for the flavors to meld. Do not boil hard, and stir periodically to prevent scorching.

- If your cumin seeds have lost their flavor or you think they may be old, slowly and gently toast them on a low flame in a sauté pan for 2 to 4 minutes or until you can smell them. Shake or stir the pan constantly. Toasting draws out the natural oils of seeds and spices.

Nutrition Facts per Serving: 130 calories, 8 g protein, 1 g total fat (0 g saturated fat), 26 g carbohydrate, 8 g fiber, 0 mg cholesterol, 450 mg sodium, 31 weighted glycemic index

Tomatoes with Crispy Bread Topping

A basic herb of French cuisine, thyme is commonly used to add flavor to vegetables. Here its small leaves contribute a strong, somewhat minty flavor to roasted tomatoes.

Start to Finish: 30 minutes   Yield: 4 servings

8 Roma tomatoes, cored and cut in half lengthwise (about 1⅓ pounds)	1 tablespoon fresh flat-leaf parsley, chopped
Kosher salt	1 tablespoon fresh tarragon, chopped
Freshly ground black pepper	1 tablespoon extra-virgin olive oil
½ cup soft whole-wheat bread crumbs	2 cloves garlic, minced (1 teaspoon minced)
¼ cup scallions, thinly sliced	1 tablespoon parmesan cheese, grated (optional)
2 tablespoons fresh thyme, chopped	

1. Preheat oven to 400°F. Sprinkle the cut sides of the tomatoes with kosher salt and pepper. Arrange tomatoes, cut sides up, in a shallow baking pan. Set aside.

2. In a small bowl, combine the bread crumbs, scallions, thyme, parsley, tarragon, olive oil, garlic, and parmesan cheese. Sprinkle over tomato halves. Bake, uncovered, for 15 to 20 minutes or until the tomatoes are heated through and the bread crumbs are browned and crisp.

Nutrition Facts per Serving: 95 calories, 3 g protein, 4 g total fat (.5 g saturated fat), 13 g carbohydrate, 3 g fiber, 0 mg cholesterol, 20 mg sodium, 54 weighted glycemic index

Sautéed Artichokes and Potatoes

Artichokes are one of my family's favorite vegetables. They are versatile and can easily be added to many salads, pastas, and grains. This delicious recipe was inspired by the cuisine of the Italian region of Liguria.

Start to Finish: 30 minutes   Yield: 4 servings

2 russet or Yukon Gold potatoes, 5 ounces each	2 cups baby spinach
1 tablespoon extra-virgin olive oil	1 teaspoon lemon juice
5 ounces baby artichokes, frozen	1 tablespoon parmesan cheese, grated
2 teaspoons garlic, minced	Salt and pepper to taste

1. Scrub potatoes and place in a saucepan. Add water to cover and heat to a low simmer. Season the water with salt; cook until the potatoes are cooked through. Remove from pan and let sit until cool enough to handle. Cut the potatoes in ⅛-inch-thick pieces.

2. Heat a cast-iron skillet or nonstick Teflon pan over medium-high heat. Add ½ tablespoon extra-virgin olive oil and the potatoes. Cook over medium-high heat until they are golden brown. Season with salt and pepper. Remove from pan and keep warm. Add remaining ½ tablespoon extra-virgin olive oil to the sauté pan; add the artichokes and brown slightly on each side. Add garlic; cook until aromatic. Return potatoes to the pan and add the spinach. Toss to wilt the spinach. Season with lemon juice, salt, and pepper.

3. Serve with a sprinkle of grated parmesan cheese.

Variations

- Use chard or kale in place of spinach.
- Add ½ teaspoon Spanish paprika and grated Spanish manchego cheese in place of the parmesan.

CULINARY NOTE

Cook the potatoes over medium heat, never boiling hard. Boiling hard causes the potato exteriors to break apart, causing the potatoes to absorb more water during the cooking process.

Nutrition Facts per Serving: 115 calories, 3.5 g protein, 4 g total fat (.7 g saturated fat), 17 g carbohydrate, 3 g fiber, 1 mg cholesterol, 60 mg sodium, 69 weighted glycemic index

Roasted Asparagus
with Toasted Bread Crumbs and Eggs

This is an easy recipe that will complement any meal. Enjoy the crisp, tender texture of the roasted asparagus with the flavor combinations of parmesan cheese, lemon zest, and extra-virgin olive oil. This is a favorite recipe I like to prepare when entertaining dinner guests.

Start to Finish: 20 minutes   Yield: 4 servings

1½ tablespoon extra-virgin olive oil	2 boiled eggs, peeled
¼ cup whole-wheat bread crumbs	1 pound asparagus, peeled, ends trimmed off
1 tablespoon parmesan cheese, grated	1 tablespoon lemon juice
1 tablespoon parsley, chopped	Salt and pepper to taste
½ teaspoon lemon zest (optional)	

1. Preheat oven to 450°F.

2. Heat a sauté pan over medium-low heat. Add 1 tablespoon of the extra-virgin olive oil and bread crumbs, stirring over low heat until the bread crumbs are golden brown and toasted. Remove to a bowl and cool. Mix in parmesan cheese, parsley, and lemon zest.

3. Grate the eggs.

4. Place a sheet pan in the hot oven. Heat for 5 minutes. Toss asparagus with the remaining ½ tablespoon extra-virgin olive oil, salt, and pepper. Place asparagus on hot sheet pan and bake 10 to 15 minutes or until tender and lightly blistered. Transfer to a platter. Drizzle with lemon juice. Sprinkle grated egg and bread crumbs on top. Serve warm or at room temperature.

Variations

- Preheat a grill and grill the asparagus instead of roasting.
- Serve with a little salsa verde.

CULINARY NOTE

To trim the asparagus, hold the spear of asparagus in your hand and snap off the bottom. The asparagus will naturally break at the spot where it is tender.

Nutrition Facts per Serving: 115 calories, 7 g protein, 6.5 g total fat (1.5 g saturated fat), 8.5 g carbohydrate, 3 g fiber, 105 mg cholesterol, 60 mg sodium, 43 weighted glycemic index

CULINARY NOTE

The acid in the vinaigrette will discolor the green beans if allowed
to sit overnight. To prepare ahead of time, combine all ingredients
except the green beans; then add the green beans just before serving.

Corn, Bean, and Tomato Salad

Red tomatoes, yellow corn, and green beans make a colorful mosaic for your plate. This stunning side salad can be served at room temperature or chilled.

Start to Finish: 25 minutes   Yield: 4 servings

½ cup dried multigrain rotini, elbow macaroni, and/or penne pasta (such as Barilla Plus)	½ cup canned cannellini beans (white kidney beans), rinsed and drained
8 ounces fresh green beans or frozen whole green beans, halved if desired	2 tablespoons white wine vinegar
1 cup frozen whole-kernel corn, thawed	2 tablespoons extra-virgin olive oil
1 cup cherry tomatoes, halved	2 tablespoons red onion, finely chopped
	1 tablespoon Dijon mustard
	1 tablespoon fresh tarragon, chopped Fresh dill (optional)

1. In a large saucepan, bring 2 quarts of lightly salted water to boiling. Add pasta and, if using, fresh beans. Cook according to pasta package directions, adding frozen green beans (if using) for the last 5 minutes of cooking. Drain pasta and beans.

2. In a large bowl, combine the pasta, green beans, corn, tomatoes, and cannellini beans; set aside.

3. In a small bowl, whisk together the vinegar, olive oil, red onion, mustard, and tarragon until well mixed. Pour dressing over vegetables; toss well to combine. If desired, garnish with fresh dill.

Variations

- Replace cannellini beans with chickpeas.
- Roast or grill the corn.
- Replace white wine vinegar with red wine or balsamic vinegar.

Nutrition Facts per Serving: 205 calories, 7 g protein, 8 g total fat (1 g saturated fat), 30 g carbohydrate, 5.5 g fiber, 0 mg cholesterol, 100 mg sodium, 39 weighted glycemic index

Roasted Ratatouille

This popular French dish is loaded with Mediterranean veggies that have been roasted for intensified flavor. Ratatouille tastes great served warm or cold and pairs perfectly with almost any entrée.

Start to Finish: 50 minutes   Yield: 4 side-dish servings

3 ½ cups eggplant (1 small eggplant), cubed	1 tablespoon extra-virgin olive oil
Nonstick olive oil cooking spray	2 cloves garlic, minced (1 teaspoon minced)
1 cup yellow summer squash or zucchini (1 small), cubed	⅛ teaspoon kosher salt
8 pearl onions, halved	⅛ teaspoon freshly ground black pepper
1 medium yellow bell pepper, cut into 1-inch strips	2 large tomatoes, chopped
2 tablespoons fresh flat-leaf parsley or regular parsley, chopped	1½ teaspoons lemon juice

1. Place eggplant in a single layer on a baking pan. Sprinkle with salt. Let sit for 10 minutes. Rinse and pat dry.

2. Preheat oven to 450°F. Coat a 15 x 10 × 1-inch baking pan with nonstick cooking spray. Place eggplant, squash, onions, bell pepper, and parsley in the prepared pan.

2. In a small bowl, stir together olive oil, garlic, kosher salt, and black pepper. Drizzle over vegetables in the baking pan; toss gently to coat. Spread in an even layer.

3. Roast about 20 minutes or until vegetables are tender and lightly brown, stirring periodically. Stir in the tomatoes and lemon juice. Roast, uncovered, for 8 to 10 minutes more or until tomatoes are very soft and start to release their natural juices. Adjust seasonings with salt and pepper.

CULINARY NOTE

For even cooking, cut vegetables the same size, about ½-inch cubes, and periodically stir the vegetables.

Nutrition Facts per Serving: 100 calories, 2.5 g protein, 4 g total fat (.5 g saturated fat), 15 g carbohydrate, 4.5 g fiber, 0 mg cholesterol, 75 mg sodium, 19 weighted glycemic index

Oven-Dried Tomatoes

Oven-dried tomatoes are sweeter than sun-dried.
There are many ways to enjoy these delicious treats. You can layer them with
sliced mozzarella cheese, mint leaves, olive oil, and crushed red peppers on
toasted whole-wheat country-style bread, sprinkle with parmesan cheese,
and broil for a few minutes. You can also toss the tomatoes in your favorite
pasta dishes, adding some fresh herbs and a drizzle of extra-virgin olive oil.

Start to Finish: 1½ hours   Yield: 12 servings, 2 pieces per serving

12	Roma tomatoes	2	teaspoons garlic, chopped
½	tablespoon extra-virgin olive oil	1	tablespoon herbs (basil, oregano, or thyme), chopped

1. Preheat oven 300°F.

2. Remove core from tomatoes. Slice in half lengthwise. Toss with remaining ingredients.

3. Place in a single layer on a parchment-lined sheet pan, cut side down. Bake until they have shrunk in size by 50 percent and are soft but still hold their shape, about 1 hour and 15 minutes.

4. Remove skin and store in a single layer in a container.

CULINARY NOTES

- The skins will peel easily from the tomatoes when they are cooked through. The tomatoes should be soft, but not falling apart. Slow roasting concentrates their flavor.

- You can make oven-dried tomatoes ahead and store in an airtight container in the refrigerator for up to five days.

Nutrition Facts per Serving: 20 calories, 1 g protein, 1 g total fat (.5 g saturated fat), 3 g carbohydrate,
5 g fiber, 0 mg cholesterol, 1.5 mg sodium, 29 weighted glycemic index

SNACKS

Flavorful and easy to make snacks to energize and satisfy are a must when eating the Sonoma Way. Try our favorite agua frescas with the essence of fruits and herbs to quench your thirst and revitalize. Spice rubbed almonds and soy ginger nuts are perfect on-the-go snacks. And when you are in the mood for something salty and crunchy, try our Crispy Kale Chips or Pita Wedges with a Creamy Artichoke Dip.

Agua Frescas

Spanish for "fresh water," *agua frescas* are fresh fruit drinks that are customary in Mexico. You will see varieties of brightly colored beverages served in large barrel-shaped glass containers lining the shelves of quaint markets. Some of the traditional flavors are watermelon, tamarind, cantaloupe, and strawberry. The beverages here are inspired by the traditional Mexican agua fresca, but are much lighter in sugar and have a natural essence of fruit and herb flavors. Cucumber in these beverages gives a very fresh and light flavor.

Sparkling Concord Grape and Lemon Verbena Water

Start to Finish: 10 minutes   Yield: 4 servings, 1 cup each

1 cup cucumber, peeled, seeded, and chopped	2 tablespoons agave syrup
2 cups Concord grape juice	1 pinch salt
½ cup lemon verbena, leaves only	2 cups sparkling water such as Perrier or Crystal Geyser

1. Combine all ingredients except sparkling water in blender. Blend until smooth.

2. Strain through a mesh strainer. Chill.

3. When ready to serve, add 2 cups sparkling water.

Variation

• Replace lemon verbena with mint.

CULINARY NOTE

The grape juice mixture can be made in advance and held in the refrigerator for several days. Add an equal part of sparkling water when serving. The sparkling water and grape liquid should be ice cold when combined or the bubbles in the sparkling water will become flat.

Nutrition Facts per Serving: 120 calories, .5 g protein, 0 g total fat (0 g saturated fat), 35 g carbohydrate, 1 g fiber, 0 mg cholesterol, 15 mg sodium, 15 weighted glycemic index

Pineapple Cinnamon Water

Start to Finish: 10 minutes   Yield: 4 servings, 1 cup each

1	cup cucumber, peeled, seeded, and chopped
1½	cups pineapple, peeled and chopped (can include core)
¼	teaspoon cinnamon
2	tablespoons agave syrup
2	cups water
1	pinch salt

Combine all ingredients in blender.
Blend until smooth.

Variation

- Replace cinnamon with ½ cup fresh mint or lemon verbena.

CULINARY NOTES

- Remove the peel and seeds from the cucumbers because they can be bitter.

- The amount of agave syrup added will depend on the sweetness of the pineapple. If the pineapple is ripe, less syrup will be needed.

- For a sparkling beverage, add some sparkling water when serving. This will dilute the flavor, but be refreshing. The sparkling water and pineapple liquid should be ice cold when combined or the bubbles in the sparkling water will become flat.

Nutrition Facts per Serving: 125 calories, 4 g protein, 7 g total fat (1 g saturated fat), 13 g carbohydrate, 2.5 g fiber, 1 mg cholesterol, 25 mg sodium, 46 weighted glycemic index

Lemon Ginger Tea

Start to Finish: 30 minutes plus cooling time   Yield: 4 servings, 1 cup each

2	tablespoons ginger, chopped
4	cups water
1	lemon
2	tablespoons agave syrup
1	pinch salt

1. Place ginger and water in a small pot. Cut lemon in half; squeeze juice into pot; add lemon halves. Bring to a simmer; cook 5 minutes. Remove from heat. Let sit for 10 minutes. Remove lemon halves.

2. Stir in agave syrup and salt. Let cool. Strain before serving.

Variations

• Replace agave syrup with honey.

• Replace the lemon with a lime.

Nutrition Facts per Serving: 50 calories, 0 g protein, 0 g total fat (0 g saturated fat), 14 g carbohydrate, .5 g fiber, 0 mg cholesterol, 10 mg sodium, 15 weighted glycemic index

BUSH'S®
Black Bean Guacamole

Here is an interesting addition to an all-time-favorite avocado dip—
black beans! A great snack that packs in as much nutrition as it does flavor.

Start to Finish: 20 minutes   Yield: about 5 cups

5	avocados, diced
3	scallions, chopped
2	limes, juiced
½	cup tomatoes, chopped
1	tablespoon cilantro, chopped
1	can (15 ounces) BUSH'S® Black Beans, drained and rinsed
	Salt and black pepper to taste

1. Place avocados, scallions, and lime juice in a large bowl.

2. Mash avocados to a coarse puree.

3. Stir in tomatoes, cilantro, and beans.

4. Season with salt and pepper.

Nutrition Facts per Serving: 100 calories, 3 g protein, 8 g total fat (1 g saturated fat), 8 g carbohydrate, 5 g fiber, 0 mg cholesterol, 90 mg sodium

Festive Pita Wedges

These wedges make amazing appetizers for your holiday feast. With grain, vegetables, and protein all included, they are substantial enough to hold any guest until the main meal.

Start to Finish: 25 minutes   Yield: 32 wedges, 16 servings, 2 per serving

4 large whole-wheat pita bread rounds	Kosher salt
⅓ cup bottled roasted red bell peppers, drained and chopped	Freshly ground black pepper
3 tablespoons pitted kalamata olives, chopped	1 cup lightly packed arugula leaves, coarsely chopped
1 tablespoon extra-virgin olive oil	2 teaspoons lemon juice
2 cloves garlic, minced (1 teaspoon minced)	4 ounces thinly sliced roast beef, cut into thin strips
1 teaspoon fresh thyme, chopped	2 tablespoons small shavings parmesan cheese or Asiago cheese
1 teaspoon sherry vinegar	

1. Preheat broiler. Cut each pita round into 4 wedges. Split each wedge in half horizontally. Place wedges on one very large or two large baking sheets. Broil 4 to 5 inches from the heat for 2 to 3 minutes or until lightly toasted, turning once. Cool pita wedges on a wire rack. (If using two large baking sheets, broil one sheet at a time.)

2. In a small bowl combine roasted bell peppers, olives, olive oil, garlic, thyme, and sherry vinegar. Season to taste with kosher salt and black pepper.

3. In another small bowl, toss together the arugula and lemon juice. Season to taste with kosher salt and black pepper.

4. Divide arugula mixture among toasted pita wedges. Top with roast beef. Top with roasted pepper mixture. Top with cheese. Serve immediately.

Variations

- Replace roast beef with thinly sliced roast turkey or pork.
- Prepare as a pita salad: Split pita bread into half, cut into two wedges, and toast in a 350°F oven until golden brown. Increase the arugula to 4 cups or use a mix of baby greens. Combine all ingredients and toss well. Add more lemon juice if necessary.

CULINARY NOTE

Do not prepare too far in advance because the roasted pepper mixture can make the pita bread soggy if left to sit for a while.

Nutrition Facts per Serving: 140 calories, 8 g protein, 4 g total fat (1 g saturated fat), 20 g carbohydrate, 2.5 g fiber, 13 mg cholesterol, 200 mg sodium, 56 weighted glycemic index

Carrot Hummus

Made of ground sesame seeds, tahini is commonly found in dishes of the Middle East, such as hummus. The addition of chopped carrots gives this hummus intensified color and sweetness.

Start to Finish: 20 minutes   Yield: 2 cups, 2 tablespoons per serving

1 cup chopped carrots	¼ teaspoon kosher salt
1 15-ounce can garbanzo beans (chickpeas), rinsed and drained	2 tablespoons fresh flat-leaf parsley, chopped
¼ cup tahini (sesame seed paste)	Assorted dippers (such as toasted whole-wheat pita bread triangles, fresh vegetable dippers, and/or whole-grain crackers)
2 tablespoons lemon juice	
2 cloves garlic, quartered	
½ teaspoon ground cumin	

1. In a covered small saucepan, cook carrots in a small amount of boiling water for 6 to 8 minutes or until tender; drain. In a food processor, combine cooked carrots, garbanzo beans, tahini, lemon juice, garlic, cumin, and kosher salt. Cover and process until smooth. Transfer to a small serving bowl. Stir in 1 tablespoon of the parsley. Sprinkle top with remaining parsley.

2. Cover and chill for 1 hour to 3 days. If necessary, stir in enough water, 1 tablespoon at a time, to make dipping consistency. Serve with assorted dippers.

Variations

- Replace carrots with parsnips.
- Replace half the carrots with peeled cooked celery root.

CULINARY NOTE

Make sure the carrots are cooked until you can pierce them easily with a fork, so they will be sweet and puree to a smooth consistency.

Nutrition Facts per Serving: 60 calories, 2 g protein, 2 g total fat (0 g saturated fat), 18 g carbohydrate, 1.5 g fiber, 0 mg cholesterol, 110 mg sodium, 41 weighted glycemic index

Sweet Potato Chips

Guilt-free and loaded with rich beta carotene nutrients, these chips are perfect for the Sonoma Way of eating. The base recipe also works well for other root veggies so your creative flavor possibilities are endless.

Start to Finish: 30 minutes   Yield: 4 servings

1 pound sweet potatoes, peeled Coarse sea salt to taste	Nonstick cooking spray or extra-virgin olive oil in mister Lime wedges (optional)

1. Preheat oven to 250°F. Line 2 sheet pans with a silpat or parchment paper. Spray generously with nonstick cooking spray or olive oil in a mister.

2. Using a wide vegetable peeler or mandolin, slice the sweet potatoes paper-thin in 1½-inch strips. Lay the strips in a single layer on the silpat. Do not overlap or let the chips touch each other. Sprinkle with salt and spray with nonstick cooking spray or mister.

3. Place sheet pan in preheated oven and bake for 50 minutes or until the potatoes are crisp and slightly golden. Remove from sheet pan and place in a single layer on a clean sheet of parchment.

4. Finish with a squeeze of fresh lime over the potato chips.

CULINARY NOTES

- Using a wide vegetable peeler or mandolin will allow you to make thin, uniform slices that will bake evenly.
- Using a silpat (silicon baking sheet) will allow the sweet potatoes to cook and crisp evenly without coloring them.

Variation
- Use other root vegetables such as carrots, parsnips, and red and yellow beets.

Nutrition Facts per Serving: 102 calories, 2 g protein, .5 g total fat (0 g saturated fat), 22 g carbohydrate, 3.5 g fiber, 0 mg cholesterol, 62 mg sodium, 44 weighted glycemic index

Creamy Artichoke Dip

A most delicious spread to serve with wholesome warm flatbreads or crunchy pita chips. The white beans give this spread more than just another vegetable serving—they lend a rich, creamy texture that allows you to spread the great flavors of artichoke, celery, chives, and garlic.

Start to Finish: 15 minutes   Yield: 1 cup, 8 servings, 2 tablespoons each

1 tablespoon extra-virgin olive oil	½ can white beans, drained (reserve liquid)
½ teaspoon garlic, chopped	1 tablespoon lemon juice
4 tablespoons celery, diced small	2 tablespoons chives
1 cup frozen artichoke hearts, cooked	1 pinch cayenne or Tabasco (optional)
4 ounces low-fat cream cheese at room temperature	Salt and pepper to taste

1. Heat the olive oil in a small sauté pan over medium heat. Add garlic and celery and cook until garlic is aromatic, about 20 seconds. Add artichokes and sauté until the artichokes are slightly browned, about 5 minutes. Cool in refrigerator.

2. Combine the cream cheese and white beans in a food processor. Process until smooth. Add cooled artichoke mixture. Puree until slightly chunky. Season with lemon juice, salt, and pepper. Add chives and cayenne.

Variations

- Replace chives with tarragon and scallions.
- Replace chives with basil.

CULINARY NOTES

- If the mixture is too stiff, add 1 tablespoon of the white bean liquid.

- Use as a spread on sandwiches or crostini with oven-dried tomatoes and basil.

Nutrition Facts per Serving: 60 calories, 2 g protein, 4 g total fat (1.5 g saturated fat), 5 g carbohydrate, 2 g fiber, 6 mg cholesterol, 75 mg sodium, 29 weighted glycemic index

Crispy Kale Chips

Light, crunchy, and guiltfree. You can't eat just one.
For the best flavor, use a good-quality extra-virgin olive oil in a mister
instead of the nonstick cooking spray.

Start to Finish: 30 minutes   Yield: 4 servings

8 ounces kale leaves, stems removed Nonstick cooking spray or olive oil in a mister	Salt and pepper to taste

1. Preheat oven to 250°F. Line 2 sheet pans with a silpat or parchment paper. Spray generously with nonstick cooking spray.

2. Lay kale leaves in a single layer on the sheet pan; press on surface of silpat and turn over. Sprinkle with salt and pepper. Spray lightly with nonstick cooking spray or olive oil mister.

3. Place sheet pan in preheated oven and cook for 20 minute or until the kale is crisp. Remove from sheet pan; place in a single layer on a clean sheet of parchment. Do not mound.

Variation

- Use thin leafy greens such as chard, spinach, or mustard greens.

CULINARY NOTE

Using a silpat (silicon baking sheet) will allow the vegetables to cook and crisp evenly.

Nutrition Facts per Serving: 35 calories, 2 g protein, 1 g total fat (0 g saturated fat), 5.5 g carbohydrate, 1.5 g fiber, 0 mg cholesterol, 25 mg sodium, 15 weighted glycemic index

Pomegranate, Pear, and Granny Smith Applesauce

In this creative rendition of traditional applesauce, the pomegranate and pears give delicate, sweet flavors that are perfect pairings to tart Granny Smith apples.

Start to Finish: 30 minutes   Yield: 4 servings, ½ cup each

2	Granny Smith apples, peeled, cored, and cut in 1-inch chunks	2	tablespoons agave syrup
1	Bartlett pear, peeled, cored, and cut in 1-inch chunks	½	vanilla bean, split, seeds scraped and reserved
½	cup pomegranate juice	1	small pinch salt
		½	teaspoon lemon juice

1. Combine apples, pear, pomegranate juice, agave syrup, vanilla bean and seeds, and salt in a small saucepan. Bring to a simmer; cover and reduce heat to a low simmer.

2. Stir occasionally until the apples and pears become a puree, about 20 minutes. Adjust seasoning with lemon juice and cool.

CULINARY NOTE

The apples will become a puree before the pears. Once the pears are tender, you can slightly mash them with the back of the spoon to help them become a puree.

Variations

- Use all pears.
- Replace vanilla bean with cinnamon.

Nutrition Facts per Serving: 145 calories, 1 g protein, 1 g total fat (0 g saturated fat), 38 g carbohydrate, 4 g fiber, 0 mg cholesterol, 43 mg sodium, 34 weighted glycemic index

Spice-Roasted Almonds

This savory snack showcases a Sonoma Power Food.
These almonds are given a treatment of spices and a short baking time
for amazingly rich flavor and intense crunch.

Start to Finish: 20 minutes   Yield: 2 cups, 32 servings, 1 tablespoon each

1 tablespoon chili powder	¼ teaspoon ground cinnamon
1 tablespoon extra-virgin olive oil	¼ teaspoon freshly ground black pepper
½ teaspoon kosher salt	2 cups whole almonds
½ teaspoon ground cumin	
½ teaspoon ground coriander	

1. Preheat oven to 350°F. In a medium bowl, combine chili powder, olive oil, kosher salt, cumin, coriander, cinnamon, and pepper. Add almonds and toss to coat. Transfer mixture to a 13 × 9 × 2-inch baking pan.

2. Bake about 10 minutes or until almonds are toasted, stirring twice. Cool almonds completely before serving. Store in an airtight container for up to 5 days.

Variations

- Pine nuts: toast 8–10 minutes total.
- Pepitas: toast 12–15 minutes total.
- Almonds: toast 15–20 minutes total.
- Hazelnuts: toast 15–20 minutes total.

CULINARY NOTES

- Use any spice mixture.
- During baking, check the nuts periodically because toasting times will vary due to the type of nut selected, the size of the nuts, the calibration of the oven, and the number of times the oven door is opened.

Nutrition Facts per Serving: 55 calories, 2 g protein, 5 g total fat (.5 g saturated fat), 2 g carbohydrate, 1.5 g fiber, 0 mg cholesterol, 30 mg sodium, 12 weighted glycemic index

Soy-Ginger Roasted Pecans

Not all fats are created equal. Although this snack has a high fat content, it is primarily polyunsaturated fats from the pecans. Pecans are cholesterol-free and a good source of fiber, iron, and ellagic acid, which has been found to have anticancer properties.

Start to Finish: 15 minutes   Yield: 2 cups, 16 servings, 2 tablespoons per serving

2	cups pecan halves	1	teaspoon toasted sesame oil
2	tablespoons reduced-sodium soy sauce	½	teaspoon ground ginger
		⅛	to ¼ teaspoon cayenne pepper

1. Preheat oven to 350°F. Line a 15 × 10 × 1-inch baking pan with foil; set aside.

2. In a medium bowl, combine pecans, soy sauce, sesame oil, ginger, and cayenne pepper. Spread pecans in a single layer in prepared baking pan. Bake for 10 minutes, stirring once. Spread pecans on a sheet of foil; cool completely. Store in an airtight container for up to 2 weeks.

Variations

- Replace ground ginger with wasabi powder.
- Replace pecans with almonds.

CULINARY NOTE

Make sure the nuts are in a single layer in the baking pan. You can line the baking pan with parchment paper.

Nutrition Facts per Serving: 175 calories, 2.5 g protein, 18 g total fat (1.5 g saturated fat), 4 g carbohydrate, 2.5 g fiber, 0 mg cholesterol, 130 mg sodium, 11 weighted glycemic index

Quick Cucumber Pickles

The all-American pickle, in a tasty home-style recipe that will be a favorite in your family. Great as a side to sandwiches or part of a salad.

Start to Finish: 20 minutes   Yield: 8 servings, 2 tablespoons per serving

2	cups cucumber, sliced 1⁄16 inch thick	¼	cup rice wine vinegar
2	teaspoons salt	1	teaspoon agave syrup

1. Toss sliced cucumbers with salt. Let sit for 10 minutes.

2. Add vinegar and agave syrup. Toss. Let sit for 10 minutes.

Variations

- Add 1 pinch chile flakes for spicier pickles.
- Add 1 teaspoon chopped cilantro or parsley.

CULINARY NOTE

Use a Japanese mandolin to slice the cucumbers. It will give a thin, even slice. Just be careful: the blades are extremely sharp.

Nutrition Facts per Serving: 50 calories, 1 g protein, 0 g total fat (0 g saturated fat), 12 g carbohydrate, 1 g fiber, 0 mg cholesterol, 250 mg sodium, 15 weighted glycemic index

Whole-Wheat Pizza Dough
for Flatbreads

This delicious and easy recipe featuring wholesome grains is perfect for hummus or other creamy spreads. This is a great side to the Gigi Salad.

Start to Finish: 3 hours, includes rising time   Yield: 10 servings

1 teaspoon agave syrup	1 teaspoon salt
1½ cups water at room temperature	1 tablespoon extra-virgin olive oil
1 tablespoon yeast	1 tablespoon parmesan cheese
2 cups whole-wheat flour	Parchment paper
1½ cups all-purpose flour	Nonstick cooking spray

1. Combine agave syrup, water, and yeast. Allow to sit for 5 minutes until yeast starts to bloom. Add flours, salt, and extra-virgin olive oil. Mix in stand mixer with dough hook for 3 minutes on low. Turn to medium and mix for 8 minutes. Add 1 to 2 tablespoons of flour if the dough is sticky. It should not stick to your hands if you handle it. Transfer the dough to a large oiled bowl. Cover with plastic wrap and let rise for 1 hour or until doubled in size.

2. Punch down dough and portion into ten 3-ounce balls. Spray a parchment-lined sheet pan with nonstick pan spray. Place balls evenly spaced on the sheet pan. Cover with parchment. Keep refrigerated until ready to bake. Fifteen minutes before baking, remove the dough from the refrigerator and bring to room temperature.

3. Preheat oven to 500°F. If using a pizza stone or baking tiles, place on lowest rack in oven. If not, place a sheet pan on lowest rack in oven.

CULINARY NOTES

- The dough will be slightly wet but should easily leave the bowl.

- Do not add salt directly into the yeast mixture. Place the salt on top of the flours. Salt will kill the yeast and prevent it from rising.

Nutrition Facts per Serving: 165 calories, 6 g protein, 2 g total fat (.5 g saturated fat), 32 g carbohydrate, 4 g fiber, .5 mg cholesterol, 220 mg sodium, 78 weighted glycemic index

4. On a lightly floured surface, pat dough into flat circles with your fingers, being careful to keep your hands flat so as not to poke holes in the dough. The circles will be about 6 inches across.

5. Season dough with salt and pepper; sprinkle with parmesan cheese if desired. Place on pizza stone, baking tiles, or sheet pan. Bake until just puffed and slightly browned, about 5 minutes.

6. Serve topped with salads or use as flatbreads for sandwiches.

Variations

- Preheat the grill. Lay pizza dough on grill, cook to establish grill marks, flip and finish cooking on other side.
- Replace agave syrup with sugar or honey.

DESSERTS

Perfect endings Sonoma style means a healthy indulgence with the best ingredients—seasonal ripe fruits, sweet spices, rich wholesome ingredients, and a little touch of the wine country. Chocolate almond biscotti, a beautiful sweet peach and raspberry galette, or a fabulous bittersweet chocolate soufflé cake— no guilt here, just flavor in the spirit of Sonoma!

Bittersweet Chocolate Grand Marnier Soufflé Cake

This is a showy dessert, perfect for special occasions. Chocolate and orange are a delicious flavor pairing, especially with Grand Marnier. Cocoa powder and bittersweet chocolate give this light and airy soufflé a deep, rich chocolate taste.

Start to Finish: 1 hour   Yield: 1 9-inch cake, serves 12

1 teaspoon whole-wheat all-purpose flour	½ cup sugar
8 ounces bittersweet chocolate	3 tablespoons cocoa powder, sifted
1 cup nonfat yogurt	¼ teaspoon salt
2 tablespoons Grand Marnier	¼ teaspoon cream of tartar
2 tablespoons half-and-half cream	Nonstick cooking spray
1 tablespoon orange zest	Parchment paper
6 eggs, separated	Powdered sugar for dusting

1. Preheat oven to 350°F. Spray a 9-inch springform pan with nonstick cooking spray. Place a parchment circle in bottom of pan. Lightly dust with 1 teaspoon all-purpose whole-wheat flour.

2. Combine chocolate, yogurt, Grand Marnier, half-and-half, and orange zest in double boiler over low heat. Let melt, stirring periodically to prevent scorching the chocolate. Set aside.

3. In a large bowl, combine egg yolks and sugar. Whip for 5 to 8 minutes on high speed or until light in color and fluffy; the mixture should form ribbons when lifted from the bowl.

4. Gently fold in the chocolate mixture. Gently fold in cocoa powder.

5. In a clean bowl with a whisk attachment, whip the egg whites until frothy. Add salt and cream of tartar. Use high speed to whip egg whites just to stiff peaks.

6. Using a rubber spatula, gently fold egg whites into the chocolate mixture, adding

Nutrition Facts per Serving: 175 calories, 6 g protein, 10 g total fat (6 g saturated fat), 20 g carbohydrate, 1.8 g fiber, 107 mg cholesterol, 100 mg sodium, 44 weighted glycemic index

⅓ of the egg whites first, then gently folding in the remaining ⅔ just until mixed.

7. Pour batter into prepared pan. Bake in preheated oven for 30 minutes, or until the center is set.

8. Let cool. The cake will fall slightly when cooled. Run a knife around the edges of the pan to remove from springform pan. Gently invert to remove paper from the bottom of the cake.

9. Serve with a light dusting of powdered sugar.

Variation

- Replace Grand Marnier with rum, brandy, cognac, Bailey's Irish Cream, or Kahlua.

CULINARY NOTES

- Whip the egg yolks and sugar with a whisk attachment on high until thick, light, and fluffy.

- Make sure that the egg whites are yolk-free and that the bowl and whisk are free from any fat. The tiniest bit of fat or egg yolk interferes with the formation of the foam. If there is any trace of yolk, do not use the egg whites. The presence of egg yolk will prevent the egg whites from whipping to a light fluffy meringue.

- Once the eggs are separated, let them sit at room temperature for 30 minutes. Room temperature egg whites will whip up faster.

- Once you start beating the eggs, do not stop halfway through the process or the meringues will be flat.

- Soft peaks: when the beaters are lifted from the egg whites, the whipped egg whites will form peaks with tips that curl over.

- Stiff peaks: when the beaters are lifted from the egg whites, the whipped egg whites will stand straight up.

- If you do not have a springform pan, use a 9-inch cake pan.

- Do not slam the oven door when placing cake in oven. The egg whites are delicate and will lose volume if overfolded or banged on the counter.

- The cake will yield slightly to pressure after baking.

- Slice the cake with a hot dry knife. Dip the knife into hot water, wipe dry, and slice. Repeat after each slice for clean cuts.

Chocolate Zucchini Bread

Everything tastes better with chocolate! Dark chocolate pairs nicely with the flavors of zucchini and cinnamon. This is a very moist and delicious bread that will be sure to become a favorite. If you have a garden, this is a great way to cook your extra zucchini and squash.

Start to Finish: 50 minutes   Yield: 1 9-inch bread (12 servings)

1½ cups unbleached all-purpose flour	3 eggs, lightly beaten
1 cup whole-wheat all-purpose flour	1 cup low-fat yogurt
½ cup sugar	2 teaspoons vanilla extract
1 teaspoon salt	3 cups zucchini, small or medium size, raw, grated
1 teaspoon ground cinnamon	½ cup mini semisweet chocolate chips
2 teaspoon baking soda	Nonstick cooking spray
¼ teaspoon baking powder	Parchment paper
½ cup cocoa powder	

1. Preheat oven to 350°F. Spray a 9 inch x 13 inch cake pan with nonstick cooking spray. Line with parchment paper, spray again, and dust lightly with flour. Shake off excess flour.

2. Combine flours, sugar, salt, cinnamon, baking soda, baking powder, and cocoa powder. Sift if necessary to remove lumps.

3. Combine eggs, yogurt, and vanilla. Add zucchini and chocolate chips. Gently mix into dry ingredients. Do not overmix.

4. Pour into prepared pan, and spread in an even layer. Bake in preheated oven for 35 to 40 minutes or until a toothpick inserted in the center comes out clean. Cool on a rack.

Variations

- Add ½ cup chopped toasted walnuts or almonds.
- Replace zucchini with summer squash or yellow crookneck squash.
- You can also use two 4½-inch thick x 8 inch loaf pans. Bake for 40 to 50 minutes or until a toothpick inserted in the center comes out clean.

Nutrition Facts per Serving: 200 calories, 6.5 g protein, 4 g total fat (2 g saturated fat), 37 g carbohydrate, 3 g fiber, 53 mg cholesterol, 400 mg sodium, 64 weighted glycemic index

Ginger Peach Sorbet

A perfect balance of sweet and tart flavors from peaches and ginger makes this a refreshing and delicious dessert.

Start to Finish: 1 hour   Yield: 6 servings, ½ cup each

3	cups peaches, peeled and sliced
2	teaspoons fresh ginger, grated
¼	cup agave syrup
¼	cup water
1	pinch salt
1	tablespoon lemon juice

1. Place all ingredients in a blender. Blend until smooth.

2. Strain through a mesh strainer. Place in refrigerator and chill.

3. Process in ice cream machine according to manufacturer's directions.

Variations

- Substitute nectarines or mangos for the peaches.
- For a slightly tart, creamier sorbet, add ¼ cup non-fat yogurt in place of the water.

CULINARY NOTES

- If you were not able to remove all the peach skin, it will strain out after you blend the mixture. The skin on ripe peaches will peel off easily using a knife. If the fruit is not quite ripe, heat a pot of boiling water. Fill a bowl with ice and water. Cut an "x" at the end of each peach. Drop the peach into boiling water for 10 to 30 seconds or until you can easily peel the fruit. Drop into the ice water to stop the cooking process. Remove from water and peel.

- You can use unsweetened frozen peaches as an alternative.

- If you do not have an ice cream machine, freeze sorbet mixture in ice cube trays until solid. Unmold cubes and place in a food processor with a chopping blade. Process in batches until fairly smooth, but still icy. Scrape down sides periodically while processing. Store batches in freezer.

Nutrition Facts per Serving: 70 calories, 0 g protein, 0 g total fat (0 g saturated fat), 18 g carbohydrate, 1 g fiber, 0 mg cholesterol, 26 mg sodium, 24 weighted glycemic index

Almond Chocolate Biscotti

Biscotti are twice-baked cookies from Italy. Baking them twice gives them a nice, crunchy texture. There are hundreds of recipes for biscotti throughout Italy, but my favorite version combines two great ingredients, chocolate and almonds. They are delicious dipped into coffee, tea, or a glass of port or Vin Santo. This is a wonderful recipe for the holiday season!

Start to Finish: 45 minutes   Yield: 3 dozen cookies, 2 cookies per serving

1¼	cups unbleached all-purpose flour	½	cup sugar
¾	cup whole-wheat pastry flour	½	teaspoon lemon zest
1½	teaspoon baking powder	1	egg
1	pinch salt	1	egg white
¼	cup almonds, slivered and toasted	½	teaspoon vanilla extract
¼	cup mini dark chocolate chips	4	tablespoons yogurt
4	tablespoons butter		Parchment paper

1. Preheat oven to 325°F. Line a sheet pan with parchment paper.

2. Combine flours, baking powder, and salt in a bowl. Add almonds and chocolate chips.

3. In a mixer using a paddle or with a hand mixer, beat the butter, sugar, and lemon zest on medium-high until fluffy, about 2 to 3 minutes. Add the egg, egg white, and vanilla, beating well after each addition. Pour half of the flour mixture into the butter mixture, mixing well. Add yogurt and stir; then add remaining flour mixture and mix until just incorporated.

CULINARY NOTE

You can use regular chocolate chips in place of mini chocolate chips. Chop them fine with a knife or in a food processor. The smaller the chocolate chip, the more chocolate you will perceive in each bite.

4. Divide dough into 3 logs, each 6½ inches long by 2 inches wide. Place on the parchment-lined sheet pan and bake for 25 minutes, or until golden brown on top. Let cool for a few minutes.

5. Transfer to a cutting board, removing them from the parchment with a large metal spatula if necessary. Using a serrated knife, trim ¼ inch off each end; then cut the logs crosswise into ½-inch slices. Return the slices to the baking sheet, arranging them cut side down.

6. Bake until the biscotti are golden brown and dry, about 20 minutes. Transfer to a rack to cool. They will crisp up as they dry. Store in an airtight container.

Variations

- Replace chocolate chips with dried fruits.
- Replace almonds with other nuts such as pine nuts, hazelnuts, cashews, or pecans.

Nutrition Facts per Serving: 60 calories, 1 g protein, 2 g total fat (1 g saturated fat), 9 g carbohydrate, .5 g fiber, 9 mg cholesterol, 42 mg sodium, 70 weighted glycemic index

Warm Figs

with Yogurt and Honey Port Glaze

Port is a sweet fortified wine named after the Portuguese city of Oporto, where these wines are shipped from. This dessert combines port with honey and lemon juice to make a sweet glaze.

Start to Finish: 40 minutes   Yield: 6 servings

½	cup port	18	dried Mission figs, halved lengthwise (about 1¼ cups)
2	tablespoons honey	6	ounces plain low-fat yogurt
½	teaspoon lemon juice	⅓	cup chopped walnuts or almonds, toasted
	Dash kosher salt		

1. In a small saucepan, combine the port, honey, lemon juice, and kosher salt. Bring to boiling; reduce heat. Boil gently, uncovered, for 15 to 20 minutes or until thickened and syrupy. Stir in figs to coat. Cover and let stand for 10 minutes.

2. Serve warm fig mixture topped with yogurt and walnuts.

Variations

- Replace figs with plum halves or quarters.
- Replace figs with red seedless grapes cut in half.

CULINARY NOTE

The figs are gently warmed in the honey port glaze. Rotate the figs after 5 minutes while they sit in the warm liquid.

Mini Pumpkin Swirl Cheesecakes

The holidays are the perfect time to serve these traditional pumpkin cheesecakes. Rich flavors of pumpkin, cinnamon, allspice, and nutmeg make for a delicious dessert.

Start to Finish: 40 minutes, refrigerate 3 to 24 hours   Yield: 12 servings

1 cup pumpkin puree, canned	2 8-ounces packages low-fat cream cheese at room temperature
1 tablespoon whole-wheat all-purpose flour	½ cup sugar
¾ teaspoon ground cinnamon	1½ teaspoons vanilla
¼ teaspoon allspice	⅛ teaspoon salt
⅛ teaspoon nutmeg	2 eggs, beaten

1. Preheat oven to 300°F. Line muffin cups with paper or foil liners.

2. Combine the pumpkin with flour and ½ of the spices. Set aside.

3. Using a stand mixer fitted with a paddle attachment, beat the cream cheese on medium speed until smooth. Scrape down sides as needed. Add sugar, vanilla, the remaining spices, and salt. Mix for 1 minute. Pour in eggs in 2 batches, mixing after each addition. Do not overmix when adding the eggs or the cheesecakes will crack during baking.

CULINARY NOTE

To create the swirled look, use only a few strokes or the mixture will lose the swirled pattern.

4. Remove ⅓ of the cream cheese mixture. Fold remaining cream cheese mixture into the pumpkin mixture. Divide the pumpkin mixture among the muffin cups. Then divide the reserved cream cheese mixture among the cups. Using a skewer or paring knife, drag the tip through the mixture to form a swirling pattern or marbled look.

5. Bake in preheated oven for 15 minutes. The mixture should not be completely set; the centers will move slightly when jiggled. The cheesecakes will continue to cook once removed from oven.

6. Set on wire rack and cool completely. Cover and refrigerate.

Variations

- Replace pumpkin with butternut squash puree.
- Replace pumpkin with pureed apples.

Nutrition Facts per Serving: 130 calories, 4 g protein, 6.5 g total fat (3.5 g saturated fat), 14 g carbohydrate, 1 g fiber, 55 mg cholesterol, 250 mg sodium, 59 weighted glycemic index

Peach, Raspberry, and Almond Galette

Lemon zest and almonds add a wonderful taste to the baked sweet flavors
of raspberry and peach. You can use this galette recipe as a base
for many other fruits—apricots, nectarines, berries, or plums in the summer,
apples or pears in the fall. It's rustic homestyle, with a natural flowing
wide rim crust that makes it a beautiful dessert.

Start to Finish: 1½ hours   Yield: 12 servings

3	cups peaches, washed, seed removed, cut into ¼ inch wedges	1	pinch salt
1	cup raspberries	1	tablespoon ground almonds
2	ounces unsweetened applesauce	1	tablespoon sliced almonds, lightly toasted
2	tablespoons brown sugar	1	11-inch Whole-Wheat Almond Galette Crust (following page)
1	teaspoon lemon zest	1	tablespoon agave syrup
½	teaspoon vanilla		Nonstick cooking spray
1	tablespoon cornstarch		

1. Preheat oven 425°F.

2. Combine peaches, raspberries, applesauce, sugar, lemon zest, vanilla, cornstarch, and salt in a bowl.

3. Lightly spray 2 half sheets of parchment paper (12 inches by 14 inches) with nonstick cooking spray. Place pie dough between the 2 sheets of parchment and roll ⅛ inch thick. To prevent sticking, periodically peel the parchment papers from the dough and then replace dough between them. Once the dough is the desired thickness, remove top sheet, keeping the pie crust on the bottom sheet of parchment paper. Place on a sheet pan.

4. Sprinkle 1 tablespoon ground almonds in a 10-inch circle on the pie crust. Scoop the fruit mixture into the center of the pie crust, leaving a 1-inch rim around the outside. Be sure to capture all the juice. Using the parchment paper, gently fold the 1-inch

Nutrition Facts per Serving: 130 calories, 2 g protein, 5.5 g total fat (1.5 g saturated fat), 17 g carbohydrate, 2 g fiber, 5 mg cholesterol, 50 mg sodium, 61 weighted glycemic index

rim over the edge of the fruit all around the galette. Sprinkle the 1 tablespoon sliced almonds on top.

5. Bake galette on the bottom rack of the oven for 50 minutes, turning half way through the cooking time. The fruit juices should bubble and thicken; the crust should start to lightly brown.

6. Remove from oven, brush edge of tart with 1 tablespoon agave syrup, and let cool for 20 minutes.

Variation

- Replace fruit with any seasonal fruits: nectarines, strawberries & rhubarb, raspberries, apricots, plums, or peaches. Apples and pears may be used in the winter but will need to be peeled and sliced ⅛ inch thick.

CULINARY NOTE

This pie crust is a delicate dough. Rolling the pie crust between the 2 pieces of parchment paper makes it easier to transfer to the baking sheet and also prevents the dough from sticking to the rolling pin.

Nutrition Facts per Serving: 130 calories, 2 g protein, 5.5 g total fat (1.5 g saturated fat), 17 g carbohydrate, 2 g fiber, 5 mg cholesterol, 50 mg sodium, 61 weighted glycemic index

Whole-Wheat Almond Galette Crust

This is a great recipe to be used with any of your pie recipes. The wholesome addition of whole wheat and almonds makes for a healthy indulgence.

Start to Finish: 10 minutes to mix, 60 minutes to chill   *Yield: 1 11-inch pie crust circle (serves 12)*

½ cup whole-wheat pastry flour	2 tablespoons cold butter, cut in ¼-inch pieces
½ cup unbleached all-purpose flour	2 tablespoons cold canola or safflower oil
1 teaspoon sugar	½ teaspoon white vinegar
¼ teaspoon baking powder	2–4 tablespoons cold water
2 tablespoons almonds, ground	
1 pinch salt	

1. Mix the flours, sugar, baking powder, almonds, and salt in a large bowl. Cut in the cold butter with a pastry cutter or fork until it is the size of mini chocolate chips.

2. Stir in oil and vinegar. Add just enough cold water to bring the dough together; it will still be a little dry.

3. Gather dough into a ball and form a flat disk. Wrap in plastic wrap and chill in refrigerator for 30 minutes or overnight.

4. To roll: Lightly spray 2 half-sheets of parchment paper (12 inches by 14 inches) with nonstick cooking spray. Place dough between the 2 sheets of parchment and roll ⅛ inch thick. To prevent sticking, periodically peel the parchment papers from the dough and then replace dough between them. Once the dough is the desired thickness, remove top sheet, keeping the pie crust on the bottom sheet of parchment paper. Place on a sheet pan for a galette, or flip dough over into a pie pan and peel off the parchment. Gently press into the pie pan. Chill for 30 minutes before baking.

CULINARY NOTE

Do not overwork the dough or the crust will be tough. Add only enough water so the dough comes together. It should barely hold together and not be wet.

Nutrition Facts per Serving: 80 calories, 1 g protein, 5 g total fat (1.5 g saturated fat), 8 g carbohydrate, 1 g fiber, 5 mg cholesterol, 37 mg sodium, 78 weighted glycemic index

Gluten-Free Pie Dough

This delicious, gluten-free recipe does not compromise any flavor or texture you would expect from your favorite pie crusts.

Start to Finish: 10 minutes, plus 60 minutes to chill   Yield: 1 15-inch pie crust circle, serves 12

½   cup brown rice flour
½   cup white rice flour (Asian, nonglutinous)
½   cup tapioca starch
¼   cup potato starch
1   pinch salt
1   teaspoon sugar
2   teaspoons xanthan gum

2   tablespoons cold butter, cut in ¼-inch pieces
2   tablespoons canola or safflower oil, cold
1   egg
1   teaspoon white vinegar
3   tablespoons cold water
    Parchment paper
    Nonstick cooking spray

1. Combine the rice flours, starches, salt, sugar, and xanthan gum. Cut in the cold butter with a pastry cutter or fork until it is the size of chocolate chips, not too small.

2. Combine oil, egg, vinegar, and water; add to flour mixture. Mix just enough to bring the dough together. Knead 1 minute. Gather dough into a ball and form a flat disk. Wrap in plastic wrap and chill in refrigerator for 30 minutes or overnight.

3. To roll: Lightly spray 2 half-sheets of parchment paper (12 inches by 14 inches) with nonstick cooking spray. Place pie dough between the 2 sheets of parchment and roll ⅛ inch thick. To prevent sticking, periodically peel the parchment papers from the dough and then replace dough between them. Once the dough is the desired thickness, remove top sheet, keeping the pie crust on the bottom sheet of parchment paper. Place on a sheet pan for a galette, or flip dough over into a pie pan and peel off the parchment. Gently press into the pie pan. Chill for 30 minutes before baking.

CULINARY NOTE

Do not overwork the dough or the crust will be tough.

Nutrition Facts per Serving: 120 calories, 1 g protein, 5 g fat (1.5 g saturated fat), 17 g carbohydrate, 1 g fiber, 23 mg cholesterol, 35 mg sodium, 91 weighted glycemic index

Almond Tart Crust

This is a great recipe you can use for any pie or galette.
The subtle flavor of almond is delicious and the whole grains used
in this recipe mean that you do not sacrifice health for flavor.

Start to Finish: 90 minutes   Yield: 1 9-inch tart shell

¼	cup almond flour	1	pinch salt
¼	cup oat flour	¼	cup powdered sugar
½	cup all-purpose flour	¼	cup cold butter
½	cup whole-wheat pastry flour	1	egg, beaten

1. Combine flours, salt, and powdered sugar in a large bowl. Cut in cold butter until pieces of butter are the size of oatmeal. Stir in beaten egg and mix until just combined. Do not overmix or the dough will be tough.

2. Form into a round disk, ½ inch thick. Wrap tightly in plastic and allow dough to rest in refrigerator for 30 minutes to 1 hour.

Variations

- Replace almond flour with hazelnut flour.
- Replace oat flour with almond or hazelnut flour.

Nutrition Facts per Serving: 125 calories, 4 g protein, 7 g total fat (1 g saturated fat), 13 g carbohydrate, 2.5 g fiber, 1 mg cholesterol, 25 mg sodium, 46 weighted glycemic index

Ricotta Mousse with Berries

The combination of fresh, sweet berries served over a spoonful of ricotta cheese is the perfect ending to a meal. Orange liqueur such as Grand Marnier or Bauchant adds rich citrus flavor to the recipe.

Start to Finish: 30 minutes, plus 1 to 24 hours for chilling   Yield: 4 servings

1 cup light ricotta cheese	½ cup fresh raspberries
2 tablespoons orange liqueur	½ cup fresh blackberries
2 tablespoons agave syrup	1 teaspoon lemon juice
1 teaspoon orange zest	1 teaspoon honey
½ cup sliced fresh strawberries	Fresh mint leaves (optional)
½ cup fresh blueberries	

1. In a small bowl, whisk together ricotta, 1 tablespoon of the orange liqueur, agave syrup, and orange zest. Cover and chill for 1 to 24 hours.

2. In a medium bowl, combine the berries, lemon juice, and the remaining 1 tablespoon orange liqueur. Cover and let stand at room temperature 15 minutes to develop flavors.

3. To serve, divide fruit mixture among four dessert dishes, spooning any juices over fruit in dishes. Top with ricotta mixture. Drizzle with honey. If desired, garnish with mint.

Variations

- Replace orange zest with lemon or lime zest.
- Replace orange liquor with brandy or rum.
- Replace honey with agave syrup.

CULINARY NOTES

- Use a microplane to grate the orange zest. Do not include any of the white pith of the orange, which is bitter.

- Add a small pinch of salt to the berries with the lemon juice and liqueur. The salt will help draw the juices out of the berries and balance their sweetness.

Nutrition Facts per Serving: 125 calories, 7.5 g protein, 3 g total fat (2 g saturated fat), 15 g carbohydrate, 2.7 g fiber, 20 mg cholesterol, 150 mg sodium, 23 weighted glycemic index

Pomegranate and Vanilla Poached Pears

with Greek Yogurt

Poaching in a delicate, tart pomegranate syrup and infusing with vanilla bean give the pears a wonderful flavor, even better when they're served with a thick creamy yogurt and a sprinkle of toasted almonds. This dessert is great for entertaining, especially since you can make it ahead of time.

Start to Finish: 45 minutes   Yield: 4 servings, ½ pear per serving

1   cup pomegranate juice

2   tablespoons agave syrup

½   vanilla bean, split, seeds scraped and reserved

1   small pinch salt

2   Bartlett pears, peeled, cut in half, cored

1   teaspoon lemon juice

1   cup thick Greek yogurt

1   tablespoon almonds, toasted and chopped

1. Combine pomegranate juice, agave syrup, vanilla bean and seeds, and salt in a small saucepan. Bring to a simmer; add prepared pears. The liquid should cover the pears. Reduce heat to a low simmer, and poach the pears until tender, about 20 minutes. Carefully remove pears from the pan onto a plate. Return liquid to medium heat and reduce by one half to the consistency of maple syrup, about 15 minutes. Stir in lemon juice and adjust seasoning.

CULINARY NOTES

- The pears must be submerged below the liquid. If they are not submerged, transfer the mixture to a smaller saucepan. You can also place a piece of parchment paper directly on top of the pears to prevent the exposure to air and stop the pears from turning brown.

- If you do not have Greek yogurt, which is thicker and richer than regular yogurt, you can drain regular yogurt overnight in a cheesecloth-lined colander to remove some of its liquid.

- The poaching syrup can be prepared the day before; it will thicken when chilled in the refrigerator overnight. Bring the syrup to room temperature before drizzling over pears.

- Use mature pears so that the flavors infuse easily and the pears cook well.

2. Slice poached pear halves in ¼-inch-wide slices, leaving them connected at the top of the pear. Place ¼ cup of the drained yogurt in a mound on a chilled plate. Fan the sliced pear leaning against the yogurt. Drizzle with the reduced sauce and sprinkle with chopped almonds.

Variations

- Replace vanilla bean with a cinnamon stick.
- Replace Greek yogurt with ricotta cheese mixed with 2 tablespoon plain yogurt.

Nutrition Facts per Serving: 170 calories, 6 g protein, 1 g total fat (0 g saturated fat), 35 g carbohydrate, 4 g fiber, 0 mg cholesterol, 65 mg sodium, 29 weighted glycemic index

TASTE OF THE
WINE
COUNTRY

Enjoy these rich flavors of the California wine country and Sonoma. Create your own experience with these recipes inspired by local Sonoma inns, restaurants, wineries, and well-known chefs.

Argentinian Grilled Flank Steak

with Chimichurri Salsa

Enjoy the spicy flavor combinations of this recipe with award-winning 2005 *Pursued by Bear,* a blend of three different Washington grapes, cabernet, merlot, and syrah. This wine has great balance and bright flavors of berry, plum, and Bing cherry.

Start to Finish: 20 minutes plus 1 hour or overnight to marinate   Yield: 8 servings

2 pounds flank steak or hanger steak	1 tablespoon smoked paprika
1 tablespoon red wine vinegar	2 teaspoon brown sugar
3 cloves garlic, minced and mashed to a paste with a pinch of salt	Salt and pepper to taste
2 tablespoon fresh oregano, chopped	1 recipe Chimichurri Salsa (page 309)
1 tablespoon freshly ground black pepper	

1. Season meat with salt and pepper; let sit for 10 minutes. Score both sides of steak in a diamond pattern by making shallow cuts at 1-inch intervals; set aside.

2. Combine vinegar, garlic, oregano, black pepper, paprika, and brown sugar. Rub meat with marinade and let sit for 1 hour to overnight in the refrigerator.

3. Remove the steak from the marinade (discard the marinade).

4. For a charcoal grill, place meat on the rack of an uncovered grill directly over medium coals. Grill the steak for 4 to 5 minutes per side for medium-rare. For a gas grill, preheat grill. Reduce heat to medium. Place meat on grill rack over heat. Cover and grill as above.

5. Transfer grilled meat to a cutting board. Cover and let stand for 10 minutes. To serve, slice very thinly across the grain. Serve with Chimichurri Salsa.

Chimichurri Salsa

One of the most delicious and versatile sauces traditionally served with grilled steak. This bright and spicy sauce is an essential ingredient to any Argentinian *parilla* or grill.

Start to Finish: 15 minutes plus 2 hours to sit   Yield: 1¼ cup (8 servings)

1 cup fresh Italian parsley, packed	¼ cup red wine vinegar
¼ cup fresh cilantro, packed	1 tablespoon lemon juice
1 tablespoon fresh oregano leaves	¾ teaspoon dried crushed red pepper
2 tablespoon shallots, minced	½ teaspoon ground cumin
3 garlic cloves, peeled and chopped	Salt and pepper to taste
½ cup olive oil	

1. Finely chop parsley, cilantro, and oregano leaves. Place in a bowl and add remaining ingredients. Mix well.

2. Let sit for at least 2 hours before serving.

Nutrition Facts per Serving: 230 calories, 25 g protein, 13 g total fat (3.3 g saturated fat), 2 g carbohydrate, 0 g fiber, 37 mg cholesterol, 68 mg sodium

Ahi Tuna
with Southern Italian Salsa

For over thirty-five years, St. Francis Winery has produced top-quality wines from superior mountain and valley vineyards in Sonoma County. Chef David Bush recommends pairing this Mediterranean-inspired dish with St. Francis Winery's Zinfandel.

Start to Finish: 45 minutes   *Yield: 4 servings*

1	tablespoon minced garlic	44-ounce ahi tuna steaks	
1	tablespoon olive oil	Sicilian Salsa (below)	
1	teaspoon chopped rosemary	Salt and pepper to taste	

1. Combine the garlic, olive oil, rosemary, salt, and pepper. Marinate the tuna in the mixture for 1 hour.

2. Grill tuna over medium-hot coals about 5 minutes on each side. Do not overcook the tuna or it will become dry. Spoon salsa over tuna steaks and serve.

Sicilian Salsa

2	tablespoons extra-virgin olive oil	2	tablespoons black Greek olives, pitted and chopped
½	cup red onion, chopped	1	tablespoon fresh parsley, chopped
1	red bell pepper, seeded and chopped	2	tablespoons extra-virgin olive oil
1	tablespoon minced garlic		Salt and pepper to taste
½	cup homemade (or canned) diced tomatoes		

1. Heat olive oil in a saucepan over medium-high heat. Add onion, pepper, and garlic. Cook 5 minutes, until the onion is soft, stirring often. Remove from heat.

2. Place in a mixing bowl and add the remaining ingredients. Season to taste.

Nutrition Facts per Serving: 310 calories, 28 g protein, 18 g total fat (2.5 g saturated fat), 6 g carbohydrate, 1.5 g fiber, 50 mg cholesterol, 83 mg sodium

Beer Can Chicken

Located on First and Main in the heart of downtown Napa and housed in a historic 1880s building, the Bounty Hunter Wine Bar & Smokin' BBQ has been voted "Top 100" restaurant and "Best Wine Bar in Napa Valley" by the *San Francisco Chronicle* two years running.

In this recipe, the whole bird comes to the table on its Tecate beer can perch, ready to be carved. And to accompany this fine meal, try a glass of 2008 *Pursuit* Pinot Noir from the Sonoma Coast.

Start to Finish: 2 hours   *Yield: 6 servings*

2 tablespoons pre-mixed Cajun spice	½ teaspoon Coleman's dry mustard powder
1 tablespoon fennel seed	½ teaspoon turmeric
1 tablespoon coriander seed	1 4-pound whole chicken
1 tablespoon white sesame seeds	1 can of Tecate beer
½ tablespoon dried thyme	1 lime, cut in half
½ tablespoon dried oregano	Aluminum foil
½ tablespoon smoked paprika	Beer can chicken holder

1. Toast all the seeds in a skillet over medium heat. Swirl the seeds around for 3 to 4 minutes until you see a little steam coming off the spices and the aroma begins to intensify. Allow to cool 5 to 10 minutes and grind in a spice grinder or coffee grinder.

2. Combine all the spices with the Cajun spice mix.

3. Clean the chicken and rub with the spice blend 20 to 30 minutes before cooking the chicken.

4. Place aluminum foil on grill; then place beer can chicken holder on top.

5. Open and pour out (or drink) about a quarter of the Tecate; then place in holder.

6. Place chicken, cavity down, over can and holder and pin wings back so they don't burn.

7. Squeeze half a lime in the neck of the chicken and use it to cork the neck to trap in the moisture.

8. Grill over low to medium heat for about one hour and fifteen minutes or until a thermometer measures 165°F between the thigh and backbone.

9. Pull chicken off the beer can and serve on a large round plate.

Nutrition Facts per Serving: 350 calories, 38 g protein, 12 g total fat (2 g saturated fat), 15 g carbohydrate, 0 g fiber, 118 mg cholesterol, 450 mg sodium

BUSH'S®
Smoky White Bean & Tomato Soup

Two varieties of creamy white beans lend a rich hand to this delicious home-style soup. Your family is sure to love this one, which is a perfect meal to serve on a cold, wintry day.

Start to Finish: 30 minutes   Yield: 6 servings

3 slices smoked bacon	1 cup canned tomatoes, chopped
1 cup onion, diced	1 15.5-ounce can BUSH'S® Cannellini Beans, with liquid, or BUSH'S® Great Northern Beans
1 tablespoon garlic, minced	
1 tablespoon mixed oregano and thyme, minced	3 cups chicken stock
1 pinch chile flakes	¼ teaspoon salt
	1 pinch black pepper

1. Heat a 2-quart saucepan over medium heat; add raw bacon and cook 4 minutes until crispy. Crumble bacon.

2. Add the onion and cook 3 to 4 minutes until translucent.

3. Add the garlic, herbs, and chile flakes; cook for 1 minute.

4. Add the tomatoes and cook for 2 minutes.

5. Add the beans with their liquid, chicken stock, salt, and pepper, and bring to a simmer. Cook for 15 minutes.

Nutrition Facts per Serving: 150 calories, 9 g protein, 4 g fat (1 g saturated fat), 19 g carbohydrate, 4 g fiber, 10 mg cholesterol, 640 mg sodium

Fig, Arugula, and Pecan Salad
with Fig and Port Vinaigrette

This fig salad encompasses wine country simply by combining ingredients that are significant alone and when combined create a uniquely delicious flavor. These are the flavors of the earth and of the wine country territory. This recipe has become the most popular signature dish of the fabulous Sonoma restaurant, *the girl & the fig*.

Start to Finish: 50 minutes Yield: 8 servings

2 ounces pancetta, chopped	½ cup pecan halves, toasted
1 tablespoon extra-virgin olive oil	4 ounces semisoft goat cheese, crumbled
12 fresh figs, halved, or 6 plums (2 pounds), pitted and quartered	¾ cup Fig and Port Vinaigrette (page 317)
8 cups arugula	Freshly ground black pepper

1. In a 10-inch skillet, cook and stir the pancetta over medium heat until crisp. Remove with a slotted spoon and set aside, reserving drippings in skillet. Add olive oil to skillet. Add the figs or plums. Cook the figs about 2 minutes or until slightly softened and browned, turning once. (Cook the plums about 5 minutes or until slightly softened and browned, turning once.)

2. In a very large bowl, toss together the cooked pancetta, arugula, pecans, goat cheese, and Fig and Port Vinaigrette. Divide the greens mixture among eight salad plates; surround greens with figs or plums. Sprinkle individual servings lightly with pepper.

Fig and Port Vinaigrette

Yield: 1½ cups

---

3 dried Mission figs

1 cup port

¼ cup red wine vinegar

¾ cup canola oil

2 teaspoons shallots, finely chopped

¼ teaspoon kosher salt

⅛ teaspoon freshly ground
    black pepper

---

1. In a small saucepan, combine figs and port; let stand at room temperature for 30 minutes. Using a slotted spoon, transfer figs to a blender; set aside.

2. Heat port to boiling over medium-high heat; reduce heat. Boil gently, uncovered, for 8 to 10 minutes or until reduced to ½ cup. Cool slightly.

3. Add port to blender along with red wine vinegar. Cover and blend until figs are very finely chopped. With the blender running, add canola oil in a slow, steady stream; blend until well mixed and thickened.

4. Stop blender. Add shallots, kosher salt, and freshly ground black pepper; cover and blend for 5 seconds more. Serve immediately or cover and chill for up to 5 days.

Nutrition Facts per Serving: 308 calories, 5 g protein, 22 g total fat (4 saturated fat), 21 g carbohydrate, 4 g fiber, 12 mg cholesterol, 219 mg sodium

Curried Tuna Salad

with California Almonds

Curry flavors are a perfect combination with California almonds
in this light and refreshing salad. This is a delicious meal that is
heart-healthy and rich in many nutrients.

Start to Finish: 20 minutes   Yield: 4 servings

6 ounces canned tuna in water, drained and flaked	1 tablespoon scallions, sliced
½ cup red apple or pineapple, diced	3 tablespoons unflavored yogurt
¼ cup celery, sliced	½–1 teaspoon curry powder
¼ cup slivered almonds, toasted	Almonds for garnish

In bowl, combine all ingredients, blend thoroughly. Serve in lettuce cups or sandwich between
slices of whole-grain bread. Sprinkle with almonds, if desired.

Nutrition Facts per Serving: 300 calories, 8 g protein, 13 g total fat (2.5 g saturated fat), 42 g carbohydrate,
5.5 g fiber, 10 mg cholesterol, 280 mg sodium

Spanish Rioja Wine Country Soup

This is one of the most simple, yet fabulous soups you will ever taste. My family enjoyed this soup during a memorable lunch with dear friends in the Spanish Rioja wine country. Prepared by my good friend, Pepe Saenz, this country-style recipe, served with rustic fresh-baked bread, locally harvested greens, and a glass of red Spanish wine, brings back memories of how great a meal can be when prepared with fresh ingredients and of course enjoyed with the best of friends.

Start to Finish: 1 hour   Yield: 6 servings, 1 cup each

2 tablespoons extra-virgin olive oil	2 cups potatoes (1 to 1½ potatoes), peeled and quartered
2 ounces spicy Spanish chorizo sausage, chopped	1½ cups tomatoes, chopped
2 cups onions, chopped	4 cups chicken broth or water
1 cup green bell pepper, chopped	1 teaspoon lemon juice
1 tablespoon garlic, chopped	1 tablespoon parsley, chopped
1 bay leaf	Salt and pepper to taste
1 pinch dry red pepper flakes	

1. Heat a large stock pot over medium heat. Add 1 tablespoon of the olive oil, chorizo, onions, green peppers, and garlic; cook 4 minutes or until aromatic.

2. Add bay leaf and red pepper flakes; cook 1 minute.

3. Stir in potatoes, tomatoes, and stock. Bring to a simmer and cook for 45 minutes or until the potatoes are meltingly tender. Adjust seasoning with salt and pepper.

4. Serve soup with a drizzle of the remaining extra-virgin olive oil, a squeeze of lemon, and chopped parsley.

Nutrition Facts per Serving: 185 calories, 8 g protein, 9 g total fat (2 g saturated fat), 20 g carbohydrate, 2.5 g fiber, 8 mg cholesterol, 175 mg sodium

Frozen Fruit Sorbet

Toni Sakaguchi, Chef Instructor at The Culinary Institute of America, suggests using fresh, ripe fruit for these recipes. The taste of the ripe fruit will be so sweet that you won't miss the sugar in this creamy, light dessert.

IN HONOR OF CHEF CATHERINE BRANDEL

Start to Finish: 10 minutes, plus freezing for 1½ hours   Yield: 4 servings, ½ cup each

2	medium bananas	1	tablespoon lemon juice
1	cup sliced strawberries		Fresh strawberries (optional)
2	tablespoons water		Waxed paper

1. Peel bananas and cut into 1-inch pieces. Place banana slices and strawberries in a waxed-paper-lined 15 x 10 x 1-inch baking pan. Cover and freeze for 1½ to 2 hours or until completely frozen.

2. In a food processor, combine frozen fruit, water, and lemon juice. Cover and process until smooth. If desired, garnish with fresh strawberries.

Nutrition Facts per Serving: 65 calories, 1 g protein, 0 g total fat (0 saturated fat), 17 g carbohydrate, 2 g fiber, 0 mg cholesterol, 1 mg sodium

CULINARY NOTES

- Ripe bananas that have a speckled skin will be extra sweet in the sorbet.

- Use any ripe frozen fruits for the sorbet. The riper the fruit, the sweeter the sorbet.

Banana-Chocolate Sorbet

Peel 3 medium bananas and cut into 1-inch pieces. Place banana slices in a waxed-paper-lined 15 x 10 x 1-inch baking pan. Cover and freeze for 1½ to 2 hours or until completely frozen. In a food processor, combine frozen bananas, 2 tablespoons water, and 1 tablespoon bittersweet chocolate pieces. Cover and process until nearly smooth, leaving some small bits of hard chocolate. If desired, garnish with fresh mint leaves.

Nutrition Facts per Serving: 90 calories, 1 g protein, 0 g total fat (0 saturated fat), 22 g carbohydrate, 3 g fiber, 0 mg cholesterol, 1 mg sodium

Peach-Raspberry Sorbet

Place 2 cups peach slices and 1 cup raspberries in a waxed-paper-lined 15 x 10 x 1-inch baking pan. Cover with waxed paper and freeze about 45 minutes or until partially frozen. In a food processor, combine fruit, 1 tablespoon honey, and 1 tablespoon lemon juice. Cover and process until smooth. If desired, garnish with fresh raspberries.

Nutrition Facts per Serving: 70 calories, 1 g protein, 0 g total fat (0 saturated fat), 18 g carbohydrate, 4 g fiber, 0 mg cholesterol, 0 mg sodium

Grilled Beef Tenderloin
with Balsamic Mushroom and Pepper Salad

Grilled beef tenderloin is always a favorite to enjoy with a great bottle of red wine. The rich savory flavors of beef and wild mushrooms are perfect with the Reynolds Family Winery *Persistence* Cabernet Sauvignon. A signature blend of cabernet sauvignon, cabernet franc, merlot, syrah, and petit verdot, *Persistence* is excellent paired with this fabulous wine country recipe.

Start to Finish: 45 minutes, plus overnight for marinating   Yield: 8 servings

2 pounds beef tenderloin	½ cup roasted red pepper, seeded and cut into small dice
1 tablespoon thyme, chopped	
1 teaspoon garlic, chopped	½ cup roasted yellow pepper, seeded and cut into small dice
Salt and pepper to taste	
1 ounce extra-virgin olive oil	4 tablespoons balsamic vinegar
2 tablespoons garlic, sliced thin	1 tablespoon lemon juice
1 pound assorted wild mushrooms (chanterelles, shiitakes, morels, oysters)	2 tablespoons parsley, chopped
	Salt and pepper to taste
	Olive oil in a mister

1. Season the beef with salt and pepper. Let sit for 15 minutes or longer. Cut into 4-ounce medallions. Combine thyme and the 1 teaspoon garlic, mash to a paste, and spread on beef. Cover and let sit overnight in the refrigerator.

2. Preheat a medium grill.

3. Place the olive oil and the 2 tablespoons garlic in a small sauté pan. Cook over low heat until the garlic is translucent and soft, about 5 minutes. Drain well, reserving the garlic and oil separately. Heat a sauté pan over medium-high heat. Add 1 tablespoon of the reserved oil and mushrooms. Sauté until the mushrooms are slightly caramelized and cooked through; season with salt and pepper. Add the garlic and 1 tablespoon of the balsamic vinegar. Sauté 1 minute; then place in a large bowl.

4. Add the peppers and parsley to mushrooms. Add remaining balsamic vinegar, lemon juice, and any oil remaining from cooking the garlic. Season with salt and pepper.

5. Bring meat to room temperature. Spray or brush with olive oil. Place the seasoned meat on a hot grill; cook, turning periodically to evenly cook on all sides until the meat reaches 130° F on an instant-read thermometer (medium-rare). Transfer to a platter, tent with foil to keep hot, and let rest for 10 minutes until ready to serve.

6. To serve, place a spoonful of the mushroom salad slightly off center on the plate. Lean the beef against the salad.

Nutrition Facts per Serving: 250 calories, 30 g protein, 11 g total fat (2 g saturated fat), 12 g carbohydrate, 4 g fiber, 60 mg cholesterol, 180 mg sodium

Mediterranean Pasta Salad
with California Avocado

Avocados and artichoke hearts give this pasta salad a unique flavor profile that everyone is sure to enjoy. Light, colorful, and, above all, delicious!

Start to Finish: 25 minutes   *Yield: 4 servings*

3	tablespoons extra-virgin olive oil		1	ripe fresh California avocado, peeled, seeded, and cut into ½-inch cubes
1	tablespoon fresh lemon juice		1	cup cherry tomatoes, cut in quarters
¼	teaspoon salt		¼	cup pitted kalamata olives, cut in half
2	tablespoon loosely packed fresh dill		½	medium hothouse cucumber, cut lengthwise in quarters and sliced
½	pound orecchiette or small pasta, cooked, drained, and cooled		1	cup artichoke hearts, cut in half

1. Place olive oil, lemon juice, and salt in a food processor or blender; blend until creamy. Add dill and pulse just until incorporated. Pour over pasta and toss to coat.

2. Add remaining ingredients and toss to combine. Serve immediately or cover and chill until ready to serve.

Nutrition Facts per Serving: 300 calories, 7 g protein, 19 g total fat (2.5 g saturated fat), 30 g carbohydrate, 8 g fiber, 0 mg cholesterol, 270 mg sodium

Grilled Lamb Chops
with Balsamic Red Onions, Asparagus, and Polenta

The savory sweet flavors in this delicious, spice-rubbed lamb recipe
pair beautifully with Kyle MacLachlan's wine, *Pursued by Bear,*
a blend of three different Washington grapes, cabernet, merlot, and syrah.
The wine has great balance and bright flavors of berry, plum, and bing cherry.

Start to Finish: 15 minutes   Yield: 4 servings

1	lamb rack, fat removed, cut into 8 chops		Balsamic Red Onions, plus their juice (page 327)
1	teaspoon garlic, minced		Grilled Asparagus (page 327)
1	tablespoons thyme, chopped		Polenta (page 328)
2	teaspoons Spanish paprika	1	tablespoon extra-virgin olive oil
1	teaspoon ground coriander		Salt and pepper to taste

1. Preheat a grill to medium-high heat.

2. Season lamb with salt and pepper. Let sit for 15 minutes. Combine garlic, thyme, paprika, and coriander in a small bowl. Rub all over the lamb chops. Let sit for 30 minutes.

3. Prepare the Grilled Asparagus.

4. Warm the Balsamic Red Onions.

5. Prepare the Polenta.

6. Drizzle the olive oil over the lamb to lightly coat. Place lamb on clean hot grill; cook 1 to 2 minutes on each side, turning 90 degrees when the meat is browned to create grill cross marks. Cook lamb to 130°F for medium-rare. Remove from heat and let rest for 10 minutes in a warm spot.

7. Place ½ cup polenta in a mound on the plate. Place red onions just slightly off to the side. Lay asparagus leaning on the red onions. Lean chops against the polenta and drizzle with some of the juice from the balsamic onions.

Nutrition Facts per Serving: 550 calories, 36 g protein, 18 g total fat (5 g saturated fat), 59 g carbohydrate, 10 g fiber, 85 mg cholesterol, 375 mg sodium

Balsamic Red Onions

Start to Finish: 15 minutes   *Yield: 2 cups*

1	tablespoon extra-virgin olive oil	2	teaspoons sage, chopped
1	pound red onions, sliced in ¼-inch rings	4	tablespoons balsamic vinegar
			Salt and pepper to taste

1. Heat a sauté pan over medium-high heat. Add olive oil and place the concentric red onion rings flat in the sauté pan. Season with salt and pepper. Cook until the surface is golden brown. Turn and cook on other side until golden brown. Stir to separate the rings.

2. Add sage. Sauté for 1 minute. When the onions are slightly soft, add balsamic vinegar; it should evaporate immediately. Adjust seasoning with salt and pepper.

Grilled Asparagus

Start to Finish: 30 minutes   *Yield: 4 servings*

1	tablespoon extra-virgin olive oil	2	tablespoons herbs, chopped (choice of parsley, thyme, oregano)
1	teaspoon garlic, chopped	1	teaspoon lemon zest
1	tablespoon low-sodium soy sauce	2	pounds asparagus, with the ends trimmed off
1	tablespoon lemon juice		

1. Preheat a clean grill over medium-high heat.

2. Combine olive oil, garlic, soy sauce, lemon juice, herbs, and lemon zest. Toss with asparagus.

3. Grill asparagus until it starts getting tender and grill marks are visible. Turn and finish cooking on the other side. Pencil-thin asparagus will cook in 5 minutes; thicker spears will take up to 10 minutes.

Polenta

Start to Finish: 30 minutes   Yield: 4 servings

1	tablespoon extra-virgin olive oil	5	cups water, boiling
1	cup onions, chopped	½	cup parmesan cheese, grated
1	tablespoon garlic, chopped		Salt and pepper to taste
1	cup cornmeal		

1. Preheat oven 350°F.

2. Heat a Dutch oven or deep sauté pan over medium heat. Add olive oil and onions. Season with salt and pepper. Cook until onions are translucent. Add garlic and cook until aromatic. Add cornmeal; stir to mix with onions. Add boiling water in a steady stream, whisking constantly. Bring to a simmer, stirring until the mixture looks homogenous, about 10 minutes. Cover tightly and place in preheated oven; cook for 50 minutes.

3. When the polenta is tender and no longer grainy, stir in parmesan cheese and season well with salt and pepper.

Asparagus Soup
with Chervil Crème Fraiche

The delicious soups offered at *the girl & the fig,* a famous restaurant in Sonoma that shuns capital letters, are representative of what is in season and always taste like an enhanced version of the actual vegetable.

From Start to Finish: 30 minutes   Yield: 6 servings

2½ tablespoons unsalted butter	1½ quarts water
1 small yellow onion, chopped	½ cup heavy cream
3 celery stalks, chopped	Salt and white pepper
1 leek, white only, cleaned and chopped	
2 shallots, chopped	*For the Chervil Crème Fraiche*
4 garlic cloves, crushed	1 bunch chervil, picked; reserve 12 stems for garnish, and chop the rest
2 bunches green jumbo asparagus, peeled and cut in ¾-inch rounds; reserve the tips	½ cup crème fraiche
	1 tablespoon heavy cream
	Salt and white pepper

1. Melt the butter in a medium saucepan over medium-low heat. Add the onion, celery, leek, shallots, and garlic and sauté until the vegetables are soft, about 7 minutes.

2. Add the asparagus and stir. Add 1½ quarts of water and season with salt and pepper. Bring to a boil. Reduce the heat and cook until the asparagus is tender, about 5 minutes. Add the heavy cream. Remove from the heat.

3. Puree the mixture. Strain the puree through a fine mesh sieve into a container over an ice bath. Adjust the seasoning if necessary.

4. Mix the chopped chervil with the crème fraiche and the heavy cream. If too thick, adjust the consistency with a little more heavy cream (or water).

5. Garnish each serving with the chervil crème fraiche and the reserved asparagus tips and chervil leaves.

WINE SUGGESTION: *Roussanne*

Nutrition Facts per Serving: 235 calories, 4 g protein, 21 g total fat (13 g saturated fat), 11.5 g carbohydrate, 2.5 g fiber, 70 mg cholesterol, 50 mg sodium

Bodega Bay Salmon

with Slow-Roasted Beets and Heirloom Apples

The reason Sonoma is such a wonderful playground for chefs is that its local ingredients are so pristine—they come to a chef just hours out of the earth or ocean. This recipe combines salmon fresh from Bodega Bay with lavender from the garden and heirloom apples picked just down the road. This recipe was created by Chef Duskie Estes at Café ZaZu.

Start to Finish: 60 minutes   Makes: 6 servings

6	6-ounce fresh or frozen skinless salmon fillets, about 1 inch thick	2	tablespoons fresh flat-leaf parsley, chopped
1½	pounds baby beets or medium beets	1	tablespoon dried lavender, crushed
4	tablespoons extra-virgin olive oil	2	teaspoons fennel seeds
	Kosher salt	1	teaspoon fresh thyme, chopped
	Freshly ground black pepper	½	teaspoon kosher salt
3	medium heirloom apples or cooking apples, cored and cut into 6 wedges	½	teaspoon freshly ground black pepper
3	medium shallots, peeled and cut into 8 wedges	1	5-ounce package baby arugula or arugula, torn (about 6 cups)
		3	tablespoons lemon juice

1. Thaw salmon, if frozen. Rinse salmon; pat dry with paper towels.

2. Preheat oven to 400°F. Trim greens from beets. If using medium beets, peel beets and cut into 1-inch wedges. Place baby beets or beet wedges in a 2-quart baking dish. Drizzle with 1 tablespoon of the olive oil; season with kosher salt and pepper. Cover with foil. Roast for 45 to 50 minutes or until tender. If using baby beets, cool slightly; peel beets. Season beets with kosher salt and pepper. Set aside.

3. Meanwhile, in a very large skillet, heat 1 tablespoon of the remaining olive oil over medium-high heat. Add apples and shallots; cook about 7 minutes or until golden brown. Remove from skillet; cover and keep warm.

4. In a small bowl, combine parsley, lavender, fennel seeds, thyme, ½ teaspoon kosher salt, and ½ teaspoon pepper. Sprinkle mixture evenly over one side of each salmon fillet; rub in with your fingers.

5. In the same skillet, heat 1 tablespoon of the remaining olive oil over medium-high heat. Add salmon; cook for 8 to 12 minutes, turning once halfway through cooking, or until golden brown and fish flakes easily when tested with a fork.

6. In a large bowl, toss the arugula with lemon juice and the remaining 1 tablespoon olive oil. Season with additional kosher salt and pepper. Divide arugula among six dinner plates. Top with beets, apple, shallot mixture, and salmon.

Nutrition Facts per Serving: 500 calories, 37 g protein, 28 g total fat (5 g saturated fat), 24 g carbohydrate, 6 g fiber, 99 mg cholesterol, 520 mg sodium

Pan-Roasted Wild Salmon
with Meyer Lemon Vinaigrette

Cole's Chop House, located in historic downtown Napa, happens to be one of our family's favorite restaurants in Napa. We have shared many special occasions and enjoyed some great meals at Cole's.

Start to Finish: 45 minutes   *Yield: 4 servings*

1 pound small fingerling potatoes	1 tablespoon shallots, minced
6 ounces yellow wax beans, stems removed	4 wild salmon fillets, about 6 ounces each
6 ounces romano green beans, stems removed	Meyer Lemon Vinaigrette (page 333)
8 tablespoons extra-virgin olive oil	1 Meyer lemon, cut into wedges for garnish
2 garlic cloves, minced	Kosher salt and fresh ground black pepper to taste
2 teaspoons fresh thyme, chopped	
2 tablespoons fresh chives, chopped	

1. In a two-quart saucepan, boil the potatoes in salted water for 15 to 20 minutes until fork-tender. Drain, cool slightly, peel, and cut in half.

2. While the potatoes are cooking, bring 3 quarts of salted water to a boil and blanch the beans; do this in two batches as the varieties may have different cooking times. After about 2 minutes, check doneness; beans should be al dente. Remove to an ice bath to stop the cooking and lock in the color. Set aside.

3. In a 10-inch heavy-bottomed sauté pan over medium heat, heat 2 tablespoons of the olive oil. Add the potatoes and cook until golden brown. Add garlic, thyme, chives, and shallots. Cook for an additional thirty seconds, remove from heat, and season to taste with salt and black pepper.

4. Season the salmon fillets with salt and pepper. While the potatoes are browning, heat two more sauté pans; heat 2 tablespoons of the remaining olive oil in each pan.

Carefully place 2 seasoned salmon fillets in each pan, belly side down, and sear for 3 to 4 minutes. Turn and cook for an additional 3 minutes. Set aside and keep warm.

5. Heat one more sauté pan, add the remaining 2 tablespoons of olive oil, add beans, and sauté until warm; season with salt and black pepper and remove from heat.

While the pan is still hot, add the Meyer Lemon Vinaigrette.

6. On four warmed plates, divide the potatoes and arrange in the center. Place the salmon fillets on top of the potatoes. Place the beans on top of the salmon and drizzle the warm vinaigrette over the fish. Garnish with reserved lemon wedges.

Meyer Lemon Vinaigrette

1 Meyer lemon	1 tablespoon shallots, minced
6 tablespoons extra-virgin olive oil	Kosher salt and fresh ground black pepper to taste

Zest the lemon. In a stainless steel bowl, combine the zest and juice of the lemon with the extra-virgin olive oil and shallots. Season with salt and pepper to taste.

Nutrition Facts per Serving: 600 calories, 40 g protein, 37 g fat (6 g saturated fat), 27 g carbohydrate, 5 g fiber, 76 mg cholesterol, 98 mg sodium

Pan-Seared Scallops
with Fennel Slaw and California Avocado-Papaya Relish

Crunchy Fennel Slaw and the fruity flavors of Avocado-Papaya Relish are a perfect combination with scallops. This recipe really reminds me of what California cuisine represents. Wonderful fresh bright flavors!

Start to Finish: 45 minutes   Yield: 4 servings

16	scallops, rinsed and patted dry	Fennel Slaw (below)
¼	teaspoon salt	California Avocado-Papaya Relish
⅛	teaspoon white pepper	(page 336)
1	tablespoon olive oil	

1. Season scallops with salt and pepper.

2. Heat oil in skillet over medium-high heat. Place scallops in skillet and cook for 2 to 3 minutes on each side.

3. Divide Fennel Slaw evenly among 4 plates. Place 4 scallops on each plate. Spoon California Avocado-Papaya Relish over scallops.

Fennel Slaw

1	teaspoon grated lemon peel	1	clove garlic, finely chopped
2	tablespoons fresh lemon juice	¼	teaspoon salt
1	tablespoon white balsamic vinegar	¼	teaspoon white pepper
1	tablespoon olive oil	3	cups fennel, thinly sliced
1	teaspoon fresh thyme leaves, chopped	2	scallions, green part only, thinly sliced lengthwise

1. In a small bowl, combine lemon peel, lemon juice, vinegar, oil, thyme, garlic, salt, and pepper; stir until well mixed.

2. In a medium bowl, combine fennel and scallions. Add lemon dressing. Mix well, cover, and set aside.

California Avocado-Papaya Relish

1 ripe fresh California avocado,
   peeled, seeded, and cut into
   ¼-inch cubes

⅔ papaya, peeled, seeded, and cut into
   ¼-inch cubes

⅓ red bell pepper, cut into
   ¼-inch cubes

2 tablespoons fresh lime juice

In a small bowl, combine avocado, papaya, and bell pepper. Add lime juice and gently stir to coat; set aside.

Nutrition Facts per Serving: 220 calories, 14 g protein, 14 g total fat (2 g saturated fat), 19 g carbohydrate, 6 g fiber, 10 mg cholesterol, 370 mg sodium

Cinnamon Apple Pork Tenderloin

Perfect for the harvest celebrations, this recipe uses seasonal apples and dried fruit to add a sweet essence to an all-time favorite, roasted pork tenderloin. Enjoy this delicious recipe with a unique varietal blend of *Daviana Cabernache.*

Start to Finish: 45 minutes   Yield: 4 servings

1 pound pork tenderloin	2 cooking apples, peeled, cored, and sliced (Golden Delicious, Granny Smith, Jonathan, Pippin, McIntosh)
2 tablespoons cornstarch	
1 teaspoon ground cinnamon	
1 tablespoon brown sugar, packed	2 tablespoons dried cranberries or raisins

1. Preheat oven to 400°F.

2. Place tenderloin in roasting pan or casserole dish.

3. Combine remaining ingredients and mix well. Spoon the apple mixture around the tenderloin.

4. Cover and bake for 30 minutes.

5. Remove cover and spoon apple mixture over the tenderloin. Continue to bake 15 minutes or until the pork tenderloin is browned and cooked through, about 150°F on a meat thermometer.

Nutrition Facts per Serving: 225 calories, 24 g protein, 2.5 g total fat (1 g saturated fat), 26 g carbohydrate, 2 g fiber, 75 mg cholesterol, 60 mg sodium

Brown Basmati Pilaf
with Almonds and Raisins

Lundberg Family Farms is a family-owned and -operated rice company that is committed to producing the finest quality rice and rice products. From the heart of California's Sacramento Valley, Lundberg rice varietals offer many inspirations for wholesome, delicious meals. This recipe features aromatic and fluffy brown basmati rice with Moroccan flavors.

Start to Finish: 1 hour   Yield: 6 servings, ½ cup each

2   cups water
1   cup Lundberg Family Farms Brown Basmati
1   tablespoon butter
    Juice of one lemon
1   teaspoon lemon zest
½   teaspoon ground cumin
¼   cup golden raisins
¼   cup scallions, sliced
2   tablespoons slivered almonds

1. Bring water to a boil in a medium saucepan with lid, and add Lundberg Brown Basmati, butter, lemon juice, lemon zest, cumin, and raisins. Cover and reduce heat to simmer; cook 50 minutes.

2. Remove from heat and let steam 10 minutes with lid on. Fluff with fork, stir in scallions, and serve garnished with slivered almonds.

Nutrition Facts per Serving: 110 calories, 2 g protein, 3 g total fat (1 saturated fat), 21 g carbohydrate, 2 g fiber, 5 mg cholesterol, 150 mg sodium

Roasted Wine Country Tri Tip

with Whole-Grain Mustard and Wild Mushroom Ragout

This recipe uses typical ingredients of northern California's wine country—wine, mustard, and mushrooms. During the month of February, beautiful bright yellow mustard flowers grow in between the grapevines, making for the most amazing landscape. Local mustard festivals celebrate this event with an endless variety of different mustard blends.

I suggest pairing this recipe with *Freedom Estate* Napa Valley Red Wine. This is a favorite of my husband, Shawn. *Freedom Estate*, a wine produced in limited quantities, is a classical blend that showcases Napa Valley's finest cabernet sauvignon. An elegant rich wine that pairs wonderfully with your best steaks to your most casual barbecues.

Start to Finish: 45 minutes, plus up to 24 hours for marinating   Yield: 8 servings

Marinade

- 2 pounds beef tri tip, fat removed
- ¼ cup red wine
- 1 tablespoon Dijon mustard
- 1 tablespoon thyme, chopped
- 1 tablespoon garlic, chopped fine
- Salt and pepper to taste

Ragout

- 1 tablespoon extra-virgin olive oil
- 2 cups wild mushrooms, cut in quarters
- 1 16-ounce can low-sodium beef stock
- 1 cup onions, chopped
- 1 tablespoon garlic, chopped
- 2 teaspoons thyme, chopped
- ½ cup red wine
- 1 tablespoon whole-grain mustard
- ½ teaspoon cornstarch
- 1 teaspoon water
- 1 teaspoon balsamic vinegar
- Salt and pepper to taste

1. Season meat well with salt and pepper. Let sit for 10 minutes.

2. Combine remaining marinade ingredients in a sealable plastic bag. Add seasoned meat and marinate in refrigerator up to 24 hours.

3. Preheat oven 350°F. Remove tri tip from refrigerator. Bring to room temperature. Wipe off excess garlic.

4. Heat a large, heavy-bottomed sauté pan over medium-high heat. When hot, add oil and tri tip. Sear on one side, and then flip and sear on the other. Remove to a baking pan and place in preheated oven. Reserve sauté pan. Roast for 15 to 20 minutes or until meat reaches 125°F on an instant-read thermometer. Remove from oven and let rest for 15 minutes.

5. Check sauté pan for burned garlic. If the garlic is burned, use a clean pan. If the garlic and bottom of the pan are not burned, use it to prepare the sauce.

6. Heat the pan to medium heat. Add the mushrooms and 2 tablespoons of the beef stock. Bring to a simmer, and reduce until the pan is dry and the mushrooms start to sauté. When mushrooms are slightly browned, add onions, garlic, and thyme. Cook for 5 minutes or until the onions slightly caramelize. Add red wine to deglaze the pan and cook until almost dry. Add remaining beef stock and whole-grain mustard. Bring to a simmer; reduce by half. Combine cornstarch and water. Stir into reduced ragout. Bring back to a simmer; adjust seasoning with salt, pepper, and balsamic vinegar.

7. Thinly slice beef against the grain; serve with 3 tablespoons of ragout on top.

Variations
- Replace tri tip with sirloin steaks, pork loin chops, or chicken breast.
- Replace thyme with oregano.

Nutrition Facts per Serving: 250 calories, 25 g protein, 12 g total fat (4 g saturated fat), 6 g carbohydrate, 1 g fiber, 73 mg cholesterol, 140 mg sodium

Salmon with Rock Shrimp
on a Bed of Fresh Corn

Executive Chef at St. Francis Winery, David Bush recommends pairing the rich flavors of salmon and this unique saffron-infused salsa with a *St. Francis Sonoma County* Chardonnay.

Start to Finish: 45 minutes   Yield: 4 servings

4 ears of corn	Caviar Cream (page 343)
4 3-ounce pieces of salmon	Chervil for garnish
1 teaspoon extra-virgin olive oil	Salt and pepper to taste
Rock Shrimp Salsa (page 343)	

1. Cut the corn kernels off the ears of corn. Blanch corn in boiling water for 30 seconds. Drain and place in water bath to preserve the crispness.

2. Season the salmon with salt and pepper on both sides. In a very hot pan with just a little oil, sear the salmon quickly, about 1 minute on each side. Remove the salmon from the pan.

3. Place a mound of corn on each plate and top with the salmon. Divide the Rock Shrimp Salsa among the 4 pieces of salmon. Spoon Caviar Cream over the salmon; garnish with chervil and serve.

Rock Shrimp Salsa

1	cup rock shrimp, cooked		Pinch saffron threads
½	cup red onion, diced	1	teaspoon parsley, chopped
1	red bell pepper, diced		Salt and pepper to taste
3	tablespoons extra-virgin olive oil		

Mix all ingredients thoroughly.

Caviar Cream

1	tablespoon milk or as needed	2	tablespoons American sturgeon caviar
½	cup sour cream		Salt

Use the milk to thin the sour cream to a pourable consistency.
Add the caviar and season with salt to taste.

Nutrition Facts per Serving: 490 calories, 38 g protein, 29 g total fat (7 g saturated fat), 23 g carbohydrate, 3 g fiber, 215 mg cholesterol, 345 mg sodium

Rustic Garbanzo Bean, Spelt, and Kale Soup

This flavor-rich soup recipe comes from Chef Mary Karlin of the Ramekins Culinary School, located in the heart of Sonoma Valley. Served with a slice of whole-grain bread, this soup makes a hearty meal.

Start to Finish: 1 hour, 15 minutes   Yield: 6 to 8 servings

8 cups vegetable stock or vegetable broth	3 sprigs fresh thyme
¾ cup whole spelt, farro, or regular pearl barley, rinsed and drained	1 tablespoon fennel seeds, crushed
1 15- to 16-ounce can garbanzo beans (chickpeas), rinsed and drained	6 cups fresh kale leaves, coarsely chopped
1 14 ½-ounce can diced tomatoes, undrained	½–1 teaspoon crushed red pepper
1 cup dry white wine	3 tablespoons lemon juice
8 cloves garlic, thinly sliced	Freshly ground black pepper (optional)
	Fresh flat-leaf parsley, chopped (optional)

1. In a 4- to 6-quart Dutch oven, bring the vegetable stock to boiling. Add spelt, farro, or barley. Return to boiling; reduce heat. Cover and simmer for 25 minutes.

2. Add garbanzo beans, undrained tomatoes, wine, garlic, thyme, and fennel seeds to Dutch oven. Bring to boiling; reduce heat. Cover and simmer for 20 minutes. Add kale and crushed red pepper. Cook, uncovered, about 15 minutes or until kale and spelt are tender, stirring occasionally.

3. Stir in lemon juice. If desired, season to taste with black pepper. Remove thyme sprigs before serving. If desired, sprinkle individual servings with parsley.

Nutrition Facts per Serving: 200 calories, 7.5 g protein, 1.5 g total fat (2 g saturated fat), 36 g carbohydrate, 7 g fiber, 0 mg cholesterol, 430 mg sodium

Shrimp, Watermelon, and California Avocado Salad

The bright flavors of lime and cilantro complement the mild flavor of watermelon and the richness of avocado. Hass avocados, the most common variety consumed worldwide, are actually native to California. California avocados are known for their exceptional flavor, adding a delicious, creamy texture and beautiful color to many dishes.

Start to Finish: 20 minutes   Yield: 4 servings

2 cups arugula	¼ cup red onion, sliced thin and rinsed
½ cup Simple Spicy Lime Cilantro Vinaigrette (page 347)	1 tablespoon cilantro
1 pound shrimp, cooked	2 California avocados, cut in ½-inch pieces
4 cups watermelon, cut in 1-inch cubes	Salt and pepper to taste

1. Toss arugula with salt, pepper, and ¼ cup of the vinaigrette.

2. Combine shrimp, watermelon, red onion, and cilantro in a large bowl. Gently toss. Add avocado and the rest of the vinaigrette. Toss just to mix, being careful not to mash the avocados. Place on top of the arugula.

CULINARY NOTE

For a quick and easy meal, use thawed frozen cooked shrimp.

Variations
- Replace watermelon with oranges or grapefruit during the winter.
- Replace watermelon with mango.
- Add ½ cup sliced radishes.

Simple Spicy Lime Cilantro Vinaigrette

Start to Finish: 10 minutes   Yield: ½ cup, 4 servings

¼ cup lime juice

¼ teaspoon garlic, chopped

1 tablespoon cilantro, chopped

¼ teaspoon chipotle in adobo sauce, chopped

¼ cup extra-virgin olive oil

Salt and pepper to taste

Combine all ingredients. Whisk well.

Nutrition Facts per Serving: 125 calories, 0 g protein, 14 g total fat (2 g saturated fat), 1.5 g carbohydrate, 0 g fiber, mg cholesterol, 0 mg sodium

Wine Country Minestrone

A slow-cooked minestrone is a wonderful meal to come home to. The Mediterranean flavors in this rustic-style soup are definitely comfort food on a cold day. Two kinds of beans, cannellini and red kidney beans, make this a filling and healthy meal.

Start to Finish: 6 hours in a crockpot   Yield: 8 servings, 2 cups each

1	tablespoon extra-virgin olive oil	5	cups chicken stock
¼	cup Italian turkey sausage, in small pieces	1	can (15.5 ounces) BUSH'S® Cannellini Beans with liquid
2	tablespoons tomato paste	½	can (16 ounces) BUSH'S® Red Kidney Beans, drained
1	cup onion, chopped	2	cups zucchini cut into ½-inch pieces
1	cup celery, chopped	2	cups baby spinach
2	tablespoons garlic, minced	1½	cups cooked bowtie pasta
1	cup carrots, chopped	2	tablespoons packaged pesto
1	teaspoon dried oregano	2	tablespoons fresh grated parmesan cheese
1	can (16 ounces) tomatoes, chopped		

1. Heat olive oil over medium heat in a medium sauté pan. Add sausage; brown well.

2. Add tomato paste and cook 5 minutes.

3. Add onion, celery, garlic, carrots, and oregano. Cook until garlic is aromatic, about 5 minutes.

4. Pour into a 4-quart slow cooker. Add tomatoes and chicken stock.

5. Cook on low setting for 6 to 7 hours or until the vegetables are tender.

6. Stir in beans, zucchini, spinach, and cooked pasta. Cook on high setting for 8 minutes or until beans and pasta are warmed through and spinach has wilted.

7. To serve, pour the soup into a bowl. Top with pesto and fresh grated parmesan cheese.

Nutrition Facts per Serving: 275 calories, 14 g protein, 7 g total fat (1.5 g saturated fat), 36 g carbohydrate, 7 g fiber, 110 mg cholesterol, 500 mg sodium

Sweet Potato California Almond Chipotle Soup

This soup is a perfect balance of sweet from the sweet potato, earthy from the almonds, and heat from the smoky chipotle—and good for you, too! Enjoy it as a great weekend lunch or light dinner with crusty bread and a simple salad, or serve it in little sake or espresso cups for a cocktail party.

Start to Finish: 1 hour, 15 minutes   Yield: 10 servings, 1 cup each

4–5	large sweet potatoes (about 3 pounds)	6	tablespoons ground almonds
3	tablespoons canola oil	6–8	cups vegetable or chicken stock (or water)
2	medium onions, diced	¼	cup maple syrup (or honey) or to taste
½	cup white wine		Slivered almonds, roasted, or garnish
1	chipotle pepper in adobo sauce, finely minced, adobo sauce reserved		Salt and pepper to taste

1. Preheat oven to 375°F. Line baking sheet with foil. Place whole sweet potatoes on baking sheet. Bake until soft when pierced with a knife (over 1 hour). Let cool. Peel and discard skin; rough chop the potatoes.

2. Heat oil over medium heat in large, heavy soup pot. Cook onions 7 minutes or until translucent, stirring often.

3. Add white wine. When liquid has evaporated, add chipotle and cook 2 to 3 minutes.

4. Add ground almonds. Stir. Add sweet potatoes and stir. Add enough cold stock to cover.

5. Turn heat up to medium-high. Once the soup is boiling, reduce heat and simmer, covered, for 15 minutes or until soft.

6. Remove from heat. Using a hand blender, puree soup until smooth. Stir in maple syrup to taste and season with salt and pepper. Garnish with roasted slivered almonds.

Nutrition Facts per Serving: 245 calories, 4 g protein, 7 g total fat (.5 g saturated fat), 41 g carbohydrate, 5 g fiber, 0 mg cholesterol, 900 mg sodium

Benziger Spring Lamb Loins
with Mint Pesto

The Biodynamic® estate vineyard on Sonoma Mountain is home to much more than grapevines. For owner Chris Benziger, biodiversity is a big part of managing a healthy property and growing world-class wine grapes.
Chef Ari Weisswasser prepared this recipe during the harvest of 2010.

Start to Finish: 45 minutes Yield: 8 servings

2 lamb loins	Black pepper
Salt and pepper	6 tablespoons olive oil or combined
1 bunch mint leaves	3 tablespoons olive oil with
1 bunch parsley leaves	3 tablespoons pistachio oil
1 teaspoon kosher salt	2 tablespoons butter
¼ cup pistachio nuts, shelled	2 tablespoons fig balsamic vinegar
6 figs	1 sprig rosemary
Fleur de sel salt	1 tablespoon extra-virgin olive oil

1. Season lamb loins with salt and pepper. Grill over hot coals about 10 minutes on each side. Rest 5 minutes in a warm place.

2. Blanch mint and parsley in rapidly boiling salted water for 45 seconds. Strain and transfer to a blender and purée on high for 3 minutes. Add oil, salt and pistachios. Blend 20 seconds. Set aside.

3. Preheat oven to 350°F. Cut figs in quarters lengthwise. Season with fleur de sel and pepper. Brown butter in a small sauté pan over medium-high heat. Caramelize the figs, cut side down, for 2 minutes. Deglaze pan with fig balsamic vinegar. Add rosemary. Finish in oven, about 2 minutes. Drain figs on paper towel. Add 1 tablespoon olive oil to pan. Remove rosemary and discard. Reserve juices.

4. Spoon mint pesto into center of plates. Arrange 3 fig pieces per person around pesto. Slice each loin into 4 medallions. Top pesto with medallions. Finish with fig pan juices.

WINE SUGGESTION: *Benziger's Signaterra Pinot Noir, Bella Luna Vineyard*

Nutrition Facts per Serving: 450 calories, 16 g protein, 30 g total fat (3 g saturated fat), 11 g carbohydrate, 3 g fiber, 70 mg cholesterol, 323 mg sodium

Three Bean, Lentil, and Arugula Salad

With its bright colors and fresh ingredients, this main-dish salad from the Ramekins Culinary School in Sonoma, California, is great to serve when entertaining. It tastes best when served at room temperature rather than chilled.

Start to Finish: 1 hour, 15 minutes   Yield: 8 servings

⅔	cup dry green or brown lentils		Kosher salt
2	cups water		Freshly ground black pepper
2	red bell peppers	8	cups arugula
1	pound fresh haricots verts (green beans), trimmed if desired	1	19-ounce can cannellini beans (white kidney beans), rinsed and drained
1	pound fresh haricots beurres (yellow wax beans), trimmed if desired	1	9-ounce can solid white tuna (water pack), drained and broken into chunks
1	cup fresh flat-leaf parsley leaves		
¾	cup lightly packed fresh basil leaves	4	hard-cooked eggs, peeled and cut into wedges
¼	cup lightly packed fresh mint leaves		
¼	cup white balsamic vinegar	2–3	tablespoons capers, drained (optional)
2	shallots, coarsely chopped		
¾	cup extra-virgin olive oil		

1. Rinse and pick over lentils. In a large saucepan, bring the water to boiling; add lentils. Return to boiling; reduce heat. Cover and simmer about 30 minutes or until lentils are tender; drain and set aside.

2. Cut bell peppers lengthwise into quarters, removing stems and seeds. Place pepper quarters on the rack of an uncovered grill directly over medium coals. Grill for 10 to 12 minutes or until just beginning to char, turning once halfway through grilling. Transfer pepper quarters to a cutting board. Coarsely chop peppers; set aside.

3. In a covered large Dutch oven, cook fresh beans in a small amount of lightly salted boiling water for 4 to 5 minutes or until just tender. (If using frozen beans, cook according to package directions.) Drain; immediately plunge into ice water to cool quickly. When cool, drain well.

4. For vinaigrette, in a blender combine parsley, basil, mint, vinegar, and shallots. Cover and blend until herbs and shallots are finely chopped. With blender running, slowly add the olive oil in a thin, steady stream; blend until well mixed. Season to taste with kosher salt and black pepper. Set aside.

5. To serve, place the arugula leaves down the two long sides of a large platter. Top the arugula on one side with the cannellini beans. Top the arugula on the other side with the lentils. Down the center alternately crisscross small bundles of the green and yellow beans (or arrange combined beans down the center). Top the green and yellow beans with the chopped bell pepper. Top salad with the tuna and egg wedges. Drizzle with some of the herb vinaigrette; pass remaining vinaigrette. If desired, sprinkle with the capers.

Nutrition Facts per Serving: 410 calories, 22 g protein, 25 g total fat (4 g saturated fat), 32 g carbohydrate, 13 g fiber, 119 mg cholesterol, 336 mg sodium

Sautéed Fillet of Red Snapper

with Miso and Lemon Grass, Baby Bok Choy, and Sugar Snap Peas

The ultimate wine country experience includes the beautiful setting and natural mineral hot springs of the Fairmont–Sonoma Mission Inn and Spa in the Sonoma Valley. Its signature restaurant, Santé, is a recent recipient of the prestigious Michelin Star.

Start to Finish: 1 hour   Yield: 4 servings

For the Red Snapper
- 4   5-ounce boneless red snapper fillets, skin left on
- 3   tablespoons grapeseed oil
-     Salt and white pepper to taste

For the Lemon Grass Miso Nage
- 1   piece kombu, wiped with a damp paper towel
- 1   gallon water
- 3   ounces bonito flakes
- 1   cup yellow onions, sliced
- 1   cup celery, cut in large dice

- 1   leek, green top removed, washed well and cut in large dice
- 2   kaffir lime leaves
- 1   teaspoon fresh ginger, grated
- 1   stalk lemon grass, chopped
- ½   cup miso (prepared according to package directions)

For the Garnish
- 1   1 pound baby bok choy, cut in half lengthwise and blanched
- ½   pound sugar snap peas, blanched
- ½   cup tomato, chopped

For the Miso

1. Soak kombu in water over low heat, bringing the water just to a simmer.

2. Remove the pot from the heat and add the bonito flakes.

3. Steep the bonito flakes until they sink to the bottom of the pot.

4. Strain the liquid well.

5. Add the onions, celery, leek, lime leaves, ginger, and lemon grass and simmer for about 30 minutes. Strain well.

6. Whisk in the miso and strain through a fine cheesecloth.

To Assemble

1. Prepare the miso according to directions.

2. Heat a large sauté pan. Add the grapeseed oil and heat until a slight smoke appears.

3. Season the fish with salt and pepper, and place each fillet skin down in the pan.

4. Reduce the heat to medium and sauté the fish until the skin begins to crisp and the edges begin to brown.

5. Meanwhile, in a separate saucepan, bring the miso broth to a simmer and add the bok choy, snap peas, and tomatoes.

6. Flip the fish over to finish cooking.

7. To serve, place the vegetables and broth in a large entrée bowl; then place the fish on top of the bok choy, making sure that it is not submerged in the broth.

Nutrition Facts per Serving: 415 calories, 42 g protein, 15 g total fat (2 g saturated fat), 25 g carbohydrate, 6.5 g fiber, 62 mg cholesterol, 700 mg sodium

HOLIDAY

It's time to celebrate. Holidays, tradition, family, and friends—it's all about the memories and special meals that bring us back to the table. Cherish these special occasions with memorable meals inspired by Sonoma traditions—Cornish Game Hens with Wild Rice, Pecan, and Fig Stuffing, Mustard-Crusted Rack of Lamb with Balsamic Fig Sauce, smoked salmon, or Smoky Mexican Seafood Cocktail. Serve with a wonderful wine, and enjoy!

Mustard-Crusted Rack of Lamb
with Balsamic Fig Sauce

The hearty flavor of lamb is even more delicious when bold flavors accompany it. Spicy Dijon mustard and a slightly sweet sauce made from Mission figs and balsamic vinegar are a perfect complement to this roasted lamb. Enjoy this fabulous recipe for a holiday celebration or a special evening.

Start to Finish: 1 hour plus 1 to 24 hours to marinate   *Yield: 4 servings, half a rack per serving*

2	lamb racks, frenched, fat removed	4	tablespoons balsamic vinegar
2	tablespoons Dijon mustard	2	teaspoons agave syrup
2	teaspoons thyme, chopped	1½	cups beef stock
2	tablespoons extra-virgin olive oil	2	teaspoons cold butter
1	cup whole-wheat bread crumbs	1	teaspoon lemon juice
12	Mission figs, cut in quarters		Salt and pepper to taste

1. Season lamb well with salt and pepper. Let sit for 30 minutes or, preferably, overnight.

2. Preheat oven to 400°F. Combine mustard and thyme in a small bowl. Set aside.

3. Heat a heavy-bottomed sauté pan over medium-high heat. Add 1 tablespoon of the olive oil; place lamb racks meat side down in the pan. Cook until well browned. Turn and brown on other side. The lamb will still be raw. Reserve the sauté pan.

4. Spread the mustard mixture on meat side of lamb rack. Combine bread crumbs and

2 teaspoons of the olive oil. Rub together until the bread is lightly coated. Place on a plate.

5. Roll the meat side of the lamb into the bread crumbs to coat lightly. Place lamb on a rack on a baking sheet, meat side up. Roast in a 400°F oven for 15 minutes or until the bread has browned and the lamb is 125°F (medium-rare). Remove to a warm spot. Let rest for 15 minutes.

6. While the lamb is roasting, place the sauté pan back on medium heat. Add the remaining 1 teaspoon olive oil and the figs, cut side down. Cook for 1 to 2 minutes to brown the figs, being careful not to burn the drippings in the pan. Once the figs are lightly browned, remove from the pan and reserve. Add the balsamic vinegar to the pan, reduce until almost dry. Add the agave syrup and beef stock and cook until reduced by half. Return figs to the sauce, adjust seasonings with salt and pepper, and gently stir in butter and lemon juice, stirring constantly to melt the butter.

7. Once the lamb has rested, cut each rack into double chops (4 per rack, 2 double chops per serving). Place 2 chops on each dinner plate and serve with 2 tablespoons of sauce.

Variation
- Replace figs with pitted cherries.

CULINARY NOTES

- "Frenched" means that the excess fat has been trimmed and the bones have been scraped down to expose the ribs. Ask the butcher at the meat counter to do this.

- Bring the lamb to room temperature before cooking. This will give the lamb a more tender texture than cooking it straight from the refrigerator.

- If the bread crumb crust is not browning enough once the lamb is almost done, place under the broiler and let brown for 5 minutes.

- Stirring cold butter into a sauce is a classic French method called *monte au beurre*, meaning "to finish with butter." A small amount of butter will add a creamy, rich flavor and texture to the sauce. The butter must be stirred when added so it melts into the sauce without breaking.

WINE SUGGESTION: *Cabernet sauvignon*

Nutrition Facts per Serving: 450 calories, 30 g protein, 13 g total fat (4 g saturated fat), 45 g carbohydrate, 6 g fiber, 81 mg cholesterol, 300 mg sodium, 42 weighted glycemic index

Smoked Salmon Buckwheat Beggars' Purses

This can be an impressive dish for parties.
The crepes are made from wholesome buckwheat flour. Smoked salmon,
capers, and parsley make a very rich and flavorful filling.

Start to Finish: 30 minutes   Yield: 6 servings

1 cup cucumber, peeled, seeded, and sliced paper-thin	1½ tablespoons capers, rinsed and chopped
12 chives	3 tablespoons scallions, chopped
3 ounces low-fat cream cheese at room temperature	1½ cups smoked salmon, chopped
3 ounces low-fat sour cream	12 Buckwheat Pancakes (page 363)
1 tablespoon Italian parsley, chopped	Salt and pepper to taste
	1 recipe Shaved Fennel Citrus Salad (page 369)

CULINARY NOTE

Be careful when tying the pancakes. Don't pull too hard or you may tear the chive or pancake.

1. Season cucumber with salt and pepper. Let drain in a mesh strainer.

2. Bring a small pot of water to a boil. Prepare a bowl of ice water. Drop the chives in the boiling water; as soon as they begin to wilt, place in the ice water. Drain well.

3. Combine the cream cheese, sour cream, and parsley. Mix well. Add capers and scallions; then fold in smoked salmon.

4. Place a pancake on a plate. Place 1 tablespoon cucumber in the center. Top with

smoked salmon mixture. Gather the pancake to form a little purse. Tie the top of the pancake with 2 blanched chives strips.

5. Serve with Shaved Fennel Citrus Salad.

Variations

- You can replace the chives with blanched leeks or scallions if desired, cut into ⅛-inch pieces.

- Instead of chopping the salmon, combine the cream cheese, sour cream, parsley, capers, and scallions. Place the cucumbers in the center of the crepe. Top with a slice of smoked salmon and a dollop of the cream cheese mixture.

- Use cooked smoked salmon in place of cured smoked salmon.

Nutrition Facts per Serving: 175 calories, 13 g protein, 7 g total fat (3 g saturated fat), 15 g carbohydrate, 2 g fiber, 57 mg cholesterol, 470 mg sodium, 36 weighted glycemic index

Buckwheat Pancakes

These light and fluffy pancakes are easy to prepare and have wholesome nutty flavors from the whole-grain buckwheat flour. Nourishing and delicious, perfect as a sweet breakfast dish topped with a fruit compote or with a savory filling.

Start to Finish: 45 minutes   Yield: 4 servings, 2 pancakes each

1 cup buttermilk	½ cup unbleached all-purpose flour
1 egg	½ cup buckwheat flour
1 egg white	2 teaspoons sugar
4 tablespoons applesauce	½ teaspoon salt
½ teaspoon vanilla	1½ teaspoons baking soda
½ teaspoon lemon zest	Nonstick cooking spray

1. Preheat pancake griddle over medium heat.

2. Combine the buttermilk, egg, egg white, applesauce, vanilla, and zest in a bowl. Mix well.

3. In another bowl, combine flours, sugar, salt, and baking soda. Mix well.

4. Gently incorporate the wet ingredients into the dry ingredients. Mix just enough to combine. Overmixing will make the pancakes tough.

5. Lightly spray the pancake griddle. Pour ¼ cupfuls of pancake batter on griddle, ¼ inch thick. Cook until golden brown and the edges start to set. Flip and cook on the other side.

Variations

- Blueberry Buckwheat Pancakes: Add 1½ cups blueberries to the buttermilk mixture.
- Banana Buckwheat Pancakes: Omit lemon zest; add 1 cup chopped bananas and ½ teaspoon cinnamon to the buttermilk mixture.

CULINARY NOTE

The leavening agent is baking soda, so once the wet and dry ingredients are combined, the pancakes should be cooked immediately. This batter does not hold well.

Nutrition Facts per Serving: 160 calories, 8 g protein, 2.5 g total fat (1 g saturated fat), 29 g carbohydrate, 3 g fiber, 55 mg cholesterol, 800 mg sodium, 52 weighted glycemic index

Cornish Game Hens

with Wild Rice, Pecan, and Fig Stuffing

I love the country-style flavors of this recipe and the simple presentation. Cornish game hens are flavorful and can be prepared in a similar way to chicken. This meal has a great combination of the sweet and savory flavors of wild rice, figs, and balsamic vinegar.

Start to Finish: 90 minutes   Yield: 4 servings, ½ hen per serving

2 Cornish game hens	½ cup pecans, toasted and chopped
1 tablespoon extra-virgin olive oil	1 tablespoon parsley, chopped
1 cup celery, chopped	¼ cup scallions, chopped
1 cup onion, chopped	3 tablespoons balsamic vinegar
2 cups wild rice, cooked according to package directions	2 teaspoons agave syrup
6 Mission figs, cut in quarters	½ teaspoon lemon juice
1½ cup chicken stock	Salt and pepper to taste

1. Preheat oven to 450°F.

2. Season the game hens inside and out with salt and pepper. Set aside.

3. Heat a sauté pan over medium heat. Add olive oil, celery, and onions; season with salt and pepper. Sauté over medium heat until translucent. Add cooked wild rice, 4 of the cut figs, and ½ cup of the chicken stock. Cook together for 5 minutes until the stock has reduced by half. Remove from heat. Stir in pecans, parsley, and scallions. Adjust seasoning.

4. Pour the stuffing in a 9-inch x 9-inch pan. (Reserve sauté pan.) Place game hens on top. Roast in preheated oven for 10 minutes; then reduce heat to 350° and cook for 20 minutes or until the game hens are cooked through and a thermometer reads 150°F when inserted onto the thigh.

Nutrition Facts per Serving: 450 calories, 32 g protein, 18 g total fat (2.5 g saturated fat), 44 g carbohydrate, 6 g fiber, 108 mg cholesterol, 135 mg sodium, 29 weighted glycemic index

5. Remove from the oven and allow to rest for 10 minutes.

6. Return the sauté pan to medium heat; add balsamic vinegar and the remaining pieces of fig. Reduce balsamic vinegar over low heat to a glaze; add remaining chicken stock and bring to a simmer. Reduce by half; stir in agave syrup and lemon juice. Adjust seasoning.

7. To serve: Cut the game hens in half. Divide the wild rice evenly among 4 plates. Place the game hens on top. Pour 2 tablespoons of sauce around the hen.

Herb-Roasted Turkey

Perfectly seasoned with a variety of spices and herbs and a dash of white wine, this roasted turkey breast makes an elegant entrée.

Start to Finish: 1 hour   Yield: 8 servings

1	2-pound boneless turkey breast, skinned
½	teaspoon kosher salt
½	teaspoon freshly ground black pepper
2	teaspoons lemon zest
3	tablespoons lemon juice
2	tablespoons extra-virgin olive oil
2	tablespoons fresh flat-leaf parsley, chopped
1	tablespoon fresh rosemary, chopped
1	tablespoon fresh sage, chopped
1	tablespoon fresh thyme, chopped
6	cloves garlic, minced (1 tablespoon minced)
1	cup chicken broth
¼	cup dry white wine

1. Preheat oven to 400°F. Season turkey breast with kosher salt and pepper. Place turkey in a shallow roasting pan. In a small bowl, combine lemon zest, lemon juice, olive oil, 1 tablespoon of the parsley, rosemary, sage, thyme, and garlic. Rub herb mixture over turkey breast.

2. Roast turkey for 10 minutes. Pour broth and wine over turkey. Reduce oven temperature to 350°F. Roast turkey about 25 minutes more or until turkey is tender and no longer pink (155°F), spooning juices in pan over turkey every 10 minutes. Let rest for 15 minutes before slicing.

3. To serve, slice turkey. Spoon some of the cooking juices from the roasting pan over individual servings. Sprinkle with the remaining 1 tablespoon parsley.

CULINARY NOTES

- For maximum flavor, allow the turkey to marinate in the herb mixture overnight.
- Letting the meat rest before slicing allows the juices to flow back into the meat.

Nutrition Facts per Serving: 170 calories, 28 g protein, 4 g total fat (.7 g saturated fat), 2 g carbohydrate, 5 g fiber, 70 mg cholesterol, 185 mg sodium, 12 weighted glycemic index

Variation

Prepare a brine: 1½ tablespoons kosher salt, 1 tablespoon brown sugar, 2 cups water, ½ teaspoon black peppercorns, 1 pinch allspice, ¼ teaspoon coriander, 1 sprig thyme, and 1 bay leaf. Heat just to dissolve the salt. Let sit for 10 minutes. Add 2 cups ice with water to cover. Chill. Add turkey breast; place in Ziploc bag or a container large enough to keep the turkey breast submerged (place a weight on top to keep it submerged). Let turkey sit in the brine for several hours. Remove from brine, rinse well, and dry.

WINE SUGGESTION: *Sparkling pinot noir*

Shaved Fennel Citrus Salad

Serve this winter salad as a refreshing side with seafood, pork, or duck. The crisp, sweet, thinly sliced fennel complements the delicate flavors of the salad. Citrus vinaigrette brightens the flavors and gives another layer of sweetness.

Start to Finish: 20 minutes   Yield: 6 servings

2 cups fennel, sliced paper-thin on a mandolin	1 cup orange segments, no pith or skin
¾ cup celery, sliced paper-thin on a mandolin	¾ cup Citrus Vinaigrette (page 385)
¼ cup radishes, sliced paper-thin on a mandolin	¼ cup parsley leaves
¼ cup red onion, sliced paper-thin on a mandolin, rinsed, and drained	Salt and pepper to taste

1. Combine fennel, celery, radishes, red onion, and oranges. Season with salt and pepper. Let sit a couple of minutes.

2. Mix in Citrus Vinaigrette and parsley.

Variations

- Add grapefruit segments in place of oranges.
- Add mandarin orange segments in place of oranges.

CULINARY NOTES

- Mix this salad just before serving.
- Serve this salad with Smoked Salmon Buckwheat Beggars' Purses (page 361).
- Serve with grilled or sautéed fish or shrimp on top.

Nutrition Facts per Serving: 100 calories, 1.5 g protein, 4 g total fat (.5 g saturated fat), 16 g carbohydrate, 2.5 g fiber, 0 mg cholesterol, 255 mg sodium, 30 weighted glycemic index

Smoky Mexican Seafood Cocktail

This festive appetizer is succulent and sweet, thanks to the starring ingredients, shrimp or crabmeat. It looks exquisite served in martini glasses and will take you only 20 minutes to prepare.

Start to Finish: 20 minutes   *Yield: 8 servings*

1½ cups clam-tomato juice cocktail, chilled	flaked, and cartilage removed, OR 12 ounces shrimp with tails, cooked, peeled, and deveined, OR 6 ounces of each
½ cup red onion, finely chopped	1 medium avocado, halved, pitted, peeled, and chopped
¼ cup fresh cilantro, chopped	
¼ cup lime juice	1 cup cucumber, seeded, peeled, and chopped
1 tablespoon tomato paste (optional)	
1–2 teaspoons bottled chipotle in adobo sauce or bottled hot pepper sauce	8 lime wedges (optional)
2 6 ½-ounce cans crabmeat, drained,	Fresh cilantro (optional)

1. In a medium bowl, combine clam-tomato juice cocktail, red onion, cilantro, lime juice, tomato paste (if using), and chipotle pepper sauce.

2. Add the crabmeat (if using), avocado, and cucumber. Toss gently to coat. Divide mixture among eight martini glasses. Top with shrimp (if using). Garnish with lime wedges and cilantro if desired.

Variations

- Replace crab or shrimp with shucked oysters or clams.
- Replace crab with scallops. Cut scallops in quarters and marinate in lime juice for 20 minutes. Drain well before adding.

CULINARY NOTE

Keep all ingredients chilled so the cocktail is ice-cold when served.

Nutrition Facts per Serving: 104 calories, 10 g protein, 3 g total fat (.5 g saturated fat), 9 g carbohydrate, 1.7 g fiber, 80 mg cholesterol, 310 mg sodium, 32 weighted glycemic index

Pork Loin Stuffed
with Dried Figs and Granny Smith Apples

This is a perfect dish for the fall harvest holiday season, when apples and figs are in season. Fruit flavors and balsamic vinegar complement the mild flavors in pork and make for a beautiful dish.

Start to Finish: 1 hour 15 minutes   Yield: 4 servings, 2 slices each

1 pound boneless pork loin, fat removed	1½ cup low-sodium chicken stock
2 tablespoons extra-virgin olive oil	1 teaspoon agave syrup
1 cup Granny Smith apple, peeled, cored, cut into ½-inch chunks	1 tablespoon pine nuts, toasted
	1 pound pork loin, fat removed
¼ cup dried figs, cut in quarters	1 pinch salt and pepper
2 teaspoons balsamic vinegar	1 tablespoon whole-grain mustard
	Lemon juice

1. Preheat oven to 350°F. Season pork with salt and pepper. Place the pork on a cutting board. Insert a long thin knife in the center of the pork loin so it extends through the other end. Wriggle the knife to form a 1½-inch slit down the center of the pork. Make another slit perpendicular to the original slit in the center of the pork, forming a + shape. This is where you will place the filling.

2. Heat a sauté pan over high heat. Add 1 tablespoon olive oil, then the apples. Sauté on high until the apples are golden brown. Add the figs, salt, pepper, and balsamic vinegar; cook until dry. Add ¼ cup of the chicken stock. Bring to a simmer. Cook until the apples are almost tender and the stock has reduced to a syrup, about 10 minutes. Stir in agave syrup. Place apple mixture on a plate to cool in the refrigerator. Add the remaining chicken stock to the sauté pan to deglaze. Bring to a simmer. Set aside.

3. Gently open the slit in the pork loin. Stuff the cooled apple mixture into the center of the pork loin. Compact it as tightly as possible, and fill from both sides of the pork loin. You will have a few tablespoons of stuffing left, which will be added to the pan for a sauce.

4. Heat a sauté pan over medium-high heat; add remaining olive oil and pork loin. Sear the pork loin all over until well browned. Reserve the sauté pan for the pan sauce. Place pork on a roasting rack on a baking sheet. Roast in preheated oven for 30 minutes or until the center of the roast is 150°F. Remove from oven and let rest in a warm place.

5. Return the sauté pan to medium heat; add the leftover filling to the pan. Sauté for 1 minute; then add the reserved chicken stock mixture. Stir in whole-grain mustard; reduce by half or until the flavors meld. Adjust seasonings with pepper and lemon juice if necessary.

6. To serve: Slice roast into 8 ¼-inch slices. Place 2 slices on each plate and serve with 2 tablespoons of sauce.

Variation

- Replace dried figs with dried plums or cherries.

CULINARY NOTE

For a thicker sauce, prepare a slurry using 1 teaspoon cornstarch to 2 teaspoon water. Mix together and whisk into sauce after it has reduced by half. Bring back to a simmer and adjust seasoning.

WINE SUGGESTION: *Pinot noir*

Nutrition Facts per Serving: 140 calories, 27 g protein, 15 g total fat (3.5 g saturated fat), 15 g carbohydrate, 2 g fiber, 66 mg cholesterol, 115 mg sodium, 33 weighted glycemic index

Sweet Potato and Cranberry Bake

Sweet potatoes and cranberries always have a place at the Thanksgiving table. This stunning combination of the two essentials is deliciously seasoned and full-flavored.

Start to Finish: 90 minutes   *Yield: 6 servings*

2 tablespoons coarse-grain mustard	¼ teaspoon freshly ground black pepper
1 tablespoon extra-virgin olive oil	2 pounds sweet potatoes, peeled and cut into 1 ½-inch chunks
1 tablespoon honey	½ cup fresh cranberries
1 tablespoon lemon juice	Fresh thyme sprigs (optional)
2 teaspoons chopped fresh thyme	
¾ teaspoon kosher salt	

1. Preheat oven to 350°F. In a large bowl, combine mustard, olive oil, honey, lemon juice, thyme, kosher salt, and pepper. Add the sweet potatoes; toss to coat. Gently stir in the cranberries. Transfer sweet potato mixture to a 2-quart rectangular baking dish; spread in an even layer.

2. Bake, covered, about 1 ¼ hours or until sweet potatoes are tender, stirring once. Uncover and bake about 10 minutes more or just until sweet potatoes are starting to brown. If desired, garnish with thyme sprigs before serving.

Variations

- Replace sweet potatoes with butternut squash.
- Replace cranberries with dried figs, cut in quarters.

CULINARY NOTE

Cut sweet potatoes into equal size pieces so they roast evenly.

Nutrition Facts per Serving: 180 calories, 2.6 g protein, 2.6 g total fat (.5 g saturated fat), 37 g carbohydrate, 5 g fiber, 0 mg cholesterol, 350 mg sodium, 44 weighted glycemic index

Roast Pork Tenderloin
with Sautéed Apples and Dried Cherries

Tenderloin is the leanest and most tender portion of pork. The richness of the meat is complemented by the tartness of the apples and dry cherries.

Start to Finish: 70 minutes   Yield: 4 servings

1 pound pork tenderloin, fat removed	¼ teaspoon fresh ginger, grated
½ teaspoon fresh ginger, ground	2 sage leaves
½ teaspoon Spanish paprika, smoked or plain	¼ cup dried cherries
1 tablespoon extra-virgin olive oil	½ tablespoon maple syrup
1 Granny Smith or Golden Delicious apple, peeled, cored, and cut in ¼-inch wedges	1 cup low-sodium chicken stock
	Salt and pepper to taste

1. Season pork with salt and pepper.

2. Combine ginger, paprika and ½ tablespoon of the olive oil. Spread over pork to marinate for 30 minutes or as long as overnight.

3. Preheat oven to 400°F.

4. Heat a sauté pan over medium heat. Add the remaining ½ tablespoon olive oil and pork tenderloin. Cook until lightly browned. Turn tenderloin over and continue to cook until golden brown all over. Remove from pan (reserve pan to prepare the sauce). Place on a rack on a sheet pan and roast in the oven until the pork reaches an internal temperature of 143°F. Remove from oven and allow pork to rest for 15 minutes.

CULINARY NOTES

- Use a micro plane or the smallest holes of a grater to grate the ginger. The flesh of the ginger should go through the grater holes while the stringy fibers stay on the root.

- While the pork is marinating, cut the apples. Do not place the apples in water to hold since that dilutes the flavor too much. They will be sautéed so it's okay if they turn a little brown.

5. Add apples to sauté pan. Cook over medium heat until golden brown. Flip and cook on other side until golden brown but still with a slightly firm texture. Add ginger, sage, dried cherries, maple syrup, and stock. Bring to a simmer and reduce by three quarters until apples are tender and liquid is syrupy.

6. Slice pork ¼ inch thick on the bias or against the grain. Serve on a bed of apples and drizzle with syrup.

Variations

- Replace pork tenderloin with pork loin.
- Replace apples with pears.

WINE SUGGESTION: *Merlot*

Nutrition Facts per Serving: 230 calories, 26 g protein, 6 g total fat (1 g saturated fat), 17 g carbohydrate, 2 g fiber, 73 mg cholesterol, 79 mg sodium, 33 weighted glycemic index

SEASONINGS

Vibrant spices, flavorful herbs, healthy plant oils, nuts, seeds, and interesting vinegars and wines—these are the essence of building a flavorful Sonoma pantry. Enjoy the healthiest foods in the world with inspirations from the Mediterranean, Asia, and Latin America. Try Concord Grape Balsamic Vinaigrette, Pomegranate Mint Vinaigrette, and the best Red Wine Barbecue Sauce you will ever taste.

Apple Cider Brine for Turkey

The apple cider and Granny Smith apples in this simple brine give a pleasing, mellow flavor that complements the flavors of the brown sugar, cinnamon, and juniper berries.

Start to Finish: 30 minutes   Yield: 4 servings

½	teaspoon juniper berries	1	small bunch thyme
1	stick cinnamon	1	quart water
1	tablespoon peppercorns	3	quarts ice water
1	cup salt	2	cups Granny Smith apples, peeled, cored, and cut in chunks
1/3	cup brown sugar	12	garlic cloves, peeled
2	bay leaves	½	gallon fresh apple cider

1. Place juniper berries in a large sauce pan. Heat in dry pan until aromatic and shiny, about 30 seconds. Add cinnamon, peppercorns, salt, brown sugar, bay leaves, thyme, and 1 quart water. Bring to a simmer and cook for 5 minutes until the salt and sugar have dissolved. Add ice water, stir together, and set aside.

2. Place apples, garlic, and 2 cups apple cider in a blender. Blend until smooth. Add apple mixture and remaining cider to the ice mixture. Whisk together until the ice is melted, but the mixture is still ice-cold.

3. Place turkey into brining bag and pour brine over. Close tightly. Refrigerate for 1 hour for each pound of turkey.

4. When ready to roast, remove turkey from brine, rinse, and bring close to room temperature before roasting.

CULINARY NOTES

- Keep all ingredients cold when brining. The brine must be cold (approximately 40°F) before adding turkey.

- The turkey must be completely submerged in the brine. If brining in a large pot, place turkey in the pot, breast side down, and place a plate or weight on top to keep it submerged.

Variation

- Replace juniper, bay leaves, and thyme with ¼ teaspoon ancho chile powder, 1 teaspoon Mexican oregano, and 1 tablespoon chipotle in adobo sauce.

Apple Cider Vinegar Barbecue Sauce

Start to Finish: 20 minutes   Yield: 2 cups, 16 servings, 2 tablespoons each

1	cup cider vinegar	1	tablespoon molasses
½	cup ketchup	1	pinch chile flake
3	tablespoons brown sugar		Salt and pepper to taste

Combine all ingredients. Bring to a simmer to dissolve sugar. Do not boil or reduce.

CULINARY NOTES

- For a quick coleslaw, combine 2 cups of shredded cabbage and ½ cup grated carrots with ¼ cup of the barbecue sauce.

- Slice leftover roast pork loin thin and mix with barbecue sauce. Serve on a thin multigrain bun with cabbage slaw.

- Shred leftover roast chicken and mix with barbecue sauce and sautéed onions. Serve on a thin multigrain bun with cabbage slaw.

Nutrition Facts per Serving: 20 calories, 0 g protein, 0 g total fat (0 g saturated fat), 4.5 g carbohydrate, 0 g fiber, 0 mg cholesterol, 0 mg sodium, 47 weighted glycemic index

Brine for Chicken or Pork

This brine and the variation will tenderize your meats and concentrate the brine spices and flavors, producing meat that is moist, tender, and flavorful.

Start to Finish: 30 minutes   Yield: 4 servings

1	cup water	1	bay leaf
¼	cup salt	½	teaspoon thyme, chopped
2	tablespoons sugar	1	pinch of allspice
1	tablespoon garlic, roughly chopped	1	juniper berry
½	teaspoon cracked peppercorns	4	cups ice water

Heat 1 cup of water; add remaining ingredients except ice water. Bring to a simmer and remove from heat. Stir in ice water.

Variation

- Replace bay leaf, thyme, allspice, and juniper with 2 pieces star anise, 2 cloves, 1 teaspoon fennel, and 1 tablespoon chopped ginger.

CULINARY NOTES

- Use to brine chicken or pork. Pour brine into Ziploc bag. Place desired meat portions in brine; mix well. The meat should be completely submerged in the brine. If the meat floats, place a weight on top to keep it submerged. Marinate overnight.

- If brining a whole chicken, you may need to double the recipe. The chicken must be covered completely by the brine. Place in a large Ziploc bag and press to remove all the air.

- To roast, remove meat from the brine; rinse and drain well. Pat dry and roast in a 350°F oven.

Caponata

A Sicilian recipe made from cooked vegetables, such as eggplant
and celery, highlighted by sweet vinegar, nuts, raisins, and capers.
This zesty Mediterranean sweet and sour recipe is a perfect complement
to grilled fish and makes a delicious filling for a sandwich.

Start to Finish: 55 minutes   Yield: 8 servings

2 pounds eggplant, sliced into ¾-inch slices	3 cups tomatoes, cored and coarsely chopped
2 tablespoons extra-virgin olive oil	2 tablespoons raisins
2 cups onions, chopped	2 tablespoons oregano or basil, chopped
1 cup celery, sliced into ¼-inch half moons	3 tablespoons green olives, chopped
2 tablespoons garlic, chopped	2 tablespoons pine nuts
1 cup red or yellow pepper, julienne	Salt and pepper to taste
3 tablespoons red wine vinegar	Nonstick cooking spray
2 tablespoons agave syrup	Parchment paper
2 tablespoons capers, rinsed	

1. Preheat oven 400°F.

2. Lay slices of eggplant on parchment-lined
baking sheet. Spray both sides with nonstick
cooking spray. Bake in hot oven for 15 minutes
or until slightly golden. Cool and cut into
¾-inch cubes.

3. Heat a large sauté pan over medium heat.
Add olive oil, onions, and celery. Season with
salt and pepper. Sauté until golden brown, about
5 minutes. Add garlic and cook until aromatic.
Add peppers; sauté 2 minutes. Add vinegar and
agave syrup; reduce by half.

CULINARY NOTES

- The eggplant will start to fall apart
  at the end of the cooking process.

- Caponata is always best if given a
  chance to sit overnight. This allows
  the flavors to meld.

- Serve with roasted meats such as
  lamb, beef, or pork.

- Toss with whole-wheat pasta and
  cooked meats.

Nutrition Facts per Serving: **140** calories, **3** g protein, **6** g total fat (.7 g saturated fat), **21** g carbohydrate, **6** g fiber,
0 mg cholesterol, **220** mg sodium, **23** weighted glycemic index

4. Add tomatoes and bring to a simmer. Cook for 8 to 10 minutes, stirring periodically until the tomatoes have reduced by one quarter. Add eggplant, capers, and raisins; cook for 20 minutes until the vegetables are tender and the mixture is thick, slightly sweet, and fragrant. Stir in herbs, olives, and pine nuts. Adjust seasonings with salt and pepper.

Variations

- Add 1 cup chopped fennel in place of celery and ¼ teaspoon crushed fennel seeds with the garlic.

- Replace raisins with dried cherries.

Citrus Vinaigrette

The beauty of this dressing is its bright and refreshing flavors from orange, lemon, and grapefruit juice. A touch of heat from the chile flakes and the tang of red wine vinegar are a wonderful combination with the essence of citrus. This will be a dressing you will pair with many different salads.

Start to Finish: 10 minutes   Yield: 4 servings

½	cup orange juice	1	tablespoon soy sauce
¼	cup grapefruit juice	1	tablespoon agave syrup
1	tablespoon lemon juice	1	pinch chile flakes
1	tablespoon red wine vinegar	1	tablespoon extra-virgin olive oil
1	tablespoon orange zest		Salt and pepper to taste

Combine all ingredients in a blender.

Variations

- Replace grapefruit juice with orange juice.
- Replace red wine vinegar with white balsamic vinegar.
- Add 1 shake of Tabasco.

CULINARY NOTES

- Soy sauce gives depth to the dressing.
- This dressing will hold for up to 1 week.

Nutrition Facts per Serving: 70 calories, 0 g protein, 3.5 g total fat (0 g saturated fat), 9.5 g carbohydrate, 0 g fiber, 0 mg cholesterol, 220 mg sodium, 30 weighted glycemic index

Concord Grape Balsamic Vinaigrette

Two wine country staples, grapes and balsamic vinegar, make a sensational flavor combination. This dressing is very easy to prepare.

Start to Finish: 25 minutes   Yield: 4 servings   1 tablespoon each

½	cup unsweetened Concord grape juice	2	tablespoon extra-virgin olive oil
1	tablespoon balsamic vinegar		Salt and pepper to taste

1. Place grape juice in a small sauce pot. Reduce by half. Remove from heat and cool.

2. Stir in balsamic vinegar and whisk in extra-virgin olive oil. Season with salt and pepper.

Variation

- Use red wine vinegar in place of balsamic vinegar.

CULINARY NOTE

Keep an eye on the reducing grape juice. It will burn if it reduces too far.

Nutrition Facts per Serving: 80 calories, 0 g protein 6.5 g total fat (0 g saturated fat), 4.5 g carbohydrate, 0 g fiber, 0 mg cholesterol, 10 mg sodium, 47 weighted glycemic index

Cranberry Orange Relish

This is a holiday essential! The delicious sweet and tart flavors of these ingredients are a perfect accompaniment to your holiday roasted turkey. My favorite way to prepare this recipe is to add a touch of fresh grated ginger and orange zest.

Start to Finish: 45 minutes   Yield: 16 servings   1 tablespoon per serving

1 cup cranberries	1½ tablespoons agave syrup
½ cup orange juice	1 pinch salt and pepper
½ teaspoon apple cider vinegar	

1. Combine all ingredients except ¼ tablespoon agave syrup in a small saucepan. Cover and cook over low heat until the cranberries are tender and bursting apart, about 30 minutes. Stir frequently to prevent the mixture from burning.

2. Stir in remaining agave syrup; remove from heat and cool.

Variations

- Add toasted almonds.
- Add orange zest or lemon zest.
- Add grated fresh ginger.
- Add vanilla or cinnamon.

CULINARY NOTE

Use this relish as a spread for pancakes or crepes or as a dessert with fresh yogurt.

Nutrition Facts per Serving: 10 calories, 0 g protein, 0 g total fat (0 g saturated fat), 3 g carbohydrate, .5 g fiber, 0 mg cholesterol, 5 mg sodium, 31 weighted glycemic index

Pomegranate Mint Vinaigrette

Pomegranate molasses is a syrupy reduction of pomegranate juice with a beautiful deep reddish purple color. It has both sweet and sour flavors that combine the best of balsamic vinegar with tart fruit. Fresh mint adds a wonderful touch to this dressing.

Start to Finish: 15 minutes   Yield: 1 cup, 16 servings, 1 tablespoon each

4 tablespoons extra-virgin olive oil	1 tablespoon mint, chopped
4 tablespoons white balsamic vinegar	1 tablespoon lemon juice
2 tablespoons pomegranate molasses	Salt and pepper to taste

Combine all ingredients. Mix well.

Variations

- Add 1 teaspoon soy sauce.
- Replace white balsamic vinegar with red wine vinegar.
- Replace mint with chopped basil or parsley.

CULINARY NOTES

- Use as a vinaigrette for fresh fruits mixed with bitter greens such as arugula and frisée.
- Use as a marinade for grilled chicken.

Nutrition Facts per Serving: 40 calories, 0 g protein, 3.5 g total fat (.5 g saturated fat), 1.8 g carbohydrate, 0 g fiber, 0 mg cholesterol, 0 mg sodium, 25 weighted glycemic index

Red Wine Barbecue Sauce

At the heart of all great barbeque are significant regional differences, along with healthy doses of ego and pride. In true California style, this sauce combines local ingredients, such as mustard and wine, into a sweet and savory sauce that's perfect for any of your barbecue recipes.

Start to Finish: 30 minutes   Yield: 1 cup, 8 servings, 2 tablespoons each

1	tablespoon extra-virgin olive oil	½	cup ketchup
½	cup onion, chopped	2	teaspoons soy sauce
1	tablespoon garlic, chopped	1	tablespoon molasses
1	cup red wine		Salt and pepper to taste
2	teaspoons Dijon mustard		

1. Heat a small saucepan over medium heat. Add olive oil and onions. Sauté until onions are caramelized and tender. Add garlic until aromatic. Stir in red wine and mustard. Bring to a simmer and reduce by three quarters.

2. Stir in ketchup, soy sauce, and molasses. Bring to a simmer and cook for 10 minutes to meld the flavors. Adjust seasoning with salt and pepper. Blend with a handheld blender or in a blender until smooth.

Variations

- **Chipotle Barbecue Sauce**
  Add 1 tablespoon chopped chipotle in adobo sauce and 1 teaspoon ground cumin with the garlic.

- **Espresso Barbecue Sauce**
  Add ½ teaspoon ground cumin seeds and ½ teaspoon chili powder with the garlic. Replace red wine with ½ cup chicken stock and 1 tablespoon espresso powder. Reduce by three quarters. Adjust seasoning with ½ to 1 tablespoon red wine vinegar, salt, and pepper.

CULINARY NOTE

Reducing the wine removes the alcohol and eliminates the raw wine flavor. Do not overreduce once the ketchup is added.

Nutrition Facts per Serving: 27 calories, 0 g protein, 1 g total fat (0 g saturated fat), 4 g carbohydrate, 0 g fiber, 0 mg cholesterol, 0 mg sodium, 31 weighted glycemic index

Salsa Verde for Meat or Vegetables

An Italian rustic sauce that is delicious for any grilled meats or vegetables.

Start to Finish: 15 minutes   *Yield: ⅔ cup (1 tablespoon per serving)*

½	cup flat leaf parsley, leaves and thin stems only	1	teaspoon lemon zest
¼	cup combination of oregano, basil, and mint	½	teaspoon garlic, minced or mashed
2	tablespoons scallions, chopped	1	pinch red chile flakes
1	tablespoon capers, rinsed and chopped	2	tablespoons extra-virgin olive oil
		1	tablespoon water
			Salt and pepper to taste

Finely chop all herbs; place in a bowl.
Add remaining ingredients and stir to combine.
Let sit for 15 minutes; then adjust seasoning
as necessary.

Variations

- Add 1 tablespoon chopped shallots.
- Add 1 chopped anchovy fillet.
- Add 1 chopped or grated hard-cooked egg.
- Add 1 tablespoon toasted whole-wheat bread crumbs.

CULINARY NOTES

- Experiment with combinations of herbs in addition to the parsley: basil, chives, chervil, tarragon, mint, cilantro, marjoram, savory, thyme.
- Add lemon juice or vinegar to make the sauce zestier. Add it just before serving, since the acid in the lemon and vinegar will cause the herbs to discolor.
- This would be a delicious sauce to serve with a frittata or omelet. It is also a great accompaniment to grilled meats or vegetables.

Nutrition Facts per Serving: 25 calories, 0 g protein, 2.5 g total fat (5 g saturated fat), .5 g carbohydrate, 0 g fiber, 0 mg cholesterol, 25 mg sodium, 14 weighted glycemic index

Southwestern Rub

Start to Finish: 5 minutes   *Yield: ½ cup*

2 tablespoons paprika	1 teaspoon cayenne
2 tablespoons chili powder	1 teaspoon chili flakes
2 teaspoons ground cumin	1 tablespoon salt
1 teaspoon black pepper, freshly ground	1 tablespoon oregano, dried
1 tablespoon ground coriander	½ teaspoon ground cinnamon

Combine all ingredients.

Soy Sesame Vinaigrette

Start to Finish: 10 minutes   *Yield: ½ cup, 1 tablespoon per serving*

4 tablespoons soy sauce	1 tablespoon ginger, minced or grated
1 tablespoon sugar	½ teaspoon garlic, chopped
1 tablespoon rice vinegar	2 teaspoons sesame oil
½ tablespoon lemon juice	Salt and pepper to taste

Combine all ingredients. Whisk well.

Variation

- For a spicier vinaigrette, add ¼ teaspoon chile sauce (sambal oelek or chopped Thai bird chiles).

CULINARY NOTE

Use a microplane to grate the ginger. It allows you to grate the pulp from the ginger root and leaves the stringy, fibrous core behind.

Nutrition Facts per Serving: 22 calories, 15 g protein, 1 g total fat (0 g saturated fat), 2 g carbohydrate, 0 g fiber, 0 mg cholesterol, 300 mg sodium, 30 weighted glycemic index

Sun-Dried Tomato Pesto

Aromatic and delicious, this is a perfect recipe for spreading on your favorite sandwich or flatbread or adding to pasta.

Start to Finish: 15 minutes   Yield: 1 cup, 16 servings, 1 tablespoon each

1 cup basil, packed	1 tablespoon garlic, chopped
8.5 ounces sun-dried tomatoes packed in oil, drained and rinsed	⅓ cup parmesan cheese, grated
	Salt and pepper to taste

1. Heat a small pot of water to a boil. While you wait for the water to boil, set up an ice bath in a medium-sized bowl. Fill the bowl three quarters of the way with ice and add just enough water to top the ice.

2. Place basil in boiling water, stir 15 seconds, and remove from water. Place in ice bath to cool. Remove as soon as the basil cools.

3. In a food processor bowl with a blade, combine sun-dried tomatoes, garlic, and basil. Pulse to a coarse puree. Pulse in parmesan cheese. Season with salt and pepper.

CULINARY NOTES

- This pesto is a rough chop, not a smooth puree. Add a little water if necessary to facilitate the pureeing of the pesto.

- Parmesan is a salty cheese. Season the pesto after the parmesan cheese is added.

Nutrition Facts per Serving: 40 calories, 1 g protein, 2 g total fat (.5 g saturated fat), 3 g carbohydrate, .5 g fiber, 1 mg cholesterol, 65 mg sodium, 33 weighted glycemic index

Yogurt Mint Sauce

In the Eastern Mediterranean, yogurt is combined with pasta, vegetables, and meat dishes for added depth and richness. In Greece, yogurts are especially creamy and thick. Besides being delicious, Greek yogurt also helps maintain the immune system and a healthy digestion, thanks to the beneficial bacteria known as probiotics.

Start to Finish: 15 minutes   Yield: 1 cup, 16 servings, 1 tablespoon each

1 cup plain nonfat Greek yogurt	½ teaspoon lemon zest
1 teaspoon garlic, chopped	Salt and pepper to taste
½ teaspoon dried mint, crumbled	

Combine all ingredients. Let sit for 10 minutes to allow mint to rehydrate.

Variations
- Replace dried mint with fresh mint.
- Replace dried mint with chopped parsley.

CULINARY NOTE

Greek yogurt is a thick, plain yogurt. If you do not have Greek yogurt, line a colander with cheesecloth or a cotton tea towel. Pour regular yogurt in it to drain for a few hours or overnight.

Nutrition Facts per Serving: 10 calories, 1 g protein, 0 g total fat (0 g saturated fat), .5 g carbohydrate, 0 g fiber, 0 mg cholesterol, 5 mg sodium, 15 weighted glycemic index

INDEX